# TINY PUBLICS

# TINY PUBLICS

## A THEORY OF GROUP
## ACTION AND CULTURE

GARY ALAN FINE

A VOLUME IN THE RUSSELL SAGE FOUNDATION SERIES ON TRUST

Russell Sage Foundation • New York

*11-12-12*
*W*
*$32.50*

## The Russell Sage Foundation

The Russell Sage Foundation, one of the oldest of America's general purpose foundations, was established in 1907 by Mrs. Margaret Olivia Sage for "the improvement of social and living conditions in the United States." The Foundation seeks to fulfill this mandate by fostering the development and dissemination of knowledge about the country's political, social, and economic problems. While the Foundation endeavors to assure the accuracy and objectivity of each book it publishes, the conclusions and interpretations in Russell Sage Foundation publications are those of the authors and not of the Foundation, its Trustees, or its staff. Publication by Russell Sage, therefore, does not imply Foundation endorsement.

**Library of Congress Cataloging-in-Publication Data**

Fine, Gary Alan.
  Tiny publics : a theory of group action and culture / Gary Alan Fine.
    p. cm. — (Russell Sage Foundation series on trust)
  Includes bibliographical references and index.
  ISBN 978-0-87154-432-2 (pbk. : alk. paper) — ISBN 978-1-61044-774-4 (ebook)
  1. Social groups. 2. Social networks. 3. Group identity. 4. Social psychology.
  5. Social interaction. 6. Culture—21st century. I. Title.
  HM716.F56 2012
  305—dc23

                                                                2011053493

The paper used in this publication meets the minimum requirements of American National Standard for Information Sciences—Permanence of Paper for Printed Library Materials. ANSI Z39.48-1992.

Text design by Suzanne Nichols.

RUSSELL SAGE FOUNDATION
112 East 64th Street, New York, New York 10065
10 9 8 7 6 5 4 3 2 1

# The Russell Sage Foundation Series on Trust

The Russell Sage Foundation Series on Trust examines the conceptual structure and the empirical basis of claims concerning the role of trust and trustworthiness in establishing and maintaining cooperative behavior in a wide variety of social, economic, and political contexts. The focus is on concepts, methods, and findings that will enrich social science and inform public policy.

The books in the series raise questions about how trust can be distinguished from other means of promoting cooperation and explore those analytic and empirical issues that advance our comprehension of the roles and limits of trust in social, political, and economic life. Because trust is at the core of understandings of social order from varied disciplinary perspectives, the series offers the best work of scholars from diverse backgrounds and, through the edited volumes, encourages engagement across disciplines and orientations. The goal of the series is to improve the current state of trust research by providing a clear theoretical account of the causal role of trust within given institutional, organizational, and interpersonal situations, developing sound measures of trust to test theoretical claims within relevant settings, and establishing some common ground among concerned scholars and policymakers.

Karen S. Cook
Russell Hardin
Margaret Levi

SERIES EDITORS

# Previous Volumes in the Series

*Coethnicity: Diversity and the Dilemmas of Collective Action*
James Habyarimana, Macartan Humphreys, Daniel N. Posner,
and Jeremy M. Weinstein

*Cooperation Without Trust?*
Karen S. Cook, Russell Hardin, and Margaret Levi

*Democracy and the Culture of Skepticism: Political Trust
in Argentina and Mexico*
Matthew R. Cleary and Susan Stokes

*Distrust*
Russell Hardin, editor

*eTrust: Forming Relationships in the Online World*
Karen S. Cook, Chris Snijders, Vincent Buskens,
and Coye Cheshire, editors

*Evolution and the Capacity for Commitment*
Randolph N. Nesse, editor

*Streetwise: How Taxi Drivers Establish Their Customers' Trust*
Diego Gambetta and Heather Hammill

*Trust and Distrust in Organizations: Dilemmas and Approaches*
Roderick M. Kramer and Karen S. Cook, editors

*Trust and Governance*
Valerie Braithwaite and Margaret Levi, editors

*Trust and Reciprocity: Interdisciplinary Lessons from Experimental Research*
Elinor Ostrom and James Walker, editors

*Trust and Trustworthiness*
Russell Hardin

*Trust in Society*
Karen S. Cook, editor

*Trust in the Law: Encouraging Public Cooperation with the Police and Courts*
Tom R. Tyler and Yuen J. Huo

*Whom Can We Trust? How Groups, Networks,
and Institutions Make Trust Possible*
Karen S. Cook, Margaret Levi, and Russell Hardin, editors

To Robert Freed Bales (1916–2004)
and the Group Dynamics Tradition

# Contents

| | About the Author | xi |
|---|---|---|
| | Introduction: Tiny Publics as Social Order | 1 |
| CHAPTER 1 | The Power of Groups | 19 |
| CHAPTER 2 | The Dynamics of Idioculture | 34 |
| CHAPTER 3 | The Power of Constraints and Exteriority | 52 |
| CHAPTER 4 | Norms and Action | 68 |
| CHAPTER 5 | The Performance of Ideology | 89 |
| CHAPTER 6 | Wispy Communities | 107 |
| CHAPTER 7 | Tiny Publics in Civil Society | 124 |
| CHAPTER 8 | The Extension of the Local | 140 |
| CHAPTER 9 | Action and Its Publics | 157 |
| | Notes | 179 |
| | References | 185 |
| | Index | 215 |

# About the Author

**Gary Alan Fine** is professor in the Department of Sociology at Northwestern University.

# Introduction

## Tiny Publics as Social Order

All politics is local.

—Congressman Thomas P. "Tip" O'Neill,
member of the House of
Representatives, 1952 to 1987

IF ALL POLITICS is local, so, I argue, is almost everything else. Action, meaning, authority, inequality, organization, and institution—all have their roots in microstructures situated in what Erving Goffman (1983) described as the "interaction order." Although downplayed in much recent social science, small groups order and organize human life, emphasizing the power of immediate surroundings and microcultures. To revive the small group as an organizing principle of social life is my task. Further, I argue not only that these groups are discrete zones of action but that through their power in defining rights and privileges, they fit into and constitute society. As such, the small group becomes a *tiny public* for the purpose of civic engagement. The group—or tiny public—becomes not only a basis for affiliation, a source of social and cultural capital, and a guarantor of identity, but also a support point in which individuals and the group can have an impact on other groups or shape the broader social discourse. Groups are simultaneously loci of local allegiance and places in which allegiance to the larger public is generated and in which processes of change begin (Lichterman 2005).

Social awareness begins with face-to-face behavior and continues as we learn to account for and make adjustments to the presence and the demands of others. We make collective commitments to a variety of small communities, creating what the philosopher Raimo Tuomela (2007) terms "we-mode" groups.

Yet, surprisingly, in emphasizing cognition, individual agency, organizations, institutions, and societies for the past quarter-century, social scientists have neglected the meso-level of analysis. They have often ignored the local arenas where interaction is performed and institutions are inhabited, turning away from the body of research that had been so

1

prominent in midcentury social science. Social relations are organized through a *network of groups,* and these tiny publics provide the *action spaces* in which society and communities are constituted and inequality and social differentiation are created. Small associations of individuals produce industrial wares, artistic products, political struggles, familial affiliations, and personal satisfactions. As sources of integration and affiliation, these social formations are distinct from detached individuals, large institutions, and mass society.

No system can thrive without a flourishing domain of small groups. They are havens in a heartless world where faceless organizations gain a visage. The intimacy, concern, and attention of participants in small groups permit the creation of social identities and linkages to larger units (Collins 2004; Summers-Effler 2010). To the extent that these small worlds are accepting—and groups differ on this—they provide a *soft community* in which various personal styles are accepted and supported.

Social actors are neither disconnected isolates nor a flock of conformists bound by biology or structure; though we are grouped, we are able to select how we affiliate and how we divide. Groups are not homogeneous, but neither are they random gatherings—they promote association among the like-minded. The desire expressed in groups for satisfying interaction is intense, even while the ostensible purpose is to achieve instrumental goals. Over time the expressive satisfactions of group life may support task goals, but they also may challenge those goals, straining the group's capacity to continue. While structure shapes action, that shaping operates through the understandings and preferences of social actors. Constraints and socialization are important, but even constraints and socialization must be organized through an interaction order. People act in concert. Each group, a dense network of relations, constitutes an interactional field that develops and negotiates norms, provides expectations of continuity, and suggests the possibility of change. The *group space* is an arena of action that creates the predictable and ongoing relationships that are essential for a belief in social order. Predictability is not to be taken lightly; our lives depend on it.

Forged within the boundaries of small groups, society is made up of the minute publics that are necessary for a robust social order at all levels. It is for this reason that I title this book *Tiny Publics,* a phrase that highlights the link between the groups model I propose and an understanding of civil society. Groups and local communities are publics, and they are tiny, at least by the standards of mass publics. They are what Alexis de Tocqueville (1835/1966) speaks of as "minute associations." That these tiny publics are embedded in interaction orders provides them with a deeply held set of social relations, a shared past, and a belief in a common future. They are a public, but one with commitment made powerful through their smallness. The title emphasizes that such groups are not necessarily trivial or evanescent—although they may be—but rather that they can be the cornerstone of social order. It is through extensions of the local that societal life is shaped.

When we consider those relationships that matter most, our eyes and hearts are directed to the presence and influence of a handful of others: the rule of modest numbers. These are the companions who not only are *aware* of each other but are *invested* in each other. They are *significant others*. Families, cliques, fraternities, work groups, teams, and gangs reveal the importance of tight and tiny networks, the building blocks of larger networks. Within the crucible of the group, three essential explanatory domains—structure, interaction, and culture—converge to create social order.

Through the small group, social psychology confronts sociology, spawning a distinctive microsociology, a *sociological miniaturism* (Stolte, Fine, and Cook 2001; Fine and Hallett 2003) in which larger social systems are organized through an array of tiny publics, together constituting intersecting *interaction orders*. A sociology based in a group culture that recognizes shared pasts and prospective futures provides the basis for unpacking the workings of those more macro concerns that have traditionally been treated as the essence of sociology.

We organize our lives by relying on known others to create meaning and then reacting to these proffered meanings. The small group is an interactional arena through which collaboration emerges (Bales 1970; Sawyer 2007). This process, grounded in the establishment of relationships, depends on local cultural understandings—what I have previously referred to as "idioculture" (Fine 1979b). More than situational—a term that suggests a transitory quality—idiocultures are microcultures that are developed from a group's opening moments and that depend on a shared recognition of solidified meaning and perspective, what I term a "local context."

By emphasizing the pivotal role of small groups in organizing social life I do not claim that all human possibility is contained within these nodes of order. Anonymous, imaginary, routinized, and bureaucratic relationships permit instrumental goals to be met. As students of public order have argued, impersonal activities have their own forms of organization (Lofland 1973; Goffman 1963; Edgerton 1979). Social control channels the options of large populations. As Max Weber recognized, structure can be the switchman of history, encouraging some social forms, preventing others. To understand how that switchman directs both large and small forces is to recognize Weber's concern with the waves of history and the patterns of verstehen embedded within tiny publics.

I began my academic career in the early 1970s as a student of group dynamics. Although I was unaware of it at the time, this moment represented the end of an era for this vigorous and consequential branch of social science research, which would be marginalized by the rise of other approaches that eclipsed the importance of group dynamics, notably the growth of cognitive science and organizational studies.

During the 1950s and 1960s, small-group research had had an emphatic impact on social psychology. The approach was so central that in December 1954 the *American Sociological Review,* the discipline's flagship journal, devoted an entire issue to small-group research. This was the golden age of the group, a lustrous moment enriched by research support from the Office of Naval Research, military men with a stake in the dynamics of submarine crews, the archetypal isolated small group. The fate of democracy was thought to hinge on the cohesion of these groups. State support eventually ebbed, as did the role of submarines in the arsenal of American defense. At the same moment that witnessed the growth of computers and the salience of *images* of computers, social psychologists increasingly explained behavior through cognition rather than co-presence, treating humans as "information processors," while embracing a metaphor of the brain as computer. Private thoughts edged out coordinated behaviors. By the mid-1970s, the question was asked: what happened to the small group? (Steiner 1974). Admittedly, small-group experimentation is more difficult to coordinate than tests of single subjects, but the continuing paucity of small-group experimentation is striking. Even *group process theory* focuses on individual status claims rather than on the dynamics of group interaction.

By the late 1970s, two streams of sociological research were swelling: ethnographic observation and the sociology of culture. Field methods were increasingly embraced as a legitimate social science methodology, and the small group—accessible, open, observable, and easily depicted— was its natural focus. The focus on small groups should have generated greater attention to groups in situ (as in classic social psychology, such as Sherif and Sherif 1964; Festinger, Riecken, and Schachter 1956; Roy 1959–1960). However, while some studies—such as those of gang activity (Horowitz 1983), street corner life (Anderson 1979), or workplace dynamics (Burawoy 1979)—examined groups, other ethnographic examinations focused on substantive problems, forgetting that they were observing a sociological "tribe" (Fine 2003a; Maffesoli 1996). Local knowledge was shunted aside in favor of a focus on institutions and communities. With the worthy goal of examining extended cases (Burawoy 1991, 2009), linking ethnography to macrosociological concerns, the interactional basis of sociality was downplayed. Groups were studied, but they were not theorized.

A second, expanding strand of scholarship focused on culture, a topic that had been primarily the domain of anthropologists prior to the 1970s. Sociologists, with their interest in structure and inter-action, treated culture as a form of collective action and brought inno-vative concepts to the exploration of meaning and performance (Becker 1974). While the examination of culture sometimes included local arenas, the cultural turn often led to analysis of how culture creates and is created by extended communities, ethnic groups, or nations. Culture shapes group identity and cohesion, and in turn groups develop their simultaneously unique and borrowed culture through the interaction of participants. Providing frameworks of interpretation and extending personal epistemic schemas into shared understandings, groups are where enactments happen. Thoughts and behaviors become "extra-personal," and the socialness of the world is created.

In the chapters that follow, I build on an approach to social psychol-ogy, sociological miniaturism, that John Stolte, Karen Cook, and I developed in an essay in the *Annual Review of Sociology* (Stolte, Fine, and Cook 2001). We argued there that the distinguishing contribution of sociological social psychology is its ability to link social processes and institutional forces. The outcomes that are often attributed to large-scale social forces originate within small-scale domains. In part this observation reflects a choice of level of analysis, but in fact the inter-section of agency and structure—the core topic of sociology—is to be found within these contexts of interaction. Observing such action realms, my colleagues and I have employed metaphors that suggest the pres-ence of institutional and societal forces as actors engage in exchange and negotiation.

As both Georg Simmel (1898, 1902, 1950) and Charles Horton Cooley (1902/1964) recognized, situations are sites where social scientists can uncover broader forces. Microinstitutions simulate the dynamics of larger social units in their causes, processes, and effects. This is not mimicry but rather the revelation within these spaces of the core features of social organization, features that are often attributed to larger institutions. Through an interaction order—*a field of performance*—phenomena that we attribute to external, trans-situational forces have effects. Here is a world that is locally ordered and socially situated (Goffman 1983, 2). This focus on microrealms suggests that rather than embracing the *social-psychological* (that is, basing sociological social psychology on reduc-tionist psychological principles), sociologists must focus on the *micro-sociological.* How do situations and their actors create structures of interpretation and coordination? Acknowledging forces that include the epistemic, the political, and the personal, we examine not the mind in skull but the mind in place that coordinates with other minds (Zerubavel 1997; DiMaggio 1997).

The miniaturist approach posits three fundamental claims about social reality: transcendence, representation, and generalizability. First, social reality is *transcendent* in that social processes operate on multiple levels. Processes such as justice, inequality, or communion that apply to one level of analysis (for example, the interpersonal) can also be observed on other levels (for example, the institutional) but within different structural contexts.

Second, this approach treats the behavior of individuals as *representative* of social order in larger entities. The individual can stand for the group and, more important, *is taken as* standing for that group by individuals and institutions that thus recognize and respond to the individual actions of an actor as those of a *collective* actor. So, for example, the behavior of clerks can—and often does—reflect on the store or government that employs them. While experiencing bureaucracies through the individual actions of clerks, clients consider these clerks to be representations of the bureaucracy or sometimes even reflections of the states or institutions in which the bureaucracy is embedded. Thus, a citizen seeking to renew his driver's license decides—based on cultural representations and on the perceived typicality of the interaction—whether the clerk behind the desk represents herself, the Bureau of Motor Vehicles, or the entire state government. The behavioral options and motivations of individual actors have recognizable parallels in attributions of behavior to groups, organizations, and other collective units. Although individuals need not always represent organizations or be taken as such, this behavioral synecdoche is routine, comfortable, and grounded in commonsense assumptions.

The third component of the miniaturist approach is the *generalizability* of social processes. The experiment that does not apply to phenomena beyond the laboratory is of marginal value for generating knowledge; this claim, a traditional feature of concluding remarks, is critical for justifying both laboratory experiments and ethnographic inquiries. Although most ethnographic studies depict action within an idiosyncratic place, we assume that the local observations transcend the uniqueness of the setting. Data from one case stand for others. The horizontal comparison of scenes, coupled with the ability to see processes operating on vertical levels, links local action to societal effects. In this way, the miniaturist approach uses transcendence, representation, and generalizability to reveal how local action becomes linked to social order.

In any sociological treatment of the local, ethnographers have an advantage: they espy interaction scenes and understand them microscopically. Even though a focus on the local is not tied to any one methodological tradition it is inherent to ethnography, which describes how group life operates as an arena of action. Ethnography reveals social mechanisms, particularly when ethnographers focus on how participants respond to group contexts in shaping organization. However, it is not ethnography as such that provides this opening but rather a form of ethnography that privileges continuing social relations. This form of ethnography treats groups as ongoing and self-referential domains. The "corner"—*Street Corner Society* (Whyte 1943), *Tally's Corner* (Liebow 1967), *A Place on the Corner* (Anderson 1979), or *Sidewalk* (Duneier 1999)—serves as such a domain for sociologists, as the tribe serves for anthropologists. The corner is the ideal imagined place, and those who hang there are the model tight-knit imagined group. The ethnographer burrows into the group space, observing it until he or she can present the contours of corner culture, and then addresses how this culture reveals trans-situational processes (Glaser and Strauss 1967). No methodology is privileged, but in-depth ethnographies have advantages for exploring culture *as group practice*. In contrast to scattershot ethnographies, observations of public behavior, surveys of attitudes, or institutional censuses, watching culture over time provides unique insight.

In this book, I draw upon ethnographic material as appropriate, largely from my own extensive research, to argue that practices on the local group level build a meso-level perspective based on self-referential action contexts—places in which actions gain meaning for the participants who share the space (Fine 2003b). Over the past thirty-five years, I have conducted a series of ethnographic projects—nine major studies and two smaller investigations. Each of these projects had its own genesis and set of analytic concerns, yet all have been focused on the intersection of culture and group interaction in order to help build a theory of group interaction orders, idiocultures, and tiny publics. Together these projects justify a sociology grounded in microcultures and action contexts.

Since this book draws upon the analysis of these data sets, here I will briefly describe the locales and the theoretical objectives of my field studies. In doing so, I prefigure the ideas on which I elaborate in the rest of the book. These précis present a concise introduction to my scholarly intentions, as carried out in my previous work.

My first ethnographic research project was a three-year observation of Little League baseball teams (Fine 1987b). I stress that the project examined Little League *teams*, not Little League *baseball*, because my focus was on the team as a site of cultural creation (Fine 1979b). The project flowed from an interest in small-group dynamics in the laboratory. My graduate training in the Department of Psychology and Social Relations at Harvard was guided by Robert Freed Bales and Stephen Cohen (1979) and their colleagues, who were then extending interaction process analysis into a more sophisticated model of group dynamics: the systematic multi-level observation of groups (SYMLOG). They described group interaction and social meaning by means of a three-dimensional space (Osgood, Suci, and Tannenbaum 1957; Heise 1979). I chose to apply this small-group model to the analysis of culture, finding in each group a local set of meanings and traditions. Within this model, group action needed to be understood as resulting from the shared cultures that developed over time. Each team created its own customs, expectations, and proprieties, and a set of shared references had built continuing and meaningful interaction. In this project, I referred to this group culture as an "idioculture," a concept that I have extended and sharpened over three decades (and discuss more fully in chapter 2). I proposed that "idioculture consists of a system of knowledge, beliefs, behaviors, and customs shared by members of an interacting group to which members can refer and that serves as the basis of further interaction" (Fine 1987b, 125). While I could have gathered data from numerous domains to demonstrate that groups establish and apply local cultures, I focused on ten baseball teams in five leagues, generalizing through the observation of similar groups. The original impetus was not to describe life on preadolescent fields of dreams but to examine how culture is created and embedded in small groups.

Despite my theoretical goals, the reality that I was examining preadolescent males and sporting behavior was central to the substantive analysis. A focus on "boy culture" was a wedge to demonstrate that a subculture is constituted by a network of small groups, a concern to which I return in chapter 8 when I consider extensions of group culture. The content of preadolescent male culture revealed a lively discourse on sex, aggression, competition, and morality. (A similar gendered scene has been evident in several of my projects.) Further, in examining not only preadolescent boys but youth baseball I was led to an analysis of the structure of preteen leisure to explore how adults organize the leisure activities of children (Adler and Adler 1998). Adult authorities impose a moral order to which groups of children respond emotionally, strategically, and sometimes, employing forms of subaltern resistance, subversively.

The topic of my second ethnographic foray stemmed from the limitations of my first project. Little League baseball teams demonstrate the existence of robust group cultures, but the temporal boundary and organizational structure of these cultures limit them as examples of the lasting and consequential influence of an idioculture. Little League teams are thin and partial cultures: they typically meet three times a week for a few hours during the spring. These groups, significant as they were to some boys, do not have the impact of other cultural domains, especially classrooms, families, and informal friendship groups. Each team establishes traditions and shared narratives, but in a thin and partial culture these are often newly established from year to year. I required a site with a more engrossing culture in order to examine the deep effects of groups on participants. I found such a niche in the world of fantasy role-playing gamers (Fine 1983). These groups consisted of adolescents (again, mostly males) who played games such as Dungeons and Dragons—a manufactured subculture (Dayan 1986)—which in those days before ready access to personal computers was played around a table. I spent approximately eighteen months with these gaming groups, observing a public club that met in the community room of a local police station and two groups of gamers who met in private homes.

These gamers expressly desired to create imaginary "worlds" or "universes." Put another way, their explicit concern was culture building; perhaps they would not have phrased it in this way, but the elaboration of the cultures of their imaginary worlds was central to their enjoyment of each other and of the collective experience. This was an idioculture, but a deep and self-conscious one that would be returned to over and over and that constituted the basis of an ongoing local sociology. Cultures need not be evanescent or peripheral but can be organizing principles of social life.

Through these gamers, I explored how the production of novel and innovative cultures is linked to extant, public cultures, given the belief that, as fantasy, any and all cultural themes are possible. Like dreams, fantasy builds on reality (Caughey 1984; Fine and Leighton 1993; Schutz 1945): it is not *just* made up. In contrast to the belief that fantasy can be anything, fantasies are socially embedded, both within the group and imported from other meaning systems. As with preadolescent sports teams, culture emerges through the small group. The young men playing Dungeons and Dragons formed tight and stable groups, and their continued interaction contributed to their robust culture. They engaged in an ongoing performance that extended their personal fantasies, creating a shared narrative that served as an alternative reality within the gaming context. Throughout the game the responses of participants mattered to all the others and, as a result, permitted the elaboration of their fantasy and an investment in its continuation. While a fantasy-gaming subculture exists—just as a preadolescent culture exists—this more extensive culture depends on allegiances within small groups, since members belong to groups simultaneously and sequentially.

Fantasy-gamers exemplify Erving Goffman's (1974) theory of frame analysis: they have to determine the register (or code) of their talk as they simulate a society with a transformed set of social relations (Hoffman 2006). In this world, imaginary selves act, but it is both a gaming world, in which players act within a system of contained rules, and a public culture, which is shaped by the gender, age, and backgrounds of participants. Sometimes participants spoke as actors, in the voice of their characters, treating the scenario within the game as their primary reality; other times they spoke as gamers, treating the game and its rules as their primary focus; and at still other times they spoke as natural persons, referring to concerns outside of the game. The challenge for participants was knowing in what normative context the interaction was being formulated—a problem that, as Goffman noted, applies to joking, play, deception, and other ambiguous domains within interaction orders. What seemed like an odd shard of interaction stood for domains in which contrasting interpretive frames abut each other.

My third and fourth projects, moving toward the analysis of idiocultures within important institutional fields, dealt with culinary training and restaurant work. This prior work is connected to chapter 3, where I examine how the concerns of an organizational analysis of the world are necessarily linked to the meanings and interactions within groups. In my first two research projects, I had neglected the power of organization, which is central to how society is structured. Little League teams and fantasy-gaming groups, while organized, float in interactional space. Organizational concerns were not entirely absent (a national Little League organization exists, and corporations, such as Hasbro, manufacture fantasy games), but organizational presence was not an insistent reality for participants. I wanted to extend my analysis of idiocultures by examining it in the context of organizations where coordination between expressive and instrumental results was crucial and by using a neo-institutional framework to see the possibility of understanding how the macrostructures of institutions provide for the foundations of a microstructure. How do small cultures fit into institutional arrangements?

For the first of these paired research projects, I observed cohorts of students training to become cooks at two hotel and restaurant cooking programs at what were then called technical vocational institutes (Fine 1985) but are now labeled, following institutional impression management, technical colleges. The program at one school lasted a year; the second lasted two years. An average of fifteen students were enrolled in each class. Following this project, I conducted ethnographic research at four restaurants for a month each (Fine 1996). Each site was constituted by a small group, once again predominantly male. Participants in these small groups addressed the challenges of producing aesthetic objects and the organizational constraints on that production while working within an economic order in which a restaurant's survival depended on ingredient prices, labor costs, and customer preferences. Beyond the obdurate organizational pressures, there were the pressures of aesthetics.

Given the limitations of language for discussing taste and smell, cooks and cooking students had to develop strategies by which they could convey shared assessments of dishes and recipes. Such aesthetic judgment is central to occupational engagement in many domains, and it depends on small-group dynamics. The interaction order of restaurants is firmly based in issues that transcend any single small organization.

The fifth project, a four-year study of mushroom collectors and the organizations to which they belong (Fine 1998), expanded on issues of aesthetic discourse but linked this subject to an important domain of civil society: the proper treatment of the environment. Here leisure was connected to ideology (a concern I address in chapter 5). I observed amateur and professional mycologists in order to investigate how groups conceptualize environmental ethics in practice, bringing cultural templates to an ideological understanding of nature. By focusing on the Minnesota Mycological Society, an organization with two dozen core members, I once again chose a small group as my primary research site. The repeated interaction of individuals, their shared talk, and their behavioral routines provided an opening to understand how environmental beliefs grow out of the ongoing interaction of these tiny publics. These groups constitute themselves as moral communities, and through their acts and their talk they develop a set of "ought" rules that guide their actions.

Based on a cultural template, the idea of nature—what I termed "naturework"—refers to how individuals define the meanings of the environment in light of cultural images. Naturework is a rhetorical resource through which people individually and collectively construct their relationship to the environment (Fine 1998, 2). These rhetorical constructions generate local norms (which I address in chapter 4). The key point is that nature can never be separate from culture; the two concepts are intertwined in multiple ways, and that reality shapes expectations within the community. First, in talking about nature—in this case, mushrooms—groups build on cultural dimensions (good, bad, pretty, ugly, male, female) as well as on elaborated cultural metaphors. They view the wild through a cultural lens. Second, entering the woods is a social occasion. Even when people traverse the wilds alone, they return with stories, and so nature becomes a platform for communal performance. Finally, nature is experienced through organizations that enable people to acquire resources for participating in the wild. These organizations permit the establishment of a domain of trust and secrecy in a world in which mushrooms are alternately treated as rare, desired objects and as dangerous, arcane ones.

Much ethnographic research depends on attention to talk, frequently more so than observations of behavior. Even though actions can be dramatic and compelling, talk can be transferred directly and effort-lessly from the scene to the page, and talk typically requires less trans-lation on the part of the researcher. I was interested in how groups conceptualize discourse as a central part of their idioculture. For my next project, I explored the local construction of talk. I searched for a group that talked about talk as a central feature of its identity. After find-ing such a scene in high school debate teams, I spent a year examining two American high school debate squads, each with about fifteen ado-lescent participants (Fine 2001). I attended classes with these teenagers and then shadowed them at local and national tournaments.

This project engaged what was then termed "the narrative turn" in social theory. How do people acquire communicative skills so that others in their scene can understand and be persuaded, given the ambi-guity of language and the uncertainty of narrative consensus? This ques-tion is particularly compelling when the talk of a group constituted as a tiny public is political (a topic to which I return in chapter 7). While as a matter of course these teenagers had to argue all sides of a topic, they also came to terms with the ways in which the topic was linked to their own beliefs, shaped by the perspectives of their teammates. Social prob-lems discourse—here and in other domains—is based on a model in which argumentation is treated as a game (Fine 2001). While debate is a dramatic example of this process, the same dynamic is evident in poli-tics, in which tiny publics engage in lively discourse, however seriously they take it (Eliasoph 1998; Walsh 2003). The particular arguments and forms of talk are constructed in the context of local activity. The judg-ment of talk is not imposed from outside but emerges from within the community, even while drawing on standards and understandings from other, more powerful institutional domains.

My seventh study examined the development of a market for self-taught art (Fine 2004). This project returned to my interest in how groups construct aesthetic value and the boundaries of this construction. Aesthetic ideology is often created in a close-knit network of relations. Self-taught art is linked to the development of norms about the value of authenticity, a value that is mirrored in other domains of contemporary society, including movements for personal growth and selfhood. In this small art world, I discovered that participants proclaimed an inverse relationship between credentials and status: value was constituted through the characteristics and identity of the creators. The embrace of this belief served as a marker of communal belonging and a reflection of socialization to the community.

This five-year study differed from previous research projects in that I observed, not a routinely interacting small group, but a dense network. Although groups existed, such as a folk art study group in Atlanta and the national Folk Art Society of America, most network venues were shows, museum openings, or auctions where attendance was open to all. These were wispy communities (as I outline in chapter 6). The arenas of local action were powerful during their activation, but they would vanish when participants departed. In contrast to other studies, this art world did not require a stable set of relations but only a shared set of values.

My next research project explored the boundaries of science within a government bureaucracy. I had moved from the voluntary and imaginary idiocultures of free-form fantasy-gaming groups to a set of local cultures linked to institutional bureaucracy, returning to some of the issues I explore further in chapter 3 (on the power of constraint and external pressures). For eighteen months, I observed operational meteorologists at three local National Weather Service offices, each of which had approximately two dozen workers (Fine 2007). In addition, I spent two weeks at the Storm Prediction Center in Norman, Oklahoma, an office of similar size that generates severe thunderstorm and tornado watches for the United States.

Weather forecasters have the collective responsibility and the authority to predict the future. Twice a day they are required to produce a forecast for the next seven days. These are occupationally based claims that the public, government, and business use to structure their activities. Further, forecasters must warn about the onset of severe weather. How are these consequential decisions made? What are the practical limits of predicting from models and from data, and how are the models and the data integrated?

The National Weather Service is a large government bureaucracy, a key reality for the local cultures created in the small, semi-autonomous offices. Although autonomy must be located in the hands of the applied scientist, personal and team judgments must also be integrated into an organization that requires both routine and immediate answers within a set of government procedures. Interpersonal authority is asserted, but such authority is always understood in light of the needs of the bureaucracy and its consequential publics.

The teamwork embedded in this bureaucracy is crucial. Forecasters do not themselves gather data, produce hypotheses, or test alternative claims. Their task is to transform the information embedded in technological inscriptions and interpret it, with the advice and oversight of others who share their space. (The National Weather Service has three daily shifts.) Even though different shifts with different personnel provide the forecasts, the office management must ensure that they are seen as collective products, not personal ones. In other words, forecasters must make their forecasts in light of what others believe. Further, each office must coordinate its forecasts with those of the offices that surround them geographically. As I discuss in chapter 8, the creations of groups that are integrated in networks are not theirs alone but are extended to publics—shared with those who are part of their institutional world.

My current ethnographic enterprise is a study of the multiple worlds of chess. I returned to my early interest in games, but with the intention of examining a complex leisure world, a layered world of organizations, networks, and casual affiliations. Over time my understanding of how local groups fit into larger communities became more nuanced, as described in chapter 8, where I examine the dynamics of local contexts and their extensions. The complexity of chess in its multiple locations makes this a particularly compelling world for field observations.

To examine chess in the United States I witnessed numerous sites of activity. These included two local clubs for adult chess players, a high school team, a club for skilled adolescents taught by a grandmaster, a collegiate team, a public park, and several meetings of a scholastic chess team at an elementary school. I supplemented these group observations with interviews and attendance at chess tournaments throughout the United States; attending some that were designed primarily for adults and some that focused on children and adolescents reconnected me with the issue of wispy communities (chapter 6).

My interest in this work is in seeing how status systems develop and how chess players situate themselves by means of a communal history (a long and complex one). Because of the numerical ratings assigned to players, according to their outcomes, chess is an activity in which status systems are explicit and public. To become a serious chess player requires an awareness of the history of the game, and chess training often entails reviewing or replaying the "classic" games of respected chess players and knowing established game "openings." Chess players situate themselves within the styles of play that have been developed over centuries, enshrining a group history. To enter the subculture of chess requires a commitment to the game and affiliation with the community. Allegiance to a shared history transforms a person who plays chess into a chess player.

Two additional studies—each less intensive than the projects described here—complete my eleven ethnographic projects. For several years I observed a group of engaged activists, volunteers for one of America's political parties, on a local, neighborhood level—a case of a tiny public (as discussed in chapter 7). These were men and women who performed basic organizational ("grunt") work such as stuffing envelopes, making phone calls, distributing leaflets, and putting up yard signs. I was interested in the salience of an ideological rhetoric, linked to the party's policy prescriptions. To what extent did the group provide a basis for public engagement? Contrary to those who suggest that activists are highly ideological, I discovered that political rhetoric was only evident on certain ritual occasions, such as at party conventions. And yet the political commitments of participants in this group did matter on those occasions when they were activated. They were political at hot moments but not in their routine interaction (Eliasoph 1998). In other words, during mundane activities a partisan belief structure was latent, and ideology held sway when politics was manifest. Yet, even if not political all the time, the group provided an entry point into a public sphere. Although volunteers had joined the party organization because of their preferred policy preferences—coupled with personal recruitment (Snow, Zurcher, and Ekland-Olsen 1980)—interpersonal affection proved more crucial in generating commitment on everyday occasions.

The final project, a brief one, involved observation of a nascent social movement made up of individuals who themselves had been accused of child abuse or neglect or who had a spouse who had been so accused, most typically by state agencies. This group, Victims of Child Abuse Laws (VOCAL), had the challenge of maintaining and defending its boundaries in the face of potential claims that the group (or some of its members) was in fact a perpetrator of such abuse. Members were seen as morally suspect by those outside the group, and even by some within. How could the organization maintain its moral legitimacy in the face of the belief that the charges made by authorities might be legitimate? What norms did they need to enforce? How and when? Should they exclude potential members who proclaimed their innocence, despite official charges or verdicts? In this case, the theoretical issue arose from the effects of the opinion of external communities on the normative structure of the movement.

Taken together, these eleven projects provide a platform from which to examine how small groups shape and are shaped by local cultures and to explore the importance of other groups and larger structures. In each project, I examined the impact of an idioculture on lived experience and local organization. To generate commitment, each group required a shared history that demonstrated that the participants *belonged* together. Despite their distinct substantive concerns, all of my studies of these groups have contributed to a theory of group cultures, local contexts, and tiny publics.

The book is divided into nine chapters, each addressing a set of themes by which a group-based analysis of the influence of local contexts explains the dynamics of an interaction order. Although they incorporate new material, these chapters draw upon writings I have published over three decades. I have reshaped, reconsidered, and reordered these writings. None of the chapters have been published in their current form, but some chapters are closer to the published texts from which they draw. I hope that by being brought together here in this way, my writings over the last thirty years justify the claim that local sociology creates a useful sociological perspective.

In chapter 1, I present an overview of the role of groups, describing how groups structure social life. Groups provide the basis for a meso-level analysis, connecting the microanalysis of persons and the macro-analysis of structures through their roles as structures of control, change agents, forms of representations, and sources of resource allocation. A theory of local contexts is necessary as a basis for understanding social order. Chapter 2 presents the theory of small-group culture I have developed over three decades: the theory of idiocultures, those microcultures that recognize their shared pasts and provide a basis for an imagined future. Chapter 3 draws out the relationship between macroanalysis and microanalysis. Three decades ago, Randall Collins (1981) proposed that macrosociology has microfoundations. True enough. However, micro-sociology equally requires a set of macrofoundations. The impact of exteriority and constraint makes behavior more than evanescent but part of a sedimented social order.

The next two chapters build on the small-group model by focusing on the particular challenges of microcultures and meso-analysis, addressing how a small-group approach incorporates norms and ideology into local culture. In chapter 4, I examine how a theory of group culture treats norms as local expectations that are tied to a shared history. In this model, norms are framed, negotiated, and narrated within interacting communities. Norms create culture just as they reflect it. Even though norms are sometimes seen as residing in our minds, they are equally at home onstage—given reality through performances. In chapter 5, Kent Sandstrom and I develop a theory of ideology as enactment, tied to interactional contexts. Although ideological formations have cognitive components, it is too limiting to suggest that ideology is only cognitive. Ideology is emotional and behavioral as well, and local contexts serve as the anchor for action.

The sixth chapter, developed from a collaboration with Lisa-Jo van den Scott, examines "wispy communities"—communities that exist for a brief period of time for events or gatherings. These communities are larger than the small groups discussed earlier in the volume, but they share a desire to create a local culture and shared past through the inten-sity of co-presence. Borrowing Benedict Anderson's (1991) construct, I argue that such "imagined communities" need not be political entities but can be cultural scenes that are based on focused gatherings. Occasions such as a chess tournament, a mushroom foray, an art fair, a political convention, or the Burning Man Festival are fleeting gatherings in which strong cultures emerge and dissipate. In some ways the flourishing of such gatherings provides an answer to scholars like Robert Putnam who worry about the decline of groups producing a society that lacks cohesion.

Chapter 7, based on a collaboration with Brooke Harrington, follows up on my attempts to connect group culture and shared history with larger social segments by developing the idea of tiny publics as a means of organizing civil society. In this chapter, I situate the analysis of groups and idiocultures in the light of political engagement. Civil society and the public sphere depend for their tensile strength on group interaction, which creates tiny publics, and tiny publics provide the platform for collective action. In chapter 8, the conclusion of my attempt to integrate a group theory with societal concerns, I describe how group cultures radiate outward. In this analysis, originally based on collaboration with Sherryl Kleinman, I present a perspective on how subcultures (cultural networks) are constituted by linked small groups. Subcultures require both the strong ties of group dynamics and the weak acquaintanceship connections by which information is diffused widely. In this sense, the book travels from a focus on small-group idiocultures to an examination of the wider social scenes that are more traditionally sociological topics.

A summary analysis of tiny publics and small-group culture is found in the final chapter, where I argue for a distinctive approach to sociological miniaturism. Here I lay out the basis of a *local sociology*, drawing on ideas developed in previous chapters and emphasizing the importance of context within an interactional arena as a means by which social organization is established in both cultural and political realms. Despite its reliance on Erving Goffman's theories, such a meso-level approach to culture and context is ultimately most crucial, not as a metaphor of improvisation to describe situations, but as a group-based theory of action in ongoing local worlds.

No project develops in isolation. As these ideas have germinated over nearly four decades, I have relied on the advice of many exceptional colleagues. I dedicate this book to Robert Freed Bales, my dissertation adviser, for inspiring me with his passion for small groups and his recognition of their importance and for his grace and kindness. I also thank Albert Pepitone, Jane Piliavin, Gregory Stone, David Karp, Amy Binder, George Psathas, Thomas Pettigrew, Harold Finestone, Randy Stoecker, Barry Schwartz, Linda Grant, Allan Teger, Thomas Hood, Gerald Suttles, Kim Elsbach, Jennifer Hunt, Dan Ryan, Robert Sutton, Leigh Thompson, Lori Holyfield, Ruth Horowitz, Tim Hallett, Michaela DeSoucey, Jessica Thurk, Michael Farrell, Lynn Smith-Lovin, Cheris Chan, Corey Fields, Diane Vaughan, Bin Xu, Nancy Whittier, and James Balkwell for discussion, criticism, and advice. In particular I give grateful thanks to my treasured writing partners, Sherryl Kleinman, Lisa-Jo van den Scott, Kent Sandstrom, and Brooke Harrington. Some of the material in this book derives from texts that each of them co-authored, although perhaps with my revisions some of the original arguments are less recognizable. Each of these mentors, friends, and colleagues belong to small groups that have provided me with intellectual and social sustenance. I also acknowledge my profound debt to four exceptional small groups: the Swedish Collegium for Advanced Studies in the Social Sciences, the Russell Sage Foundation, the Rockefeller Foundation's Bellagio Center, and the Center for Advanced Study in the Behavioral Sciences.

No small group is more important than one's family. I thank my sons Todd and Peter and wife Susan for support in our tiny public.

# Chapter 1

## The Power of Groups

It is the doubtful advantage of all incipient sciences that they must temporarily furnish refuge for all sorts of vagrant problems. The boundaries of new sciences are necessarily indefinite and indefensible. They are thus open to all the homeless. They therefore gather by degrees a miscellaneous content which can not be managed. Then the process of limitation begins. . . . If, therefore, sociology is to have a particular and independent significance its problems must consequently concern, not the contents of social life, but its form—the form which brings it to pass that all those contents which are treated by the special sciences are "societary." . . . The subject-matter of sociology is, therefore, the forms or ways in which human beings exist beside, for, and with each other. . . . I see society . . . wherever a number of human beings come into reciprocity and form a transient or permanent unity.

—Georg Simmel, "The Persistence of Social Groups" (1898, 662–64)

W E RESIDE in a universe of groups, a world of tiny publics. Through the associations we share with others—close and knotted ties—we find affiliation that allows us to conclude that others care about what we do. Small groups provide spaces where sociality operates, and sociality generates the building blocks of society. The great theorist of sociality Georg Simmel recognized that it is through social forms that personal connections emerge. It is perhaps not surprising that the best-selling work of sociology—a true best-seller and cultural icon—was David Riesman's *The Lonely Crowd* (Riesman, Glazer, and Denney 1950); this treatise, which describes how groups provide a bulwark against the ache of alienation, was the starting point for Riesman's subsequent explorations of sociability (Riesman, Potter, and Watson 1960). Riesman belonged to a genealogy of theorists from Alexis de Tocqueville (1835/1966) to Edward Banfield (1958) to Robert Putnam (2000) who believed that involvement in groups or associations generates social progress and a sense of community (Lichterman 2005; McPherson, Smith-Lovin, and Brashears 2006). In this view, groups shape individual choices by encouraging people to choose what their comrades are choosing, creating the conditions for conformity (Christakis and Fowler 2009). Extending Goffman's (1967, 3) phrase, we must examine a world not of persons and their groups but of groups and their persons.

Despite the importance of groups in establishing commitment, over time the analysis of small groups has declined within both sociology and psychology (Steiner 1974; Collins 1999), leaving a gap between individuals and collectives. This is regrettable in that the group is an arena through which generic interactional processes operate. It is on the level of the small group that *things happen*. Society should be conceptualized as an ecology of groups. Groups, overlapping like fish scales, sharing traditions and members, have distinctive ways of being. Belonging to a group provokes a communal identity, and often those identities powerfully shape a sense of self. In addition, groups make organizational life possible. Organizations survive and thrive not just because of the formal arrangement of personnel but because of the interaction among them: they are embodied and, as a result, become powerful action realms (Hallett and Ventresca 2006). From this perspective, the strength of both selves and organizations depends on the interaction order generated through the organizing properties of small groups.

Sociologists tout that their animating question is the one that was posed by the English philosopher and political theorist Thomas Hobbes some 350 years ago: How is social order possible? How does coordination among individual actors operating from personal interest come about? The answer to Hobbes's question depends on overcoming the chill reality that each individual has interests and goals and will act strategically to achieve them. It is only through enforced constraint or voluntary restraint that society is possible for Hobbes. Hobbes imagined a cold world of amoral egotists whose conflicting interests inevitably produce conflict. This heart-of-darkness imagery depicts a society lacking centralized control, mired in violence and discord. Hobbes suggested that humans in a state of nature, lacking systems of constraint, are destined to live lives that are "solitary, poor, nasty, brutish, and short (Hobbes 1886, 64)." Sociology noir. Individuals must relinquish their rights to a leader—the "Leviathan," he termed this powerful figure—who, representing them all, would tame their selfishness, preventing contentious behaviors, establishing security, and creating (docile) citizens from fighters.

We need not share Hobbes's pessimism. A rosier view is possible. The question is not why does so much social control exist, but why is so little control necessary? Social mechanisms permit humans to collaborate to achieve common interests. Even if people do not always maximize their desires, they receive sufficient benefits to be satisfied. (As economists suggest, they "satisfice" their interests; Simon 1956.) This perspective is nicely captured by the Yale law professor Robert Ellickson, who demonstrates in his book *Order Without Law* (1991) that farmers and ranchers can resolve conflicts without recourse to formal adjudication through mutual adjustments when such negotiation is supported by community expectations. Microcultures make social control less onerous, smoothing the rough edges of dispute.

My animating assumption is that society consists of a network of group cultures—an approach that stands apart from treating society as being fully explicable through selves, situations, or structures. While much has been made of networks as a world of weak ties, it is through network clumps—routinized ties imbued with emotional energy (Collins 2004)—that affiliation produces commitment and, through commitment, action. Groups and networks together—strong ties as well as weak ones—help explain how social order is possible even in the absence of powerful and intrusive external constraints. The small group provides internal and external mechanisms that prevent the need for routine physical, economic, and psychological coercion. Such a perspective treats the chalice of authority as half empty rather than half full. The small group is a mediating form, moderating individual interests in the face of group goals and conflicting desires.

## The Small Group

Although never as prominent a construct as the individual or the society, the small group has been the topic of theory and research for well over a century. Small groups are cognitive, affective, and behavioral domains. By "small group" I refer to aggregations of persons who recognize that they constitute a meaningful social unit, interact on that basis, and are committed to that social unit. These actors may know each other as discrete persons or through their social roles. Interaction may be long-lasting or flickering and transient, and it can be primarily face to face or evident through other modalities, including cyber-communication. Whatever the case, participants recognize that they have interests in common and share a history.

Although size helps define a *small* group, the term refers to a set of persons who recognize each other as belonging to an interdependent community. Robert Freed Bales (1950, 33) defined a small group as "any number of persons engaged in interaction with each other in a single face-to-face[1] meeting or series of meetings, in which each member receives some impression or perception of each other member distinct enough so that he [or she] can, either at the time or in later questioning, give some reaction to each of the others as an individual person." Paul Hare (1976, 4–5; see also Sherif 1954) suggests that the recognition of similar goals, behavioral expectations or norms, interaction rituals, differentiated roles, and networks of attraction distinguishes a group from a population of individuals. A group requires an interaction scene, an identification of the unit as meaningful, and a differentiation of participants into positions.

Special note should be taken of the dyad, a distinctive form of the group. The dyad has many qualities of the small group (Oring 1984). It is an interaction system and, as couples recognize, can generate a robust and powerful culture that enforces social control and mutual dependency. The partners are both deeply knowledgeable and concerned about each other's responses; lacking awareness and joint commitment, the dyad is subject to dissolution. As a consequence, dyads are structurally less stable than larger groups, as either participant has the power—and the moral authority—to terminate the relationship (Emerson 1962; Cook and Emerson 1978). Unlike other groups, the dyadic relationship requires mutual co-presence, even if that presence is embedded in telephonic communication or in cyberspace (Zhao 2003). A dyadic culture is fully constituted by the participants, rather than being shaped by a larger group whose members do not all have to be present for the group to exist (Gibson 2000). Although I treat dyads as a group form, Georg Simmel (1902) is persuasive that dyads have special properties and interaction systems that are fundamentally altered with the addition of a third participant. Further additions complicate group structure and politics but do not fundamentally change how a group is organized.

Similar to dyads is what might be labeled "role relations." These ties are found within focused gatherings and can be conceptualized as temporary groups. They derive not from a commitment to continuity but rather from a desire to achieve a goal. Of course, some relations are disrupted because participants may have either goals that do not overlap or diverse beliefs about how goals should be achieved. Conflict is always potential in any interaction scene, and inequalities of resources are also possible. Still, orderly social life depends on these relations. When I interact with a cashier, we have momentarily formed a dyad with some of the features of group life: a small number of participants, an interactional focus, the hope for goal coordination, and social differentiation (Tolich 1993). What is lacking in transient social relations is a group history, a prospective future, and a cementing culture. Still, role relations, anonymous as they might be at first, have the structural *potential* to create collective history. Clerks and customers could establish continuing interaction. The reality that social relations do not always or routinely generate a past, future, and significant present reminds us that behavioral ties in themselves may not be sufficient for cultural traction. Yet, even without a *specific, embedded* history, these relations have an *implicit, generalized* history that derives from the customer's previous experience with cashiers and the cashier's experience with customers. They need not create a culture because they can borrow one. These relations may be biographically empty, but the stability of role relations replaces the absence of personal knowledge. Recurring role enactments have features of an attenuated group.

## Groups and Their Kin

To appreciate the special features of a group as a social form, I contrast it with other social forms: the monad, the situation, the association, the network, and the mass. Each form reflects limiting features of the small group and so sheds light on the groupy-qualities of the group.

*The Monad:* Perhaps it is odd to conceive of a monad—a self—as a form of social relationship (for a critique of this proposition, see Garfinkel 2006, 193–95), and even stranger perhaps to think of a self as a setting for "interaction." Yet, we perform socially meaningful behavior when we are *alone.* George Herbert Mead (1934, 42–43) recognized that not only do we act when by ourselves, but we engage in "internal conversations" in which we can play several roles. In Mead's terminology, this conversation is between the "I" and the "me": the "personal self" and the "social self." We perform for ourselves and then evaluate our performance. Mead realized that we are an audience for ourselves, and sometimes our own worst critics. In the words of Lonnie Athens (2005), the self is a soliloquy, supported by a chorus of imaginary others. When self-conscious, we reflect on our own actions and may attempt to escape our self as we perceive it (Baumeister 1991). We contain within us a chorus of voices, a multiplicity of perspectives. Even though much of our behavior is performed outside of the presence of others, we try to align it with social standards, bolstering our identity. Norms and expectations influence what we judge as proper, even when others are physically absent but symbolically present. The external, judgmental world affects us because of the weight that we give it. To the extent that we know our intentions, we judge not just action but motivation.

*The Situation:* To escape the reductionist focus on the individual, theorists such as Erving Goffman and Randall Collins emphasized the centrality of situations as organizing features of social life—what Goffman (1967, 3) memorably spoke of as "moments and their men," not men and their moments. However, situations are not sufficient. Without a history, that is, a set of common references that structure interaction, situations are empty vessels. Situations are arenas in which actors are known to each other through their relations and their roles. These established relations permit a situation to become a local context: a community that recurs. Although structure can emerge from activity (Sawyer 2005, 198), a guiding set of expectations must be present. Moments and men are insufficient without shared pasts.

*The Association:* As used here, an association is a group writ large.[2] It is a set of connections that is constituted through the recognition of common interest and of coordination that cements individuals who need not be personally connected. Associations are too expansive to depend on informal, emergent organization alone. Associational life often depends on strangers congregating, suggesting that it is the perception of collective interests that motivates cohesion rather than the satisfactions from interaction itself. The reality that in associations individuals do not—and are not expected to—know all other participants suggests that the connection to the organization, rather than to particular others, is crucial—vertical coordination, not horizontal. Personal attachments exist, but only because of interactional spaces and constraints within the association. Relations in an association are grounded in instrumental demands rather than in interpersonal satisfactions. Much has been said by those who see themselves treading the Tocqueville path, venerating the importance of associations for social stability (Warren 2001; Sandel 1996; Bellah et al. 1991), but often these theorists neglect the number of participants in the form of belonging. This approach, discussed in chapter 7, conflates expansive, national associations with de Tocqueville's "minute associations," tiny publics that have effects through shared histories (Lichterman 2005).

*The Network:* Over the past three decades, networks have come to be seen as crucial forms of social organization, partially as a result of the recognition that spatial propinquity has declined as the central form of community. Social ties constitute opportunities for influence. However, differentiating networks from groups is not easy and not always desirable. Networks consist of clumps of relations, but they also consist of connections between clumps that bridge structural holes (Burt 1992). Thus, networks depend on separation, rather than being fields of interaction. In other words, networks consist of linkages among recognizable *groups* of actors who know each other and have a shared past and a prospective future (Fine and Kleinman 1983; Katovich and Couch 1992), but these linkages do not constitute a single realm of action. Through external linkages of participants—tendrils to other action scenes—a set of groups constitutes a social system. Networks gain power through the clumps of strong ties linked by weaker ties, not through weak ties alone.

*The Mass:* Like networks, masses (or crowds or publics) comprise small groups (Aveni 1977; McPhail 1991). In a mass, group cultures abut each other. However, a mass often lacks an explicit social identity that derives from committed participation. Its social structure is undefined and in flux. Individuals and groups participate in masses because such locales are compelling action scenes but typically without explicit goal direction. The fluidity and marginality of identity in a mass makes a stable and self-reflexive culture or an institutionalization of that culture difficult to establish.

In contrast to these five social forms, small groups are characterized by interpersonal collaboration, collective focus, ongoing interaction, and a shared history. Unlike the actions of an individual, a small group requires shared participation. Unlike the situation, the group depends on the continuing presence of a set of participants. Unlike the association, the group depends on immediacy of interaction. Unlike the network, the group has routinized interaction. Finally, unlike the mass, meaning is essential for small-group identity. Participants identify themselves with the group and treat it as an entity that has a history and solidity. None of these features by itself distinguishes a group from other interaction forms, but taken together they constitute what makes a group distinctive. Without them, identity and collaboration are lost as an insistent, shared reality.

My perspective overlaps with Michel Maffesoli's (1996) provocative idea of the tribe as a feature of a new modernity, whether or not with the emotional intensity that Maffesoli asserts. Sociology has the mandate to examine clusters of individuals who establish a domain of meaning (Gibson 2005), creating Goffman's (1983) interaction order. Such clusters are never isolated from the remainder of society, but in their strong ties they serve as a collective and caring haven. Through weak ties a cluster is connected to other groups, creating a society (Watts 2003).

Small groups are a natural topic—perhaps *the* natural topic—for social-psychological analysis. Groups represent an archetypal instance of an organization in which interactional processes are readily observable. Meso-level analysis, which situates individual agency and structural processes within interactional arenas, demands a focus on the group (Maines 1982; Strauss 1978). This approach, seeing groups as cementing individual and society, stands in sharp contrast to the standard treatment of the small group within sociological analysis. Too often the group is seen as a black box and ignored as a level of analysis in its own right.

I suggest that four components of a small group reveal its value as an explanatory tool. Each is analytically distinct, and though at times they are in tension—since groups may serve as vehicles for control or for change—together they justify the sociological analysis of the group as the bridge between macro and micro, between structure and agency.

First, *groups socialize individuals to communal standards,* and small groups are particularly effective for two crucial reasons. Group members are easily able to observe the actions of others. In this respect, the small group is a form of Jeremy Bentham's (or Michel Foucault's) panopticon: it facilitates effective and immediate surveillance, although in contrast to the Benthamite carceral panopticon, the seer is seen as well. Further, because groups matter to members and shape their identity, the pressures of group life often have great consequences in channeling behavior.

Second, just as they socialize members, *groups provide an arena in which communal standards and expectations are shaped.* Small groups are incubators of change and may form the nuclei of movements that contest forms of social control (Polletta 2002). Such groups are so effective as foci of commitment that social movements often are designed to be reticulated networks of small groups (Gerlach and Hine 1970)—a cell structure—as reflected in the mantra to "act local, think global."

Third, *groups provide spaces for the collective development, appropriation, and interpretation of meanings and objects,* thus permitting communities to represent themselves in symbolic terms. As I discuss in chapter 2, every small group has an associated idioculture: a set of meanings that individuals refer to in creating a collective identity. Groups are not merely interactional arenas but also cultural fields.

Fourth, *small groups are domains in which status processes and identity become concrete and individuals are allocated to positions.* In the case of ascribed characteristics, groups provide rewards or punishments that generate status, encouraging actors to manage their stigma or to advertise their honors through presentation of self. In the case of achieved characteristics, groups are fields where these achievements are collectively recognized. Simultaneously groups may become the source of active resistance to the ascription of undesired roles and identity.

Together these four processes justify the study of the group as forces of control, contestation, representation, and allocation.

## Groups and Control

The small group is an effective and efficient agent of direct constraint, a means by which collective power becomes consequential. Among the techniques by which social order is made palpable, socialization is the most immediate and influential form of control. Although socialization is not a unidirectional process by which individuals passively incorporate community expectations without challenge, it underlines how society presses itself upon the individual, forging thoughts, feelings, and behaviors (Sandstrom, Martin, and Fine 2009). Even when negotiation and resistance are permitted, the obdurate power of society is evident.

As noted by theorists from the utilitarian Jeremy Bentham (1789/1996) to poststructuralists such as Michel Foucault (1977) to rational choice theorist Michael Hechter (1987), the confined intimacy of groups facilitates the monitoring and sanctioning of individuals. The presence of others—

both role models and distributors of rewards and punishments—has intense effects on the formation of personhood. It is sociologically significant, if unsurprising, that much of childhood is organized through the arrangements of small groups: families, peer groups, and classrooms. Children must bend their emotions, cognitions, and behaviors to constraint. It is better if they believe that they do so voluntarily, but compulsion stands behind their "free choice."

The coercive potential of groups is evident not only during childhood but throughout the life course. We are continuously influenced by authorities, peers, and subordinates. As demonstrated by Stanley Milgram's (1974) laboratory drama of obedience in which naive subjects are "forced" by an experimenter's orders to shock a fellow subject (in reality a confederate) to an imagined death, the *co-presence* of the authority figure is crucial. Authorities have substantial power to monitor and sanction (Ridgeway and Walker 1994). Peers may also exert social control as individuals search for cues to acceptable behavior (Turner and Killian 1987; Corsaro and Rizzo 1988).

The group embodies a power structure on an intimate level. Small groups are sources of control not only because individuals are assigned to places within a hierarchy but because they are exposed to the control (and sometimes absence of control) associated with these positions. Decisions of representatives of larger institutions also shape individual action, influencing material and phenomenological realities (Lovaglia and Houser 1996). Stigma is made palpable within groups, disadvantaging certain participants. Persons with esteemed social characteristics find that those characteristics bring rewards and lead to preferential treatment (Berger, Rosenholtz, and Zelditch 1980). Particularly effective in providing rewards and punishments are tight-knit groups that link these outcomes to collective identity (Lois 1999).

Social control does not operate as efficiently in extended, diverse populations; rather, power is mediated through groups and relations constituted temporarily or permanently as interaction sets. This influence takes several forms and includes such relations as police interaction with juveniles, teachers' discipline in school classrooms, family traditions, and constraints in work teams. Because members observe each other, deviations can be quickly countered. For Kurt Lewin (1936), social actors operate within force fields in which others provide opportunities, constraints, and inducements. If, as Foucault (1977) argues, society depends on discipline and punishment, the small group—by virtue of surveillance and its apparent openness as a behavioral space—is an especially efficient arena for generating conformity. To theorize social control without addressing how and where it is enforced is to miss the fact that power is a social achievement.

## Groups and Contestation

Beyond enforcing socialization and social control, groups are also mechanisms of contestation and change. People are not passively socialized through participation in group life; they use social relations to challenge authority and enforced norms (Scott 1987). Groups concur and they resist. As Anthony Giddens (1984) remarks, groups are simultaneously tools of human agency and means constraining that agency. They provide the microstructure through which individuals mobilize and create transformations (Snow et al. 1986).

How do groups become the agents of structural change, given their localized character? Early work in collective action treated the group as a repository for grievances, particularly those stemming from relative deprivation (Gurr 1970; Smelser 1962). Later research raised doubts that social change could be motivated by purely psychological forces and refocused attention on resource mobilization: the ability of groups of activists to access resources such as money, recruits, media attention, or the support of elites (McCarthy and Zald 1977). These critical resources, necessary for promoting social change, are gathered and organized through patterns of social relations.

The ability of groups to mobilize resources depends on their success as microlevel control systems. As Mancur Olson (1965) argued, collective action is possible only in groups that effectively monitor, manage, and motivate participation, limiting the resource depletion of free-riders. The smaller, more exclusive, and more tightly knit the group, the greater the ease of coordinating behavior.

Most important, the act of participating in a small group builds commitment to ideologies—or frames—of social change (Gamson, Fireman, and Rytina 1982; Hirsch 1986). Ideology flows from commitments. Put differently, individuals do not require prior ideological allegiance in order to join a social movement. Rather, participating in a small group, with its associated community and identification, produces engagement. This process in which obligation supports social change—what David Snow and his colleagues (1986) term "micromobilization"—occurs through negotiation and persuasion (Polletta 2002). Social change starts with talk (Davis 2002; Fine 1995) and then extends to action (Gamson, Fireman, and Rytina 1982). As a result, the small group becomes the arena in which many social movements are formed (Benford and Hunt 1992; Fine and Stoecker 1985).

## Groups and Representations

A groups perspective argues that culture is created and enacted within groups and then may transcend the originating group. Culture can be indigenous, imported, or exported. Local cultures not only affect participants but may have effects beyond the group. It is within groups that sets of individuals draw from their cultural tool-kits (Swidler 1986; Wuthnow 1994) to create symbolic and ideological structures that constitute collective representations, but individuals also rely on representations that are part of their background culture to share within the interaction scene. Whether locally generated or borrowed, expressive symbols at their moment of creation are formulated not by masses but by colleagues—social relations that establish a shared past.

As Howard Becker (1982) demonstrates with regard to art worlds, because culture depends on collective activity that is constituted in local scenes—communities with shared interests—the narrative of art history is properly couched in terms of "schools" rather than through a parade of individual geniuses. Consider the case of the Impressionists, a group of artists who dined, drank, argued, and painted together. As a result, their works were seen as sufficiently similar that they *belonged together*, even though much stylistic variation among them was evident. And they were seen as different from Cubists or Surrealists. As Michael Farrell (2001) argues, personal ties within the group were translated into an "objective" feature of style when the differences between Manet and Monet were erased and the boundary with others outside the group was highlighted. This stylistic distinctiveness is not only an objective measure or a matter of individual taste but a function of group process. These works are identifiably products of a small-group environment: a group that shares and announces a philosophy, a set of techniques and experiences, common exhibition venues, and a social life as friends, neighbors, and occasionally lovers. The dynamics of group life affecting intellectual output is evident in intellectual worlds as well, including philosophy (Collins 1998) and sociology (Mullins 1973).

Innovation therefore depends on small-group interaction. Cultural creations become markers of belonging. Émile Durkheim (1915/1965) famously argued that religion—a set of representations that pervades social life—was established in the crucible of the small group. Durkheim contended that religion in its elementary form is a *self-portrait* of the small group. The dramaturgical (Goffman 1959) and symbolic interactionist (Blumer 1969) traditions take this line of theorizing a step further by asserting that meaning is socially constructed through the sharing of ideas and beliefs, although this approach deemphasizes the shared history from which these groups construct their worlds. Interactions and the situations in which they are embedded are neither random nor ahistorical but rather depend on ongoing relationships with acquaintances or with those who share recognizable interests or recurring roles. Although interactionist theories have been criticized as antistructural, they gain power when negotiations are situated within a continuing set of meaningful social relations. Goffman's (1959) writings on frontstage versus backstage behavior—indeed, the entire dramaturgical project (Brissett and Edgley 2005; Messinger, Sampson, and Towne 1962; Smith 2008)—become more persuasive when these interactions are based on a stable set of local expectations. In other words, self-presentation draws on understandings from past interactions.

Small groups help explain not only how culture extends from personal creation to larger social units but also how representations trickle down to individuals. Adults' concerns about monitoring children's peer groups stem from a recognition of the role of small groups in diffusing culture. The group is the mechanism by which fads and fashions as well as values and norms are transmitted. When children learn *bad* things—cultural forms from which parents wish to shield them—it is through the relentless promotion by peer groups of counter-hegemonic identities. The sexual talk of preadolescent Little League teams—even joking about rape, as I have detailed—may be noxious and nasty to adult ears, but it gains appeal not only because it is rejected by adults, while being linked to what is imagined to be adult privilege, but also because this hidden and privately held knowledge certifies the value of the group to members in acquiring this scarce resource. Its juicy tendentiousness validates the group but also serves as a valued exchange resource with those in other groups.

### Groups and Allocation

Finally, small groups are venues in which individuals negotiate their position in status hierarchies (Ridgeway and Berger 1986). In such settings, stigmas are punished and valued social characteristics are rewarded, a central insight of group process theory and symbolic interactionism alike. The group is the arena in which individuals directly confront the power structure of the social order. Not only are individuals assigned to slots within a hierarchy, but they are exposed to the expectations that these positions entail. In allocating individuals, groups reproduce and legitimate the status quo.

Although this model might appear to privilege consensus, groups can contest systems of status allocation. Many groups form for the purpose of collective support or personal transformation. Ethnic organizations or twelve-step programs share a mission of status enhancement, just as leisure groups claim that engaging in some esoteric activity makes the participant a better person—a justification for such diverse activities as mushrooming, high school debate, and scholastic chess—by pointing to the ethical, performative, or cognitive skills that the activity allegedly encourages.

Gangs, cliques, clubs, and other voluntary organizations have the dual function of providing members with identity and status. The price of this self-placement may involve embracing encouraged behaviors, such as getting a tattoo, not associating with members of rival groups, tolerating a hazing ritual, using drugs, or the like. Being a member of the popular crowd in high school often requires that one not associate with those less popular, even at the cost of being thought "stuck-up" (Eder 1985) and even if popular behaviors are not popular among adults. To participate in a fantasy game one must be willing to embrace and act out the fantasies suggested by others; membership in a political party entails proclaiming a set of beliefs, whether or not one holds all of them with certainty, and being willing to support those running for office under the party's banner. To be sure, groups are not fully able to enforce these demands, but they often have considerable suasion in setting boundaries and, if rejected, encouraging exit.

One of the most productive lines of research on the allocation of position in small groups has examined the power of gender. Research by Kay Deaux (1984; West and Zimmerman 1987; Fenstermaker and West 2002) finds that masculinity and femininity, far from being innate and fixed features of individual biology, are "performed"—shaped through the awarding of status to those who perform well. Gendered behavior is elicited within settings of interaction and shaped by local expectations. Groups simultaneously attach status to individual identity and to social categories. Studies of men and women in conversation (Aries 1976; Smith-Lovin and Brody 1989; West and Garcia 1988) reveal that women's lower social status is made manifest in mixed groups through frequent interruptions by men. In similar fashion, although high school debate rounds are structured to permit equal talk, girls still must surmount the conversational hegemony of boys, who are expected to interrupt and be verbally dominant and who often enough make demeaning remarks. The link between gender and status is established in preschool, where teachers take children who are similar in comportment, appearance, and behavior and transform them into "boys" and "girls" (Cahill 1989; Martin 1998; Corsaro 2003).

Research on expectation states demonstrates that adults joining work organizations have similar experiences. Workers who are otherwise similar in their qualifications are sorted into status groups in the course of interaction; this allocation occurs through the importing of the prestige order of the wider environment, as filtered through local interaction arenas. Status is conferred not automatically but behaviorally. The assignment appears linked to the particular characteristics of individuals, but those characteristics are only known through their position within socially endorsed microsystems.

## The Power of Groups

In this chapter, I have attempted to lay the ground for the remainder of the book by situating the study of groups within sociology. Despite the disciplinary preference for examining broad structural forces of stability and change, local interactional systems are crucial in several ways in establishing order. The group, a level between self and society, should properly have a central place in sociological theorizing. The group constitutes a local field in which meaning is created and in which action is possible. As a community of care and surveillance, it creates allegiance; members know each other, come to create a culture and shared history, and can use the group as a basis of connection to the larger society.

Because of its intimacy, the small group creates a space where individuals accommodate themselves to and negotiate with each other and collectively can accommodate themselves to larger and more powerful units. Further, groups can come to represent the face of institutional power in classrooms, offices, or churches, and in this they stand above and beyond persons. In like fashion, macrostructures such as status hierarchies are transmitted and experienced in small-group settings. The group should not be treated as separate from structures but as crucial to them. The social structure, like the network, results from the connections of local interactional contexts.

Groups exemplify Durkheimian social facts in being more than the individuals who participate. They are also facts on the ground where interaction gets done. As a result, groups are both institutional and personal sites for action: meso-level spaces that shape personal choices and channel institutional forces. Because of the local and shared knowledge that social relations require, involvement in groups avoids the tabula rasa problem of a constructionist model in which shared expectations must be created afresh in each interaction.

The group, in embodying core organizational principles, is society writ small, a form of sociological miniaturism. Because small groups remind us that society is built from the interpersonal level, they become mechanisms for social transformation. Revolutions begin in groups. The group not only serves as a vehicle for enforcing social control or sharing culture but also permits two-way transmission by which individuals recruit others to amplify aspirations and grievances.

In describing the place of the group, I emphasize a set of core social processes that are central to social organization: control, contestation, representation, and allocation. Recognizing how group action reveals these features of social life demonstrates the centrality of small communities.

The claim that small groups constitute the microfoundation of social structure directs attention to how groups stand between individuals and society. This should be our sociological agenda, but it is one that has often been lost. To create a seamless, integrated discipline, sociologists must search for locations in which the macro and the micro, agency and structure, freedom and constraint, interpenetrate. The small group serves this role, providing a platform for understanding why big society and big culture cannot stand on their own. If the small group has been ignored because it has seemed neither wholly social-psychological nor wholly social-structural, its liminal quality ultimately works to its advantage.

# Chapter 2

## The Dynamics of Idioculture

*If a serious effort is made to construct theories that will even begin to explain social phenomena, it turns out that their general propositions are not about the equilibrium of society, but about the behavior of men.*
—George Homans, "Bringing Men Back In" (1964, 818)

T HE CONCEPT of culture has become so thoroughly enshrined throughout the social sciences that it sometimes has escaped attention how little we know of culture in situ—culture as it is played out. The microclimate of culture has taken a backseat to the macroanalysis of culture as linked to society at large.[1] Social scientists have often ignored the idea that culture is a form of performance within a local context, with meaning derived from those contextual features, while treating culture as a thing in itself, separate from how it is used in practice. Even performance theorists, such as Jeffrey Alexander (2004), rarely address the doing of culture as a local achievement. In these analyses, performances must not be examined too closely because then we might see how they are shaped by local choices. Sociologists speak of the culture of a society or social segment with the expectation that their audience will share a commonsense understanding of what is meant. That audiences often have this common understanding does not eliminate the fact that we neglect the process through which culture is performed and elicits responses.

To counter this lack of specification of culture and its audiences, I propose a few simple premises:

1. Culture is revealed in behavior and its material productions.

2. Culture is performed or produced for audiences (present or implicit).

3. Audiences identify (and disidentify) with these performances and productions.

The first two premises suggest that culture is performed, while the third reminds us that a performance or production results in the creation of selves and the recognition of allegiance. To emphasize the public dis-

34

play of meaning underlines that culture is situated within an ongoing and self-referential interaction order. If we do not link the content of culture to a particular field of action, the concept may become an amorphous mist that swirls throughout a gauzy and indeterminate social system (Ghaziani 2009). To escape this trap, we must conceptualize culture in light of those behavioral domains in which it is embedded. Societies are said to "have" culture, but culture is performed and displayed to particular audiences (even through media productions, created by groups that have extended audiences). Ultimately culture is embodied. Such a perspective avoids the lack of specification that is often found in studies of national cultures or subcultures and that limits their empirical usefulness. If we do not develop firm references to what constitutes, say, American or German or Bolivian culture, the concept is usable only through our intuition.

In developing the symbolic interaction perspective, Herbert Blumer (1969) argued that meaning derives from interaction, and culture, a system of shared meaning, is at the heart of Blumer's premise. This view of culture as revealed in actions and in objects contrasts with the argument that culture is purely to be understood as a "system of cognition" (Geertz 1973) or "collective representations" (Eliasoph and Lichterman 2003) rather than a system of "referential performance." While culture is created and transmitted through interaction, culture is not behavior as such, nor is culture only an idea. In contrast, culture is a message embedded within interaction.

Specifying the cultural practices of a society is an insurmountable task. However, if we embrace Blumer's premise, taking agentic action as the basis of determining culture-in-structure (Emirbayer 1997), culture can be specified and located. It is within microcommunities with interests and resources that culture is produced. Culture should be understood as a dependent variable produced by "interested parties" rather than as an independent variable that has exogenous force separate from the conditions under which it was produced.

This conception returns us to the small group. Although shared understandings can transcend interactive fields, these fields structure much of interaction (Fine and Kleinman 1979). Despite transcending group boundaries, cultural traditions are experienced as part of a local communication system, even if known widely.[2] However wide the audience, culture is discussed and used locally.

## Creating Idiocultures

In focusing on the interaction order as a wedge for analyzing culture, I propose that every group has a unique culture, or what I have labeled an "idioculture."[3] I define an idioculture as a system of knowledge, beliefs, behaviors, and customs shared by members of an interacting group to which members refer and that they employ as the basis of further interaction. Members recognize that they share experiences, and these experiences can be referred to with the expectation that they will be understood by other members and can be used to build a shared reality. As a result, group culture is historicized. The concept of idioculture stresses that culture characterizes a group, although the content may be either borrowed or created anew.

August Hollingshead (1939, 816), the author of the classic examination of adolescent culture *Elmstown's Youth*, asserted that "persons in more or less continuous association evolve behavior traits and cultural mechanisms which are unique to the group and differ in some way from those of other groups and from the larger socio-cultural complex. That is, every continuing social group develops a variant culture and a body of social relations peculiar and common to its members." Likewise, Alfred McClung Lee (1954) and Milton Gordon (1964) argued that a group culture fills a void in sociological conceptions of culture by providing a behavioral grounding that transcends the examination of values and attitudes. Despite the occasional attention of ethnographers, who see groups up close (Erickson 2009; Furman 1997; Cravalho 1996; Whyte 1943), or experimentalists, who examine how culture can shift or remain as membership is altered over time (Rose and Felton 1955; Jacobs and Campbell 1961; Weick and Gilfillan 1971; MacNeil and Sherif 1976), attention to the analytic virtues of idiocultures has been sporadic. Notable is the pioneering work of Donald Roy (1959–1960). Roy labored as a punch-press operator with a small group of workers, and he describes in compelling detail how this group established rituals to provide structure to their mundane workday (for instance, by establishing "Banana Time," the sharing of a banana among coworkers). Eventually, as the result of ill-advised teasing by Roy, the allegiances and the culture of the workers were disrupted. Roy demonstrates that the history of the group, as revealed in its traditions, bolstered solidarity and self-esteem–based efficiency but also potentially undercut it (Gecas and Schwalbe 1983). Group culture develops from the structure of social relations and shapes those relations. The fact that participants share cultural markers provides evidence that they are meaningfully bound together in ways that support trust.

## Justifying Group Culture

How can we justify giving our attention to the small group as a primary domain of cultural analysis? What kinds of insight are possible with this analytic focus that are absent elsewhere? A small-group model has several virtues: it permits the specification of cultures, the comparative analysis of groups, a more precise understanding of cultural creation and diffusion, the recognition of groups as cultural arenas, and the appreciation of culture as a mediator between environment and action.

*Specificity of Cultures*    Since small groups can be observed and members questioned, culture need no longer remain the amorphous mist suggested by Amin Ghaziani (2009). Ethnography contributes to the analysis of local cultures in that it helps describe the cultural objects and displays that constitute a group. This ability to focus on a domain of activity provides the microanalysis of culture with an advantage that other approaches lack. Idiocultures can be specified to a much greater extent than is true of larger units, be they societies or subcultures. For instance, observing a three-person work group, Roy could describe the main contours of the traditions of this tiny band of laborers as they gave meaning to their labor during the course of their shift. The more we can link the form of interaction with the content of culture, the more likely we are to be able to use the group for understanding the choices that actors make in creating a shell of meaning around their performances.

*Comparative Analysis of Groups*    While the detailed examination of groups as cultural fields is important in understanding how idiocultures are developed, theory depends on creating contrasts across space and over time. The concept of idioculture sees groups as differentiated along analytically significant dimensions and thus allows for a systematic comparison of them (McFeat 1974). Social scientists have traditionally paid little attention to how closely related groups differ. Such groups may have similar goals, comparable memberships, and interchangeable spaces, yet they develop unique cultures and distinct styles of behavior. The cultures that groups develop result from environmental contingencies, coupled with the social definitions that emerge locally through interaction. By contrasting groups in their backgrounds, experiences, and shared references, we find the dynamics of cultural differentiation—a process that J. L. Fischer (1968) labeled "microethnography." In analyzing Little League baseball teams (Fine 1987b), I have described how two successful teams in the same league established contrasting idiocultures because of varying abilities and status among the players. The behavioral styles of their coaches and the sociometric structure of the team produced distinct and vibrant cultural traditions that generated different responses to victory and defeat. One team with a strongly hierarchical status structure and more "professional" coaches was more intensely competitive and less tolerant of the mistakes of lower-status members, whereas the other team, which had a more diffuse status hierarchy and a less competitive coach, was more accepting of defeat and error. As in any recursive system, the cultural elements that had been developed and the emotional responses of the team shaped the legitimacy of the social structure. Although the culture did not override the ability of the players, life on the team provided different models that the players could use in other groups and in their understandings of how social life should transpire. The underlying principle is that small systems that might appear similar from the outside may differ dramatically in their microstructure and culture formations.

*Cultural Creation and Diffusion*    The creation of an idioculture is in many respects not so different in its implications from cultural creation in larger social units. A group serves as a microcosm of larger systems (Stolte, Fine, and Cook 2001). Just as we can describe the settings under which groups operate, so can we detail the circumstances under which an item of culture is created. Cultural creation in a group is, at its originating moment, identical to that for cultural products that reach a wider audience. Some forms of locally crafted culture spread widely and rapidly, either through intentional promotion or through the emotional energizing of audiences to be open to diffusion. Metaphorically speaking, the process is equivalent to genetic diffusion—or what scholars speak of as the spread of "memes" (Heath, Bell, and Sternberg 2001). Many cultural products, designed to be diffused, are created in group situations, including scriptwriters' conferences, theater ensembles, and scientific work groups (Fine 1977; Stebbins 1979; Latour and Woolgar 1979; Knorr-Cetina 1999). Cultural origins are rooted in group dynamics and then spiral to outside audiences. Cultural products, such as jokes, slang, and superstitions, develop through local interaction and then may "catch on," spreading beyond the boundaries of the originating group and becoming embedded in a national culture or subculture (Fine and Kleinman 1979). Of course, few cultural items diffuse widely, but in examining the genealogy of a popular saying, one frequently finds an interacting group as the locus of creation. This pattern reveals general processes of cultural transmission, such as the recognition of the classic two-step flow of communication in which innovations are first spread among those with strong ties and subsequently spread more widely through network relations (Katz and Lazarsfeld 1955; Coleman, Katz, and Menzel 1966; Rogers 2003).

*Groups as Cultural Arenas*    A theory of idioculture emphasizes that groups do not exist in a content-free context but are continuously engaged in producing a history (McBride 1975; Rossel 1976) and a system of meaning (Berger and Luckmann 1967). Although small-group researchers who are committed to laboratory research largely treat group dynamics as separate from the content of talk and action, this is equivalent to watching a silent movie. The group is analyzed as a social form and not an arena of action. Interaction is never empty, however, but is filled with content that emerges from the social relations of the participants. Meaning is generated in action, and ongoing negotiation over cultural content defines a group as a microinstitution. The *aboutness* of talk and behavior is central to understanding how groups develop. When there is no consideration for meaning, behavior is "meaningless"—a point that most experimental examinations of small groups minimize. Influential research by Dawn Robinson and Lynn Smith-Lovin (2001) demonstrates that humor, with its themes of superiority and power, directs and mirrors group structure, making content an essential element of social relations (see also Fine and DeSoucey 2005).

*Culture as Mediator Between Environment and Action*    Idioculture mediates between constraints external to the group and the behavior of the group in dealing with these constraints. It serves in this regard as a filtering mechanism (Eliasoph and Lichterman 2003). As the medium through which collective decisions are made, culture permits an understanding of how a group establishes its "groupness"—its cohesion and commitment. As Peter Berger and Thomas Luckmann (1967, 87) suggest in *The Social Construction of Reality*, awareness of a subuniverse of meaning differentiates group members from outsiders. Group culture is essential in creating boundaries, which are so critical to identity (Lamont 1992). Varied responses to environments and to the structure of the group produce distinctive values held by small communities (Vogt and O'Dea 1953; Rogers and Gardner 1969; DuWors 1952). Research on cultural traditions in research communities in Antarctica has demonstrated how local traditions (traditions that differ from one research station to the next) address the external reality of total darkness in the depth of winter and its challenging effects on psychological and social functioning. Although each community develops its own culture, each is also attempting to solve challenges to group life presented by external reality (Cravalho 1996). The culture of a group channels options for action once the collectively shared interpretation of an event has been determined. After meaning is set, group members select responses from their cultural toolkit; in groups with strong consensus others endorse those strategies (Swidler 1986).

A small-group culture underlines the influence of local knowledge. Certainly both the structures of larger, distant, encompassing social systems and the microinteractional structures of conversation matter greatly in how groups organize themselves, but groups are also self-organizing and self-referential. This structuring results from the conditions and experiences that participants face together. The concept of local knowledge, despite earlier roots (see, for example, Polanyi 1964), owes much to the writing of Clifford Geertz (1983, 167), who asserts that legal and political systems depend on the operation of indigenous concepts. The danger in emphasizing concepts and interpretations is that such a stance privileges mind over action. A mental model of social organization marginalizes negotiation, affiliation, and collective action, which have the potential to transform the personal into the communal.

Sociologists have long had—and still have—considerable difficulty in analyzing culture because of their reluctance to see that action is at the heart of social order. Caught between the cognition and emotion of individual actors and the structure and control of the institution, action is routinely downplayed, just as George Homans (1964) warned a half-century ago. Like all domains of social life, culture is to be found in an interaction order, and so sociologists should privilege how actors produce culture in situ. We must move from "sociology as imagined" to "sociology as lived." For both theoretical and methodological reasons, examining group culture uncovers the nexus of agency and structure. This nexus is evident in those tiny publics that we as citizens, as family members, as teammates, as workers, and as friends confront every day. The choices we make while interacting with our significant others are not ours alone, but neither are they produced magically. Small groups are the organizational mechanism through which Max Weber's switch-man theory operates. Idioculture places us on tracks of action, which serve us well until the sharp shocks of disruption shake us.

## Building an Idioculture

Idiocultures do not just appear but are created through the whirr of interaction, which serves expressive and instrumental purposes. What are the effects of the creation of shared pasts on prospective futures? How do groups develop shared references that permit collective trust? Why do groups require a common culture to demonstrate the reality of their identity to themselves and others? Why is the creation of idiocultures theoretically significant?

At its outset, even if some participants are acquainted, a group is, in effect, a world of strangers. Although particular ties may be rich with content, the group lacks coherence or a shared identity. Social relations do not *mean* anything until participants develop a shared past—a domain of collective memory. This recognition transforms talk into culture. The formation of a culture and a collective identity occurs from the opening moments of interaction and draws upon background knowledge. When individuals meet, they begin to construct a culture by asking for names and other biographical markers that can be referred to later (Davis 1973). With enough collective references, idioculture becomes self-generating, and direct solicitation and reciprocal questioning are no longer required for social solidarity. Rules are established, opinions are expressed, information is exchanged, and members live through events together, creating a history—a meaningful retrospective past (Katovich and Couch 1992). Discussing their studies of children's camps, Muzafer Sherif and Carolyn Sherif (1953, 236–37) write that

> when individuals having no established relationships are brought together in a group situation to interact in group activities with common goals, they produce a group structure. . . . This group structure implies positive in-group identifications and common attitudes, and tends, in time, to generate by-products or norms peculiar to the group, such as nicknames, catchwords, ways of doing things, etc.

Not every element of a group's conversation or behavior enters its idioculture. Cultural performances do not inevitably generate group solidarity (Goffman 1967). Idioculture is augmented if an experience is shared or information is transmitted within the presence of individuals who recognize their common and meaningful social relations and who perceive the experience as an event or remark that is notable, capable of being referred to meaningfully (Garfinkel 1967, 38–41). The topic of talk or action must merit retrospective notice. Routine actions, being taken for granted, typically do not alter the group's idioculture, but they may become notable if the local context invests them with significance. A catch by a poor outfielder at a crucial moment produces a nickname on a Little League baseball team. A verbal gaffe in the final round of a tournament similarly creates a recurring joke on a debate team. A forecasting error provokes an ongoing teasing theme in a weather service office. By provoking attention, the unusual or startling event serves as a trigger for memory. Something unusual has happened that becomes sedimented in memory.

The creation of idioculture is not generated randomly through chance statements and events but is open to a sociological analysis of how local life is organized. Participants build meanings from social constraints that affect the boundaries of permissible behavior. Although the content of particular cultural elements must satisfy a set of criteria to become incorporated into an idioculture, these criteria are not external to the group but dependent on it. They are local components of sense-making systems. How these criteria affect the sharing of group culture is negotiated in interaction and eventually becomes solidified through normalization and the support of group standards (Cohen 1978). These processes, tied to the dynamics of reference groups and of conformity, operate as filters (Siman 1977; Eliasoph and Lichterman 2003), limiting options by constraining cultural selection. For a cultural element to become a part of group tradition it must have the characteristics that group members find acceptable and it must lack those characteristics that make its reception and repetition inappropriate. Although I speak of "filtering," which suggests editing out, I could equally speak of "incorporating," which involves the more positive, if implicit, selection of the acceptable.

Five filtering elements help explain the selection, stability, and salience of items in a group's idioculture. The item must be perceived as known (K), usable (U), functional (F), appropriate (A) in light of the group's status system, and triggered (T) by experience. These factors can be schematized in an ordered relationship through a Venn diagram according to the number of *potential* items that meet each criteria: K>U>F>A>T. It is not that the items pass through stages temporally but that each needs to be present. Most critically, and shaping the other four criteria, someone must sponsor a cultural item by bringing it into group life through voice or action. This action component constitutes the "trigger." Such an originating performance is unlikely unless the item is known, usable, functional, and status appropriate, but even if it is presented, its longevity is a result of the relevance of the other criteria. In exploring the creation of idiocultures, I focus on my research with Little League baseball teams, but the process by which culture is generated occurs within all groups.

## Known Culture

The first constraint on whether a potential cultural element will become part of a group's idioculture is that at least one member of the group has *known* the item or its components and, as a result, actors can access these elements in ongoing interaction. I label this pool of background information as the "known culture" of the group. As Howard Becker and Blanche Geer (1960) argued, the manifest culture of a group derives from the latent (known) cultures of its members. While cultural content emerges from group interaction, latent culture, or the recall of prior knowledge—what has been termed cultural "memes" (Heath, Bell, and Sternberg 2001)—affects the form of these cultural elements. Cultural content is synthesized from remembrances of shared experiences and known content. Since members have access to other idiocultures (latent cultures) through previous or concurrent memberships as well as through exposure to media cultures, the information retrievable by participants is extensive (Schudson 1989).

Among teams in one Minnesota Little League, a foul ball that was hit over the backstop was known as a "Polish Home Run." Such a cultural item would have been meaningless had it not been for the latent, implicit cultural knowledge of what a home run is and the symbolic opposition of hitting a ball straight over the outfield fence and hitting it backward over the backstop. But this in itself was insufficient. The term also required knowledge of ethnic stereotypes—"Polish" is an ethnic slur that implies backwardness or incompetence. In the absence of this cultural knowledge, such an identification of this kind of foul ball would not have become a stable part of the culture of these preadolescents. Likewise, referring to other players on the basis of their uniform color as a "green bean" or "Chiquita banana" suggests that cultural elements depend on prior knowledge derived from realms external to the group.

Creativity can be incorporated into this model, since culture is never created de novo; rather, actors combine elements with which they are personally familiar in novel ways (Hebb 1974; Hare 1982, 155). These combinations may be assigned meanings different from that of any constituent element. The porosity of group boundaries through the varied experiences of members causes idiocultures to be unpredictable. On one occasion prior to a team practice, several ballplayers were hanging on the backstop at the field. One of the players shook the fence vigorously, an activity that he named—apparently spontaneously—a "Chinese pain shake." Although the term was unpredictable, its content depended on team knowledge: the cultural association of the Chinese with torture (the Chinese water torture) and with the powerful earthquakes that had recently decimated mainland China. This cultural tradition, ostensibly idiosyncratic, resulted from previous knowledge. The term made sense given the web of meanings accessible to these boys.

The greater the proportion of group members who are aware of a latent cultural element, the more likely it is that this knowledge or some transformation of it will characterize the group. Since participants draw from diverse knowledge pools, the larger the number who share this knowledge and the greater their recognition that this knowledge is shared, the more likely it is that this knowledge will emerge as part of the group's culture and will characterize the group. Background knowledge allows newly created cultural items to be more readily incorporated into group interaction.

## Usable Culture

A second criterion for inclusion in a group's idioculture is that a potential item be perceived as *usable.* It must be seen as suitable for group interaction and fit the moral and psychological demands of the core participants (Munroe and Faust 1976). This criterion is distinct from whether the element is known and raises the question of whether the element is suitable for the local context: does it fit the circumstance in which it will be used? In many groups, some elements of the latent or known culture may not be shared publicly because the topic is either sacred or deviant. Such cultural forms stand outside normative boundaries.

The interpretations of members determine the usability of a known cultural element. Members' personalities, religion, political ideology, and morality influence whether a cultural tradition can be expressed. In other words, the morality of culture can be highly localized. On one Little League team, a star player objected vehemently to a teammate's reference to the "fucking umps." Another chastised a teammate for uttering the epithet "Jesus Christ!" On other teams, such usage was legitimate and was treated as a mark of maturity. Groups develop distinctive standards, a result of the tastes and proprieties of participants. Given that group membership is shaped by selection processes—determining the collective habitus—how morality is tied to behavior can differ substantially.

One of the two teams observed in a league in a heavily Catholic community emphasized religion more heavily than the other, although most players on both teams were Catholic. Possibly because of the backgrounds of the players—or perhaps the symbolism of the team name—the Angels evinced a greater interest in religion than did the Rangers. The Angels asked each other why they had missed church. The Rangers never publicly mentioned religion, but on several occasions players joked about abortion. Although it can only weakly be inferred that similar jokes could not have been shared on the Angels, such jokes felt inappropriate on that team. Rude, nasty, or sexual jokes were spread only among the Rangers (outside of the earshot of their coach) and not, in my observation, among the Angels.

Crude racial epithets were common on another team. One player referred to local blacks as "jungle bunnies," while another asserted that "all the people who live around me are niggers"; a third described a Puerto Rican adolescent as "half nigger and half white." Although other boys were surely aware of these slurs, only on this one team were they regularly expressed. Explaining why such comments were usable in this group and not in others is difficult. Two years before, this team had had an African American coach who was disliked; this experience may have accounted for the salience of racial resentment but not for the underlying attitudes, which were supported by racial strains in the community. The acceptance of racial epithets was compounded by the fact that the two adult coaches were not greatly upset by them. For instance, when a black preadolescent pitching for the opposing team hit one of their batters, this conversation ensued on the bench:

JUSTIN: Come on, you nigger.
COACH: Don't be stupid.

JUSTIN: That's what he is.
ASSISTANT COACH: You'll get thrown out of the game.
JUSTIN: I don't mind if he calls me "whitey."

The reaction of the coaches supported the usability of the slur. These adults saw racial abuse as a *strategic* problem, a problem of impression management.[4] Boys should not use such a term because other adults would sanction them. Perhaps these coaches were trying to change behavior through a pragmatic exhortation, but Justin was not punished. The adults, while not encouraging such comments, did not outlaw them, and they persisted throughout the season.

Central to usability is situational fit. Standards for both prescribed and proscribed behavior are bounded by local context. Culture may be usable in certain circumstances, such as when an authority figure is absent but not while present. On those occasions when group members are in the presence of outsiders, elements of a group's idioculture may be curtailed. Usability is as often situational as it is normative. Preadolescents are sufficiently wise to refrain from sharing dirty jokes in the presence of adults as much to protect the sensitivity of the listeners as to protect themselves. The jokes comparing aborted fetuses to ripe, red tomatoes that circulated on one team were limited to occasions when adults (other than the author, an "honorary kid") were absent. Usability is characteristic not simply of content but of time and place.

### Functional Culture

A third force that influences the likelihood of an item being incorporated into a group's idioculture is whether it is perceived as meeting the goals and needs of some or all group members and whether it is treated as facilitating the survival and successful operation of the group as a unit (Pellegrin 1953). If such is the case, the item is considered part of the functional culture. This approach is agnostic over whether any cultural form actually supports group continuation or leads to dissolution (and in a formal sense is *dysfunctional*). Potential cultural traditions that are known and usable may not enter the group's idioculture if they are not believed to support the interests of the group or of its members. In some instances of cultural innovation, especially when competing cultural elements are tied to task goals, a process metaphorically akin to natural selection may operate. Scholars refer to the small traditions that constitute a culture as "memes," drawing on the metaphor of genetic selection (Heath, Bell, and Sternberg 2001; Dawkins 1976).

Participants use cultural forms as a response to shared problems (Becker and Geer 1960; Spector 1973), implicitly proposing solutions.

This proposition is supported by examinations of microcultures in laboratory settings, thus demonstrating that problem-solving strategies that continue over time are those that have been most efficient (Weick and Gilfillan 1971).

Among Little League baseball teams, the rules and restrictions that team members enforce reflect the functional properties of group culture. One team decided that players would take batting practice (a desirable activity) in the order that they arrived at the field. Their decision encouraged players to be prompt. On occasion the entire team arrived before any of their rivals. Players on other teams respected the team for its spirit and friendship as players bonded through their pregame activity. The routine also minimized disputes about the batting practice order. The boys, rather than the coaches, organized the team's behavior, and the rule strengthened the position of the leading player, who lived a block from the field and often arrived early. Prior to the establishment of the rule, the team had determined the batting order haphazardly based on whoever was most insistent rather than through a consensual process. Players had considered the ordering of batting practice to be problematic, and the rule provided a solution.

Another team prohibited chewing gum after one player nearly choked after he ran into another player while attempting to catch a fly ball. Other teams did not establish a similar rule; for them the concern had never become salient. For an item of culture to be functional, participants must recognize a shared problem or goal and then respond with what they consider a solution.

### Appropriate Culture

Some potential elements of a group's culture, while functional for meeting group goals or personal needs, are not incorporated into an idioculture because they undermine the group's social structure by challenging the established status system or power relations. Cultural elements that members consider consistent with established patterns of interaction constitute the *appropriate culture*. A cultural element that expresses hostility toward a well-liked or powerful individual may be known, usable, and even functional (conflict can serve a social purpose), but it still may be inappropriate unless the group structure is altered.

Nicknames, which reveal local status directly or implicitly, are particularly salient in this regard (Morgan, Harré, and O'Neill 1979). A nickname must fit the target's recognized status. During the first year I observed the Beanville league, one player, Tom, was nicknamed "Maniac," a play on his last name that coupled with his physical awkwardness as an eleven-year-old substitute outfielder. When I asked players to name their three best friends on the team, only one teammate named Tom. Tom had low status among his peers, and the nickname stuck. The following year Tom, now twelve, was the team's starting third baseman, one of the team's best hitters, and firmly situated in the middle of the team's status hierarchy, being named by four teammates as a best friend. His nickname Maniac was no longer appropriate. Tom's new nickname was "Main Eye," also a play on his last name, but with dramatically different symbolic connotations. Tom's position on the team had changed, as did his nickname. Nicknames do not always change so readily, but sometimes labels that begin as critical become affectionate as their origins are forgotten.

A similar cultural change that mirrored a status transformation occurred in another league. One eleven-year-old was known as an incompetent ballplayer, having gone hitless the previous season. As a result of his marginal skills and his social isolation he was called "Smell-ton," a play on his surname. During the first week of the season, much to his teammates' shock, he smashed a grand slam home run. His harsh and insulting nickname was shelved; everyone called him Jim after that momentous hit.

Some nicknames are limited to particular occasions. One high-status player was called "Mousey" by his affectionate mother. This nickname was too juicy not to be remembered by his teammates, but they refrained from using it in his presence because of his status and his intense dislike of the name. His distaste made the nickname more precious, although teammates were cautious about its use.

Nicknames are not the only cultural items linked to status; pranks and practical jokes target low-status members (Posen 1974), and rules privilege the prerogatives of older players, such as who can coach the bases (high-status players) or who should run to the refreshment stand for water (social isolates). As William Foote Whyte (1943) observed in his examination of bowling in Cornerville, participants are likely to perform in accordance with their group status, whatever their natural ability, as those with lower status defer to those with more esteem.

In addition to the status appropriateness of its target, the group's acceptance of a cultural item depends on its sponsorship, a point made powerfully in Muzafer Sherif's account of preadolescent campers (Sherif and Sherif 1953, 252). The stature of the sponsor rubs off on local performances; the cultural item is an extension of the person who presents it. For instance, when a coach proposes a group ritual, while not invariably adopted, such a practice stands a comparatively greater likelihood of acceptance because of his endorsement. The coaches of one team suggested that before a game the team form a circle and players extend their hands into the middle. When the coach yelled, "Let's go," players buoyantly raised their arms in unison. The ritual began each game for this team. Another coach ritually asked his team what three things they needed to win. They vigorously shouted, "Hustle, pride, and class." A third coach referred to a dribbling hit as something that his grandmother could hit better than, and this middle-aged man's grandmother entered into team lore.

High-status players are advantaged in their endorsements. Several members of one team got "wiffles" (crew cuts) after Wiley, the second-most-popular player, was shorn and spoke proudly of it. The fad continued, with one or two boys newly shaved each day, until Rich, the most popular boy, claimed that he thought that the haircut looked stupid, although he excluded Wiley from his assessment. After Rich's announcement, only one low-status boy had his hair cut in that fashion. The team was highly critical of that haircut, claiming that it was not a real wiffle. Similar status processes encouraged conformity of dress, including wristbands, sneaker brands, or removing one's shirt at practice.

### A Triggering Event

The range of potential cultural items that are known, usable, functional, and appropriate is extensive. While the other criteria operate implicitly and in the background, the triggering mechanism is different. It emerges from the immediate behavior of the group. This is a process that incorporates the other criteria. An interactional mechanism or *filter* accounts for which items enter a group's cultural repertoire. The concept of a triggering mechanism helps explain the selection. Some bit of interaction, perhaps unpredictable, serves as a spark that initiates the specific content of an idioculture. This event can consist of any action or talk that produces a group response, consistent with Neil Smelser's (1962) idea of a precipitating factor for collective behavior. A haircut may be sufficient to spawn a new nickname ("Buzz Conroy," "Peach Fuzz"). A miscue may provide the impetus for a joking sequence that remains part of group life. A threat to group boundaries may inspire a legend, norm, or prescription for group action.

Although any triggering event has the potential to produce idioculture, those events that recur are particularly likely to establish traditions, and once produced, these traditions are more likely to be defined as relevant to the group. Recurrence allows the possibility that some member of the group will recognize the continuing relevance of the event and sponsor it in the group. The recurring tradition is made available as a selected event that can easily provoke further comment by its presence. Put another way, recurring events are more readily retrievable within groups (Schudson 1989). They become "super-traditions" in that they are often visible and salient within the group and frequently referred to.

The superior batting of one Little Leaguer led to him being called "Superstar," and the absence of such talent led another boy to be labeled "Strikeout King." The nicknames were sociometrically appropriate, as well as being frequently triggered within the context of team activities.

Although recurrence is an important feature of cultural incorporation, repetition is not the only way that culture is developed. Triggering events that are notable or novel are especially likely to produce idioculture. The social psychologist Harold Kelly (1967) argued that distinctiveness, uniqueness, and consistency create attributions that focus on the characteristics of the distinctive other. The anthropologist George Gmelch (1971), exploring superstitions among professional baseball players, found that rituals emerged from uncommonly good performances, while behavioral taboos resulted from incompetence. One Little League coach's beat-up, rusty Chevrolet was called a "Cadillac" after a powerful foul ball nearly dented it even more. He humorously warned the team not to hit his Cadillac. The term caught on. As Gmelch noted, notable events also affect taboos. One coach gave his team red-white-and-blue wristbands on opening day to generate unity and spirit. However, the team, expected to win the championship, lost its first game by the lopsided score of 12–3. After the game, the players decided that the wristbands brought bad luck, and from that day they were not worn. (The team won the league championship.)

Triggering events cannot easily be predicted, as they emerge directly from interaction. However, in experimental settings, triggering events can be systematically controlled by the researcher and their effects in shaping group culture examined. For instance, creativity increases in isolated groups with stronger boundaries (Rose and Felton 1955), suggesting that triggering events may be more salient when those events are seen as more salient for the group in differentiating it from others.

## The Workings of Idioculture

In arguing that the creation of local cultures is patterned, I also argue that five elements—the known culture, the usable culture, the functional culture, the appropriate culture, and the triggering event—generate the content and enactment of a group's idioculture. Each is shaped by the patterns of group interaction, and the likelihood of cultural elements characterizing a group depends on how many individuals (and what proportion of the group) see the cultural form as fitting the criteria and how often the cultural form emerges. These configurations suggest how groups differ in their culture and why specific forms appear and continue within a microculture. Local cultures result from group dynamics at the same time that they shape these dynamics. Culture is not merely an independent or exogenous force but is tied to action within a group.

A full analysis of the establishment of local cultures must examine each component of the culture production process. For example, during the middle of the Little League season the Beanville Rangers created and then enforced a rule that players could not eat ice cream while seated on the bench during a game. This rule was triggered by a combination of circumstances: it originated in the middle of a game in which the Rangers, by that time accustomed to victory, were being beaten. On the bench, a nonplaying, lower-status boy was licking an ice cream cone. Seeing this, the high-status older players decided that ice cream could not be eaten during a game, although gum was allowed.

Being drawn from the behavior of professional sports teams, the rule was known; it was usable in that it did not deal with tabooed or threatening areas of children's culture and it was comparable to rules that children frequently establish (Piaget 1932/1969; Hughes 1983; Corsaro 2003). The rule solved a group problem by relieving the frustration that the older players felt, and in focusing the attention of the younger players it generated emotional energy in group activity (Collins 2004). Further, the mere presence of the rule, by serving as a marker that the group had surveillance power as well as common purpose, generated group cohesion (Cartwright and Zander 1953; Borgatta and Bales 1953). Finally, the rule was appropriate in that it gave the high-status players a way to control their low-status teammates. Later in the season an older high-status player ate ice cream on the bench and was not reprimanded by his peers, although the rule was enforced for others, illustrating that the rules were flexible in practice.

In producing the specific content of group culture, the five elements operate through the local negotiation of members, and that negotiation depends on shared experience. Culture is a local construction that builds on consensual meanings and collective representations (Eliasoph and Lichterman 2003).

## Idiocultural Worlds

The shared understandings of small groups—whether leisure worlds, workspaces, families, or cliques—result from desires for cohesion and self-formation. Cultures produce both identities and local practices. These outcomes result from the traditions of the group, their tasks and experiences, their personnel and social relations, and the forms of social control that direct their actions. The internal character of group life shapes the local character of knowledge regimes. How individuals use their idiocultures affects both identity and the conception of moral propriety. Although some forms of culture transcend group boundaries, as I discuss in chapter 8, a local nexus of meaning provides emotional and normative control over group life, shaping what actions are deemed legitimate.

Groups can develop strong cultures that situate members in particular locations within the social world to which they belong, both separating them from others and encouraging allegiance. Idiocultures differ in strength and extent, perhaps a function of the character of their participants, the existence of a strong internal clique, a focus on the importance of boundaries, or a connection to external systems of power and constraint. Although comparative analyses of local cultures have been rare, they are vital to determine the conditions under which cultures expand and diminish. And though culture is often conceptualized as a general social good, sometimes idiocultures have destructive effects on morale or in shaping external relations, providing benefits for subgroups with their own interests. But always idioculture serves as a mediator between the structural features of group relations and interactional forces. Ultimately, the process of cultural production depends on both external pressures and internal dynamics.

Every group builds a culture that is based on and feeds back into social relations. The interaction order channels and limits a group's idioculture, but simultaneously the idioculture makes structure apparent and regulates the behaviors of participants. Local cultures as they are known and performed in particular contexts provide models for how groups are supposed to operate. In creating expectations of the shared and the proper, they influence interaction channels.

Shaping the triad of structure, culture, and interaction is the force of history. History matters in a dual sense: both because events—both internal and external to the group—impinge, and because shared history selects the events that are emphasized in a collective identity. Groups invariably have both a prospective and retrospective focus (Katovich and Couch 1992). Events that group members experience jointly set expectations for the events that they can imagine. The memory and the interpretation of shared events can either strengthen collective identity or rend social connections.

The characteristics of participants and the situations in which groups are embedded shape local cultures. Groups, seemingly similar in their environment and formal structure, can develop fundamentally distinct cultures, a result of differing known, usable, functional, appropriate cultures and triggering mechanisms. Yet, once traditions develop, a strong inertia locks them into set tracks. Change occurs, but the cultural switchman is powerful and inertia dominates. Once cultures are institutionalized, they retain their shape unless subject to new circumstances, internal reassessments, or external shocks. The desire for stability in cultural life mirrors the desire for stability in the individual's social world. Change has costs, and tradition comes to be valued in itself. As a result, local cultures are sticky to the touch.

# Chapter 3

## The Power of Constraints and Exteriority

> [A person] is free, as I conceive the matter, but it is an organic freedom, which he works out in cooperation with others, not a freedom to do things independently of society. It is teamwork. He has freedom to function in his own way, like the quarterback, but in one way or another, he has to play the game as life brings him into it.
> —Charles Horton Cooley, *Human Nature and the Social Order*
> (1902/1964, 49–50)

A S A RULE, we should avoid playing havoc with the slogans of others. Yet, in this chapter, I mischievously invert the title of Randall Collins's (1981) influential essay, "On the Microfoundations of Macrosociology." My claim is that "the macrofoundations of microsociology" is equally invigorating. Although not the first to recognize the challenge of integrating levels of analysis, Collins has been particularly influential in arguing for the necessary linkage of "macro" and "micro" sociology, and he created a sociology of completeness that incorporates meso-level perspectives.[1] The meso-level is my playground as well.[2] Collins proclaims that an adequate macrosociology depends on microsociological presuppositions and assumptions.[3] He is correct, but in emphasizing the effects of small groups on interaction, I reverse the argument to suggest that an adequate microsociology depends as much on a set of macrosociological presuppositions surrounding the interaction scene. I argue that two constructs, *constraint* and *exteriority*, both of which are fundamental to macrosociological theory, provide a basis for microsociology and together help extend the analysis of the group settings in which I have focused my observations, particularly although not exclusively my examination of the restaurant industry.

Too often microsociologists have willfully ignored the macrosociological implications of their approach, situating themselves as a social-psychological opposition. We are wiser when we can recast insights from macrosociology in terms of their influence on local contexts as action scenes. All microsociology has a macrosociology, just as Collins recognized the converse. These perspectives are not truly in opposition but depend on each other for a robust interpretation of social order. The macrosociological presuppositions inherent in microsociology arise from physical realities, social structure, institutional connections, organizational power, history, and tradition.

Images of "macro" and "micro" sociology often reflect a schism that limits the opportunities for theory-building (Ritzer 1985, 88). In one sense, smaller units compose or are *constitutive* of larger units, just as efficient behavior in restaurant kitchens depends on individual workers with their own skill sets: teams of workers, servers, and cooks must collaborate to create and distribute products in a coordinated fashion; a restaurant could not function without these smaller units generating the organization. This model properly rejects a superorganicism (Kroeber 1917; Perinbanayagam 1986), a reading of Durkheimian social facts that lacks a credible social psychology (Alexander and Giesen 1987). Microsociologists have persuasively argued that collective or institutional action requires some form of social psychology to incorporate the behavior, meaning, and context. Recognizing that social facts depend on emergent practices (Gross 2009; Sawyer 2005) and coordinated action (Blumer 1969, 58), microsociologists view intervening variables as demystifying an airy suprahuman reality.

A microinterpretation does not demonstrate causation; instead, it propounds *metaphors* of causation (Lakoff and Johnson 1980; Nisbet 1976). Metaphors are heuristic and powerful tools but must not be confused with an empirical description of *noumenal* reality. A metaphor of causation can also flow from macro to micro. For instance, the rules set by National Weather Service bureaucratic procedures "cause" the production of forecasts in local offices. Meteorologists follow the organizationally mandated procedures that are provided in heavy binders produced by the main office outside Washington, including the times when forecasts are to be issued, their form, and the necessity of collaboration with other offices. Workers treat these rules as obdurate and they are rarely ignored because they are backed by sanctions, including formal reprimands and suspensions. These sanctions mean that the rules will be questioned infrequently. Instead of seeing causation only as a constitutive metaphor ($a$ is a subset of $b$; therefore, $a$ causes $b$), a metaphor of constraint has different assumptions ($b$ has the authority to control the domain of which $a$ is a part; thus, $b$ causes what $a$ can do). Causation between levels flows in both directions simultaneously, and each depends on translation.

Despite the occasional deep chasm between macro and micro approaches, interpretations require both, a point that classic sociological theorists have long recognized. It is hard to classify Durkheim, Weber, Simmel, and Mead as macro- or microtheorists. They treated interpretations as seamless, although often their followers chose sides. Unfortunately, too many midcentury sociologists, both functional and interpretivist, ignored this bridging and instead sought self-contained theoretical edifices with walls that excluded extraneous variables and extraneous scholars. While one group disregarded agency, the other ignored structure. A tight focus made the possibility of *systematic* and *predictive* knowledge seem almost within reach, but in doing so often excluded the possibility of a messy but complete integration.

The canonical works of symbolic interactionist thought reveal that the linkage of macro- and microelements was central to the perspective. Charles Morris entitled Mead's transcribed lecture notes *Mind, Self, and Society* (1934). Likewise, Cooley named his best-known writing *Human Nature and the Social Order* (1902/1964). These scholars held macroissues as equal to their concern with self and interaction. While their societal analyses are incomplete and less subtle than their microtheorizing, they aimed for a robust analysis of society.

In parallel, the "macro" Durkheim of *The Rules of Sociological Method* (1964, 23) recognized that actors can choose how to interact, although real consequences and constraints bracket their interaction.[4] Indeed, a line of microsociology has long found inspiration in Durkheim's work, especially *The Elementary Forms of the Religious Life* (1915/1965; see Stone and Farberman 1967). Erving Goffman, especially in his early writing, was as indebted to Émile Durkheim and his ideas about ritual as he was to George Herbert Mead. Max Weber and Georg Simmel (and Auguste Comte) *as a matter of course* addressed society on the level of the individual, the group, and the social system (Fine, Harrington, and Segre 2008). Weber's emphasis on verstehen clearly reveals his focus on the local (Truzzi 1975). By being embedded in local scenes and having local affiliations, individuals are the consequence *and* the cause of society: a society writ small. It is through the meso-level that society is transformed into action and affiliation.

The argument that microsociology requires macrosociology emphasizes two central meso-level concepts: (1) perceived boundaries on action (constraint) and (2) the effects of societal infrastructure (exteriority) that transcend individual or group interpretations. Constraint implies that individual action is limited by the recognition of external (and typically social) forces, which shapes the range of decisions and closes off some avenues while opening others. So, hotel cooks are not free to act as they wish because they are monitored by others within the organization who set rules and establish expectations, which they monitor closely or at a distance. Scheduling is a good example of constraint in this context:

chefs work with a labor budget that forces them to dismiss workers on a slow evening or recall them when reservations grow. For many chefs, creating a suitable schedule that satisfies both workers and bosses is a major challenge.

Exteriority implies that the consequences of external forces, introjected or not, are real; external forces are independent of individuals, although sometimes recognized by them. Here one notes the effects of local, national, or global economies on the restaurant industry; these forces cannot easily be overcome. Much of my research was conducted during a recessionary period, so restaurant chefs had to make difficult choices as to what to serve and how much because of economic forces buffeting them, filtered through the organization. Economic headwinds led one restaurant, for instance, to decide to serve six rather than seven scallops in an entrée.

Whereas constraint operates through internal decisions and is linked to systems of authority such as laws and regulations, exteriority establishes contingencies apart from perception. Constraint is the limitation on agency stemming from the authority to set standards—the realization that within hierarchies action is not free. Exteriority is an impinging and obdurate structure whose reality cannot be changed but only adjusted to.[5]

## The Constraints of Local Hierarchy

The need to comprehend the sources and effects of social organization is central to the sociological mission. Put differently, we strive to answer the question: how is social order possible? How do individuals form collectives in which participants behave in a systematic, predictable, and effective fashion? Radical individualists argue that social organization is intensely fragile, suggesting that intersubjectivity and collective action are continually problematic. The romantic view of "man the meaning-maker" (homo creator) haunts microsociological thought (Shalin 1984, 1986; Rock 1979). Its strong form is useful only for parody. The weak form is trivially correct.

More foundational and problematic questions involve the processes by which intersubjectivity and collective action are generated and how their stability is enforced. How do persons embedded in organizations and relationships understand their world and others' positions in it through scripts and motivations? Discourse and practice combine to produce local cultures (Vaisey 2009). From a shared history, people come to believe that they share moral standards, and they recognize a similar system of authority that enforces it. These moral codes, accepted as enduring and eternal, limit what is seen as possible and when accepted build long-standing trusting relations (Ellickson 1991). The recognition of consensus (that is, consensus that suffices for group harmony) does not negate the classic interpretive concern with alternative perspectives. Divergent perspectives require negotiations and do not deny the reality of conflict, even if fundamental epistemological ruptures are rare.

Central to how interpretive microsociologists avoid rampant relativism is the construct of constraint (Maines 1977, 1988; Sewell 1992). Embedded forces determine what actions are treated as preferred or as possible without sanction or cost. Constraints may be spatial, temporal, material, social, or symbolic. They depend on *an obdurate reality of images*— a belief in collective agreement. Mead's (1934, 154–56) concept of the generalized other emphasizes this reality: it is not that individuals cannot act as they wish; rather, they typically wish to act consistent with the wishes of others, tacitly transforming the moral basis of community standards into personal standards. Given a range of motivations and goals, this explains why we ask, not why there is so much deviance but why there is so little. Recognizing that rule-breaking is something to be explained, we often rationalize it through accounts (Scott and Lyman 1968) or through aligning actions (Stokes and Hewitt 1976). Thus, even if coworkers chafe under the rules that their bosses set, they apologize when their deviance affects others—as, for instance, when cooks slack off in setting up their station and creating an adequate mise en place, thus forcing their colleagues to do their work. I was surprised that some hotel cooks who were sharply critical of organizational requirements would arrive an hour early off-the-clock to ensure that if they frittered away any time, it would not affect their coworkers. They constructed a code of conduct that incorporated slacking while still accepting organizational constraints.

Sense-making transcends the interpretation of persons and artifacts (the self-self and self-object relation) because it depends on local cultures. As Eviatar Zerubavel (1997) has argued forcefully, perception directed toward situations, institutions, and ideas is consensual. These are not material objects, but people see, hear, and feel them as real, and therefore they have real effects. We see institutions as motivated actors as we filter organizational action through values and ideologies (Ben-Yehuda 1985, 213), although this personification is a literary conceit. Even if organizations are ultimately composed of individuals, they are treated as collective. Meteorologists groused that they had to put up with foolish decisions of the National Weather Service, debaters were punished by their school for their misdeeds, and chess players complained about the incompetence of the United States Chess Federation. Interactionist writings imply this "macro" perspective in, for instance, studies of occupational socialization (for example, Becker et al. 1961;

Kleinman 1984; Cahill 1998), and it was implied in my suggestion that the students I observed in the two culinary training programs treated their intended occupation as an unquestioned material reality to which they had to adjust (Fine 1985). These culinary students had no doubt that their careers would be set by the "demands" of the food service industry, and they typically did not even consider the impact of individual restaurants. They were motivated to learn not the demands of particular employers but the general requirements of restaurants and hotels. The belief in the uniformity of constraints in this work world motivated these students to embrace the standards of their profession as their instructors proclaimed them. Even while creating strategies to handle the pressure of excess work, they accepted the moral legitimacy of their occupation and adjusted to it through anticipatory socialization.

At the heart of the interactionist perspective is the belief that objects become real when groups react to them in a systematic fashion. Meaning is local, even if it is imported from outside. As Herbert Blumer (1969, 88) wrote, "Social organization enters into action only to the extent to which it shapes situations in which people act, and to the extent to which it supplies fixed sets of symbols which people use in interpreting their situations." The irony is in the word "only." In Blumer's world, order is a residual concept, not a sensitizing one; it is present but secondary.

But this residual concept is not at all residual but rather presuppositional. Groups set constraints on action and privilege symbols that members use to understand their local worlds. This perspective is not only consistent with but necessary for microsociological analysis to prevent a random and unpredictable world.

In practice, the demand for categorization and boundaries (Rosch 1978; Lamont and Fournier 1993) makes everyone a macrosociologist. People think more comfortably in terms of groups and collectives than in terms of the shifting sands of social interaction and process. Even microsociologists see an individual's emotional life as a set of responses to organizational forces and institutional actions (Hochschild 1983; Stenross and Kleinman 1989; Smith 2008; Orzechowicz 2008).

Learning to act appropriately requires identifying the type of situation in which we find ourselves and then, as I discuss in chapter 4, knowing the expected behaviors. We continually add to our local knowledge and thus to instances from which we can generalize. As my ethnographies of children attest, adjustment to adult demands is the heart of the interpretivist analysis of childhood socialization (Denzin 1977a; Corsaro 2003; James, Jenks, and Prout 1998), and it continues throughout the life course. When a situation diverges from our experience, we review and revise our generalizations drawn from relevant situations by specifying them by place, time, or personnel. While situations are not identical in structure, we nevertheless abstract and typify them. Further, we perceive them as controlled by and constitutive of organizations, groups, institutions, and societies. Our reading of situations involves creating the typifications of macrostructures on which our responses in future contexts will be based.

Field research reveals that people reify their life worlds. Students, for instance, never doubt the authority of the school they attend, since their misbehavior (drinking, poor grades) might prevent them from participating in extracurricular activities. People treat the settings in their life worlds as real, and as a result macrosociology is a form of folk belief—it is how people commonsensically organize their experiences. Labeling theory and attribution theory, although social-psychological, describe ostensibly idiosyncratic action as "truly" the result of stable and large forces. In *The Sociological Imagination,* C. Wright Mills (1959) asserted that people think and speak about personal troubles rather than social problems, but this is true only in that people see themselves as objects of these troubles. Often they describe the cause as an impersonal force that affects many others. Any ethnographer knows that some children hate *school* and some cooks blame their *employer* and some political activists passionately oppose the *government.*

Although situations are fleeting and fluid, people perceive them as stable. This perception is made concrete through storymaking that is more dramatic than discrete facts (Martin and Powers 1983; Davis 2002; Polletta 2006). These narratives sound like *real reality,* and using them is a well-known strategy for politicians who present catchy anecdotes rather than policy analysis. People take reification for granted and act on that certainty.

Any plausible approach to social order must recognize that although actors have some authority over their interpretations, their choices are also influenced from other directions, whether corporate, collective, or metaphoric. The freedom of individual actors, closely held, is illusory, but through this profound illusion it becomes real for all intents and purposes. Authority must be imported into one's life world, and it is this that makes constraints effective. Yet, as I argue in discussing exteriority, the effects of structure are not illusory, even when the images that categorize structure are more imagined than descriptive.

## The Exterior Reality of Images

Obdurate reality—or what I label exteriority—checks the excesses of the romantic imagination. Constraints get negotiated; obdurate reality must be adjusted to. Durkheim's enduring legacy to sociology consists of recognizing that subjective morality stems from objective existence (Giddens

1978, 36). Blumer's contribution in his studies of labor policy and race relations is to admit that this real, but often unseen, obdurate quality generates the *collective* creation of meaning and the structuring of inter-action (Maines and Morrione 1990). Life has a materialist base, even if this fastness is not always consensually recognized.

What features of obdurate reality undergird the establishment of local meaning? I propose five components that bolster an interaction order by taking exteriority seriously: (1) the physical limits of the built environment, (2) temporal and spatial effects, (3) institutional linkages, (4) the obdurate reality of tradition, and (5) a belief in organizational primacy.

## The Physical Limits of the Built Environment

Physical boundaries prevent bodily action, and yet environments also open up options; this is the most compelling feature of the world's insis-tent reality (Gieryn 2000). Although in one sense this issue is trivial—we are not superhuman—at the same time it could hardly be of greater soci-ological significance. The environment is not only something that *is* but something that is made, shaped, and sometimes consciously disregarded. People carve niches in this environment and colonize other pre-made niches; these niches may be created by cascading decisions and negoti-ations in which power, authority, resources, technology, and collective action shape choices. Creating a suitable environment is an ongoing project for actors. Yet even if we determine our environs, we are limited by material reality.

Technology is, in this regard, of special interest. Human beings can-not fly, yet we *can* fly because of airplanes. While we cannot see through walls or skin, machines give us both views (as Steven Barley, 1988, demon-strates in his analysis of CAT scan interpretation). Meteorologists can see far beyond what is visible to the unaided eye because of the inscriptions of the skies that instruments provide. Technology alters the boundaries of sensory access. As a result, the environment-person relationship becomes dynamic as technologies are embraced or ignored. Still, this recognition does not alter the fact that the material environment (includ-ing the mechanical) directs the possibility of action. Insistent realities change while remaining insistent.

Ultimately, human choices are mediated through material reality. A building's construction results from the decisions of individuals and groups but also from conventional practices, aesthetic preferences, ide-ologies, social organization, institutional resources, and collective knowl-edge. Analyzing the construction of scores of buildings, microsociology loses its parsimony, and the replication of decisions suggests routinization. Architects can do what they do efficiently precisely because many options are not options in practice (Blau 1984; Latour 1988).

Deciding what should be built is negotiated on both the group level (involving the values or tastes of resource providers) and the institutional level (involving public policy demands established through other, powerful groups), but its foundation depends on what communities of builders perceive as collective needs, coupled with available technology and the accepted pools of competent knowledge held by architects, contractors, and construction workers (Thurk and Fine 2003). These accepted practices are grounded in the reality of the political economy and the accepted practices of engineering science, as filtered through the desires of those who will use the space, assuming that their advice is heeded. This became clear in my research in local offices of the National Weather Service. As new local offices were built, the central bureaucracy set rules for how those buildings would be sited and structured. For instance, each National Weather Service office had to have a safe room and backup electrical systems in case of severe weather. More striking was the central administration's attempt to prohibit windows, which it considered distracting to those using the machines inside the office. Forecasters arose in frustration and anger, arguing that observing the skies helped their forecasting by incorporating their own experience of the weather. In this case, the central administration gave in, and local offices were able to install windows. In the Chicago office, although questions about how the layout of the building promoted effective forecasting remained controversial, forecasters pointed out that they used the windows when severe weather approached. As one explained, "That's our backup—to look out the window" (Fine 2007, 24).

Once in place the built environment channels the movements and possibilities of actors (Goffman 1974, 1; Gieryn 2000). Small-group research demonstrates the symbolic power of seating arrangements and communication channels (Hare 1976, 260–77)—a point made dramatically in the symbolic structures involved in resolving political conflict (famously, the debate about the shape and size of the table at negotiations to end American involvement in Vietnam). Likewise, how restaurant kitchens are laid out determines the kinds of social relations found in them, including the amount of surveillance and the forms of worker collaboration. In restaurants in which stoves are crowded together, workers can help each other in ways that are impossible when they are spread apart in a larger space: cramped quarters sometimes contribute to mutual aid. Setting the height of a cubicle wall is not merely a technical decision but a decision that shapes work lives by affecting the level of communication in which individuals can engage. This was a source of controversy at the Chicago office of the National Weather Service, where privacy conflicted with community and adjustment was necessary. Groups must juggle the divergent meanings assigned to an environment (Lyons 1983; Purcell 1986), hoping for shared meanings and routine acquiescence.

## Temporal and Spatial Effects

Anthony Giddens's (1984) concept of "structuration" argues for the importance of temporal and spatial macrofoundations of microsociology. His emphasis on the dynamic, processual aspects of structure underlines the importance of context. Yet, Giddens often privileges action at the expense of meaning and thus treats the actor as less consequential than is warranted. A weak actor buffeted by exterior demands must somehow respond to those powerful forces, an effort that downplays the negotiation of meaning.

Giddens's most compelling insight is that action must be interpreted within a time-space continuum. Action is sedimented temporally (Busch 1980; Powell 1987; Flaherty 2000) in that what has happened previously presumes an expected future.[6] Some actions have lengthy pedigrees that are so fully accepted that it is difficult to reject these routinized expectations.

To cope with client demand efficiently, organizations solidify temporal expectations, as Zerubavel (1979) demonstrates in his examination of the creation of hospital staffing schedules. My examination of government meteorologists demonstrates the same point: the release of forecasts must be timed for media needs and so indirectly for the public, which then affects the work shifts of employees (and in the night their sleep patterns). It is not that an organization can be run only one way, but that, in any given case, one way should be privileged. An organization privileges some choices over others. My research on restaurant kitchens suggests that the obdurate demands of customers and suppliers structure how restaurants connect to their publics, which then determines work life and kitchen experience. The demands of customers for rapid service prevent some food from being served and limit food quality, given constraints set by labor and material costs. If a steak falls on the floor after having been cooked for twenty minutes, the cooks have no choice but to wipe it off and serve it rather than preparing another. The unknowing demands of customers make such choices essential. Although flexibility is possible within these temporal limits, choices are always restricted. Such limits may be more evident at a fast-food chain, but they also operate in the finest restaurants, where cooks lament customers' demands and regret what they cannot do as a consequence of customer expectations. Temporal limits are common in organizational venues, as the efficiencies of organizational life depend on the ability to process products and clients. These constraints gain force by virtue of the consequences when actors do not recognize them. In such instances, the kitchen may get "slammed": too many orders back up; poor-quality food is served as a result; and customers, servers, and cooks experience a frustrating evening.

The enactment of joint activity creates behavioral expectations that in turn shape the choices of participants. While recognizing choice, we should not bow too humbly at the altar of agency. The effects of structure can mask the ways in which its perception precludes behavioral choice. For instance, the codes of language and the need to communicate efficiently overwhelm individual options: social competency demands compliance with collective standards. Sedimented language choices, not consciously selected but built on choices previously made, have enormous ramifications as they shape how social actors hear and understand their world. Likewise, the decisions of a powerful small group within a corporate home office reverberate in small groups throughout the company (Farberman 1975; Denzin 1977b). The dramatic changes in the structure of the National Weather Service, which moved from regional offices to state offices and then to local offices, required additional hiring and changes in assignments. This bureaucratic decision from a distant headquarters, pressured by Congress, created 122 small offices as the organizational basis of forecasting, and situating radar towers near these local offices gave authority to the small office as the font of meteorological knowledge.

The power of actions to reverberate beyond the immediate context in which they are generated provides a macrofoundation for microsociology. The reality of the "world out there" circumscribes the choices that interactants can make. Not only does decision-making have effects, but its outcome and aftermath shape idiocultures. Decisions assume a life of their own and become reified, such that people respond in their local spaces. Even when the decision is not explicitly recognized, the external contingencies on which the choice is made are experienced. The meaning of a decision is grounded in actors' *responses* to that decision (Mead 1934).

The perspective that legitimizes the real-world effects of externalities was forcefully conveyed by Erving Goffman (1983) in his depiction of how the interaction order is itself a form of structuration. Although Goffman was keenly aware of the choices of actors, he contended crucially—and I think not defensively—that structure underlies all interaction. That belief led some to label him a "structuralist" (Denzin and Keller 1981). Interaction generates structure (Rawls 1987) as, in turn, structure generates interaction.

Simmelian formalism (Rock 1979, 46; Wanderer 1987) is part of the structure and macrofoundation of interpretive microsociology. It recognizes a *generalized form* and temporality in that previous events reverberate throughout time. Parodying his own metaphor, Goffman (1974, 1–2) wrote,

> All the world is not a stage—certainly the theater isn't entirely. (Whether you organize a theater or an aircraft factory, you need to find places for cars to park and coats to be checked, and these had better be real places, which, incidentally, had better carry real insurance against theft.) Presumably, a "definition of the situation" is almost always to be found, but those who are in the situation ordinarily do not *create* this definition, even though their society often can be said to do so; ordinarily, all they do is to assess correctly what the situation ought to be for them and then act accordingly. (emphasis in original)

Goffman's claim is that interaction *by itself* cannot explain the existence of social order; order is exterior to selves, not newly minted by them. The act is real, but the stage is real too. The stage, grounded in history, economics, architecture, and shared memory of other stages, circumscribes the actor and the company. As Edward Gross (1986) demonstrates, historical pageants, such as those designed by monarchs (for example, coronations) or revolutionary leaders (for example, mass rallies), reify power, and it is the accepted belief in power and resources, backed always by the threat of coercion (bolstering belief in power), that enables these demonstrations (Alexander 2006). This was readily apparent in my ethnography of political actors, where ceremonies and convocations allowed ideology and belief to be publicly shared. A political conclave with its colorful banners, bunting, and orations persuades group members that their mundane volunteering matters in establishing an improved state system and better civil society. They return to their groups with the enthusiasm that comes from witnessing a dramatic display with energized others. Stages, organized temporally and spatially and backed by institutional power, connect the actor's local world to institutional foundations.

## Institutional Linkages

Institutions are linked through bonds both meaningful and consequential. Webs extend beyond the reality that individuals in one organization may have personal contacts with those in others—a standard concern of those who examine corporate board interlocks and other elite networks. In my ethnographic research on the development of a market for self-taught art, these intersections were common and crucial. Museum curators would reach out to gallerists, to corporate and private collectors, and to journals and magazines. In addition to developing friendships, they became tied together organizationally. The art market comprises not simply isolated buyers and sellers but organizations with linked fate. This structure affects the local cultures of participants.

Institutions and associated organizations sometimes are forced, sometimes expect, and sometimes want to develop linkages within their cultural field. The interorganizational contacts that organizational survival requires imply (and facilitate) personal networks and, as a result, institutional connections.

A network that incorporates institutions—both specific organizations and more broadly conceived social institutions (church, media, school)—is built across time and space, revealing the process of structuration (Cohen 1987, 287). To note that it is individuals who act is precise but not particularly helpful. Spokespersons and their audiences *know* they speak for institutions, serving as public *embodiments.* It may be a meteorologist who forecasts or a cook who prepares food, but it is the National Weather Service and the restaurant that are evaluated, even when new workers are hired to fill these roles. A sense of agency is constrained by their role as representative. Research by Carl Couch and his colleagues on the implications of the representative's role in situations of conflict reveals the freedom lost through social control (Couch and Weiland 1986). Organizational agents are targets of suspicion not in themselves but because they serve as fronts for organizational reputation. Although the decisions originate within a local context, they radiate outward. Those affected, looking from afar, can properly wonder about the hidden motives that stand behind those decisions, which, once negotiated among representatives of organizations and then sedimented, shape local cultures.

Groups are frequently represented as "collective actors," but they often find a narrow menu of choices, especially when decisions are routinized and evaluated and overseen in other realms (Blumer 1969, 58–59). The National Weather Service is a prime example. Businesses, media organizations, and the public never see individual forecasters as determining the forecast, even though, in fact, it is a particular worker who produces the prediction, building on advice from colleagues and data gathered through technology provided by distant others.

Large entrenched bureaucracies provide representatives little leeway, and in this case reporting that the institution acts loses little analytic precision. The power relations that Peter Hall (Hall and Spencer-Hall 1982) demonstrates in school systems emphasize the effects of a web of organizations on local schools: some schools and school systems come to be seen as more effective and garner more public support and resources than others, with predictable impacts on administrators, teachers, and children. Through connections between and within systems, organizations impact each other.

## The Obdurate Burdens of Tradition

Marx wrote of how the "dead hand of tradition" shapes the present. He understood that a shared past is critical in building social reality (Flaherty and Fine 2001). Tradition shapes present behavior. Our understanding of *history* will always be channeled by how we view the present (Maines, Sugrue, and Katovich 1983; Olick and Robbins 1998).

Although present needs mold the past, the perceived past weighs heavily on the present (Schwartz 2000). Thus, we read history backwards, as current values shape what historical actors should have known. The past has an obdurate quality, both as a metaphor that structures our thought (Lakoff and Johnson 1980) and as a form of external discipline (Hobsbawm and Ranger 1983). Through our imaginings, the past becomes real, consequential, shared, used, and a guide to future behavior (Katovich 1987). In an activity such as competitive chess, players are continually evaluating their styles and moves in light of the lengthy history of the game. What is labeled "chess theory" is fundamentally an evaluation of the different styles of play associated with the heroes of the game. Actors and groups accept that traditions must not be violated if moral continuity is to be preserved (Durkheim 1915/1965). The belief in the primacy of the past is transformed into a social fact. As a result, this obdurate, consensual past has real effects in shaping behavior (that is, it is exterior to actors) and is perceived as beyond individuals' control (it constrains actors).

Since the perceived past is the compilation of actions of individuals, groups, and institutions, it is separated from those behaviors found in local contexts. Although historical events can be traced to specific interactions, such events as they are conceived are supra-individual and often transtemporal (for example, the population explosion, the AIDS pandemic, global warming, or the flood of immigrants). The collective perception of and lessons from *history* are separate from the experience of any individual (Shils 1981).

Organizations and institutions may be said to generate local situations that enmesh actors. We appear to have less control over contexts intentionally designed by organizations—although in some measure the reach of organizations affects all socially patterned behavior.[7] That children attend school is not a decision arrived at by the child, the family, or even a local school board but one that rests on the custom and labor market requirements that are sedimented into legislation and reinforced by unquestioned moral belief. Even parents who home-school find themselves resisting the omnipresent institution of the school while (often) reproducing much of the learning that occurs within it and demonstrating this commitment to the collective moral order as evaluated and credentialed by state institutions (Stevens 2001).

Interaction depends on previously set, "natural" rules of structure. We are routinely surprised when something seemingly so self-evident was not always so (for example, patterns of childhood discipline, attitudes toward nature, table manners). Negotiation is treated as marginal because of our acceptance of the traditions that underlie ordered interaction. To choose to break all the rules of a social order would be literally *unthinkable*. Studies of the life worlds of criminals demonstrate that even the vilest among them heed communal expectations with remarkable diligence (Athens 1980; Katz 1989). To achieve criminal ends a malefactor constantly bows to the social order's demands (rapists do not wander the streets naked to find victims). Unlike the image of the deviant as mad, what makes deviance troubling is its similarity to the ordinary. He is like us, a paragon of mundane normalcy; she wears a gray flannel suit. Only rarely are such actors judged insane, and only when they flout rules that even bad people will not flout (Scheff 1966). Such mad actors lack the good sense to present accounts. An absence of deference to the traditions on which propriety is built questions one's placement as a competent soul.

### Belief in Organizational Primacy

We rarely doubt the empirical primacy of organizations and routinely accept what some theorists deem a sly fiction: that organizations and other collectivities act. Yet, that people interact with *symbols* is central to sociology (Pollner 1987; Duncan 1968; Douglas 1985; Cohen 1989). We think and speak of collective action as the product of a single collective actor. Macrosociology is the common tongue of nonprofessionals who speak of social order. To say that "the government passed a law," "the company cheated me," or "I hate school" is fully and unproblematically understandable. Likewise, we recognize the reality of law and regulation without having to think about which groups created them and which groups enforce them. They are there and backed by institutional authority. We could unpack and translate these sentiments through a radical individualism, but only if we wish to separate words from thought. Organizations have direct effects once they are transformed into the reified objects of cognition (Rock 1979, 33), as labor-management relations attest (Fantasia 1988).

Public confidence in the reality of organizations is crucial, even if that confidence is not the same as agreement. Just as with the past (the locus of practices), social actors attribute an obdurate reality to organizations (the locus of power) even while acting in robust interaction scenes with their own local expectations. Those who set public agendas often have this collective character: the government, the police, the schools, the corporation, the stock market, or the media. That people never interact with collective actors may be literally true but ignores how people interpret their interactions. This also underlines Mead's crucial insight about the perceptions of the generalized other. The generalized other for Mead is a construct that inserts the institutional order into cognition, affect, and behavior. Society is interjected into mind and self. The impingement of the external world provides for the collective charter of knowledge.

Given that people routinely treat actions and actors as representing larger units, negotiated order depends on perceptions of a reified order based on individuals' routine and repetitive experiences with these collective entities. "Bureaucracy" as a social form, for instance, has meanings separate from any one agency or any one operative within that agency. Similar responses produce a collective perspective that transcends any local group, producing a solidified and stable interaction order.

## Constraints and Exteriority

Microsociology is necessary for an adequate macrosociology. But for a local sociology I argue the inverse: macrosociology undergirds microsociology. And a meso-level analysis incorporates both. The local does not stand by itself. Just as society requires the local, the local requires society in its various forms. Even when we focus on the local, if we ignore or downplay macrosociological concepts, theories, reasoning, and images, we are choosing to build a watery and cramped sociology of interaction and self-reflection. Such a stance has little to recommend it as an intellectual exercise.

Structure's reality is separate from its interpretation but must be mediated through the perception of constraints on action and the experience of external forces. This mediation occurs through the internalization of constraints and the exterior reality of institutions and stratification systems. The first focuses on how behaviors are shaped through the exercise of power, and the latter on how the behaviors are shaped without conscious power but through those realities that we take for granted. We navigate social life in light of Scylla's obdurate jaws and whirling Charybdis's constraint on free movement.

These themes of constraint and exteriority allow a local sociology to address the world's fastness and vastness: the physical limits of the built environment, time and space dimensions, institutional links, the obdurate reality of tradition, and belief in organizational primacy. Although implicit in microsociological writings, these themes have been neither explicitly addressed nor brought together. Physical reality, time, space, power, history, and organization provide for stable and predictable life worlds and a sociology that is both local and global.

# = Chapter 4 =

## Norms and Action

Moralities, ethics, laws, customs, beliefs, doctrines—these are of trifling import. All that matters is that the miraculous become the norm.
—Henry Miller, *Black Spring* (1938)

ORALITIES, ETHICS, laws, customs, beliefs and doctrines, far from trifling concerns, depend on interpersonal relations, arenas of action, and shared understandings. Perhaps the fact that we can coordinate so well is itself miraculous. Our frequent decisions to affiliate—the basis of social order—are inevitably local, contingent on our idiocultures, even as they are shaped by external structural forces.

Decisions to trust—to embrace belonging—require the predictability and the expression of commitment to shared standards. People must believe that certain behaviors and responses are expected and proper, even while the details of group life are emergent and negotiated. In short, local communities require normative cultures. To this end, groups develop behavioral strategies that organize routine interaction. Although norms have often been treated as reflections of society writ large, they are enacted in small groups and gain power from co-presence and shared culture. Norms build on local action scenes and extend beyond them through the parallel structure of groups as well as through a belief in the legitimacy of this cultural isomorphism.

If groups are to maintain stability—a durable interaction order that underlies the desire for predictability—members must fashion a robust system of expectations and controls that allows actions to be treated as routine. Despite the assumption of diversity and novelty in cultural production, the mundane, the ritual, and the foreseen make culture a collective and comfortable property of groups. A shared commitment to propriety answers the Hobbesian conundrum: how is social order possible in the face of individual interests?

As Christine Horne (2001) observes, answers to this normative question have been plentiful on both the micro and the macro levels. Some microtheorists, particularly those with a rational-choice bent, focus on the coordination of individual actions through parallel assessments of costs and benefits in light of the expected choices of others. Macrolevel theorists stress the impact of societal standards (such as values) and social formations (such as class). The seeming rightness of these arrangements results from socialization and institutional control. Each perspective has contributed to the debate on how norms channel social life. In contrast to both of these perspectives, a groups approach, emphasizing the enactment of negotiated meanings, operates from the meso-level of analysis, examining individual action within a domain of others and recognizing the importance of set routines.

## The Concept of "Norm"

The concept of "norm" is a sociological construct that has seeped into popular discourse, and as often happens when technical language is transformed into lay-speech, confusion abounds. Norms, as I use the term, involve the recognition of *rules of order*. Norms are not merely behavioral regularities but involve a collective embrace of the propriety of this regularity. Norms involve perception and commitment and, thus, are cultural choices that then become solidified. Norms have a rulelike quality but are not merely cognitive and emotive but are performed within a social surround and are justified, when questioned, in light of widely held values.

In practice, the frequency and location of normative behavior varies, despite an assumption of universality. Norms are never as universal as the term implies, and groups can disagree or divide on the applicability of any particular rule of order. As a result, while the examination of norms has often been linked to a vulgar functionalism, norms are not given but, in contrast, locally situated rules of order that can be negotiated or even serve as points of conflict. The distribution of power within a local community shapes the outcomes of these negotiations and conflict. The examination of norms must not presume that in any given situation norms *work*; they often fail to generate agreement. But the existence of an ongoing group suggests a desire for cohesion, even if that search eventually proves futile.

A theory of group culture argues that it is insufficient to note that individuals act in similar ways. Norms have an *ought* quality, and thus internalization is privileged over identification or compliance (Kelman 1973). Normative behaviors do not just occur but are *taught*. Being taught, they are not simply technical responses, but through the hope to create stability they are moral as well. They are the outcome of desire. The rules of order found in a local context are linked to collective wishes and vary according to backgrounds and interests, as well as the demands of that interactional arena. Socialization does not just *happen* but is enacted through local preferences, even as they are shaped by forces beyond the local. Norms are a frame by which individuals answer the Goffmanian question forcefully raised in *Frame Analysis* (Goffman 1974): "What is happening here?" In this, norms are tools to be selected; they are not scripts but guidelines.

## Norms and Culture

Whereas sociologists once spoke of moral regularities as central to culture (Williams 1967; Parsons 1937), today we are more likely to focus on collective representations. Perhaps these are not so very different, as both propose a transpersonal set of meanings: a macrocognitive world barely tied to interaction scenes. Yet, there are distinctions as well. Norms and values as central organizing concepts have become unfashionable for several reasons. First, used as societal forces, they relegate personal agency to the margins, suggesting an oversocialized concept of actors that lacks a clear linkage to individual choice. Second, they homogenize action, ignoring the differences among different groups. Third, since they frequently lack a behavioral referent, norms and values float mystically and majestically at the level of society. And fourth, forms of culture that apply to large-scale social systems justify functional analyses that privilege stability and consensus, marginalizing conflict.

Norms often feel divorced from the mechanisms of social life. Culture, a more fashionable, if overly used, term, provides a framework for behavior; this concept can be seen as another way of referring to norms without implying control of individual behavior by an overarching social structure. Such an approach is implicit in the attempts to develop a cognitive sociology. Eviatar Zerubavel (1997) argues in *Social Mindscapes* that how we perceive the world has been socially shaped. Categories of objects (for example, "food") may seem natural, but in fact such categories are precepts that create and reinforce moral boundaries (Douglas 1967).

Treating norms as fundamental to the cultural basis of community underlines that action is meaningful. Even habitual or ritualistic behavior, performed thoughtlessly, is interpreted in light of standards of behavior, although explanatory justifications do not by themselves describe how behaviors originated or what purposes they serve (Sewell 1992). Still, we belong to communities of interest with standards that we believe that we share. Perhaps, as ethnomethodologists suggest, we embrace the illusion of shared understanding. This illusion validates our actions. A desire to proclaim the need for consistency is central to understanding the discursive power of norms; further, instances of unexpected behaviors are treated as *notable* events and become narrative topics. Society consists of a bundle of stories (White 1987) justified by the compelling drama of violations of the moral order. By giving prominence to a "butt" who violates the normative order, jokes provoke laughter in presenting a violation and its resolution. Expectations and violations are central to understanding how narratives are generated. Such an approach is consistent with Ann Swidler's (1986) evocative metaphor of culture as a tool-kit—a set of meanings that can be enacted in light of the social order.

A central framework within the sociology of culture approach is that of the "cultural diamond," proposed by Wendy Griswold (1994, 14–16). Griswold argues that four interconnected elements are necessary for understanding cultural systems: (1) objects, including symbols, beliefs, values, and practices; (2) creators, referring to the organizations, groups, and individuals that produce and distribute cultural objects; (3) audiences; and (4) the social world or context—both local and global—in which culture is created and experienced. Perhaps more important than describing the concepts themselves is understanding their relations, both concurrently and sequentially. This model provides a framework by which the linkages among behavioral fields are emphasized. The student of social norms begins with the relationship between the social world and the cultural object, recognizing that norms exist in social space and are linked to interactional orders. To understand how norms emerge requires treating the cultural creator as a normative entrepreneur. Examining the role of receivers and their links to creators within a local community is crucial to understanding the process by which norms become framed, negotiated, and narrated.

## Norms and Interaction

A theory that situates norms within group life assumes that norms are constituted as expectations for local action. As the symbolic interaction perspective has emphasized (Stryker 1980; Blumer 1969), our choices of how to act toward other people depend on how we situate them: lover, teammate, or enemy. Identities produce expectations, what Peter Burke and Jan Stets (2009) refer to as "identity standards." These standards constitute the means by which individuals evaluate themselves and others within the context of local communities. That the process of identification is acquired through various forms of socialization does not imply that identifications are unchangeable, but they do require redefinition. Actors master the meaning of objects collectively. That is, the meanings that one person holds are likely to be similar to the meanings held by others, and the process of sharing evaluation within a group has powerful effects. As Muzafer Sherif (1935) argued in describing his autokinetic experiments, our drive for collective meaning is such that we search for consensus by establishing in our local communities norms of judgment that serve as a stable set of interpretations in the face of potential ambiguity. Although interpretations are socially generated, they are not random or unpredictable or unchangeable. Our choices have consequences, shaping our own experiences and those of others. As W. I. Thomas and Dorothy Thomas (1928) famously asserted, definitions of situations, once established, are real in their consequences, although as noted in chapter 3, these real consequences are never so powerful that they erase the effects of forces of constraint and exteriority.

To focus on the centrality of negotiation in group life is to question the power of generalized societal norms and values. Not only do individuals adopt social value orientations (Messick and McClintock 1968), but so do groups and small communities. Broad claims about the power of norms typically postulate an oversocialized conception of human actors and downplay how adjusting to local conditions can bolster agentic authority. By emphasizing expectations or rules of order, I situate the locus of action within the interaction order. Although some theorists treat norms as statistical regularities, I argue that the immediate choice of what behavior to enact is a response to local demands.

That behaviors often appear to be normative, demanded by external forces, even when strategically selected through impression management is a central point made by Goffman (1959) in *Presentation of Self in Everyday Life*. Goffman asserted that patterns of behavior exist because of the desire of individuals to be seen as morally respectable in the eyes of others and to have interactional sequences flow smoothly, avoiding disruptions (Emerson and Messinger 1977). In later writing, such as in *Frame Analysis* (1974), Goffman suggested that the establishment of collective frames of meaning helps actors determine which expectations are applicable in particular contexts. Group members develop frames of reference that direct action (Snow et al. 1986).

Although Goffman never specified how actors acquire the skills to define frameworks of interaction, childhood socialization is central to learning to be responsible public persons (Cahill 1989; Fine 1987b; Thorne 1993; James, Jenks, and Prout 1998). Children are tempted with a minuet of rewards and punishments to be sensitive to the expectations of their groups. Through the power of institutional isomorphism, these rewards and punishments are recognizably similar across families and institutions and are bolstered by expectations that transcend local scenes.

Although many norms are widely accepted, in practice their enactment is locally constituted. Norms are not provided by society; rather, they are understandings that are recognized through performance. In other words, one does not "obey" norms but "perform" them. Yet, while norms are enacted, they are also capable of being reported, justified, or inserted into group discourses, and as a result they become general and constraining. Even the act of questioning and objecting accepts that current expectations constitute standard operating assumptions. Especially in violations of the taken for granted, reference to behavioral rules becomes the basis for performances that bolster a moral argument about how social life should be organized. Alternative performances are possible, but the operating assumption in group life is that what is, should be. Given that group members are socialized similarly, norms become generalized as well as locally enacted.

To explore how norms are organized, I analyze social order through three broad social processes: framing (contextualizing meaning), negotiating (coordinating lines of action), and narrating (making claims about the nature of the "ought"). Although similar mechanisms have occurred in each of my ethnographic investigations, I focus on one group: amateur mushroomers. Examining mushroom collectors is particularly propitious in that the issue of how nature *should be* treated is never far from the surface. Mushroomers are men and women who are forced to confront their values. Mushrooming is leisure, but it also reveals moral commitments.

## Framing Norms

Social life operates on the assumption that we can predict the behavior of those around us. We assume the power of regularity. This does not suggest that we enact these expectations with full consciousness but rather that these behaviors become salient when they are violated and that they depend on cultural ideals or idioms for which we can provide accounts. Further, these behaviors are not enacted by rote but occur in situations in which they are judged to be relevant given the location, the social relations, and the shared history of the participants.

Drawing on the anthropologist Gregory Bateson's construct of frame (Argami and van den Scott 2010; Bateson 1972), Goffman (1974) argued that cognitive and behavioral definitions organize events and our subjective experience of them. By framing, Goffman suggested that groups rely on cultural templates to treat a local scene as exemplifying a category of meaning. The template provides a mechanism by which acts are linked to underlying assumptions about the motivations that generate them (Gross 2009). This answers *what* is happening and *why* individuals are acting as they are. Framing presumes shared values, recognizable motivations, and behavioral expectations.

The underlying principle that prevents a groups perspective from being individualistic and idiosyncratic is that situated interpretations and subjective experiences are not arbitrary but are routinized and knowable, tied to established idiocultures. People recognize *types* of situations and draw upon known patterns of behavior, comparing the meaning of one context with others (Fine 1992). Paul Rock (1979, 71) has argued that "situations order and direct the process of knowing," but it is not the situation as composed of aloof actors but the way that situations have been developed by engaged participants. The situation affects participants who are motivated to uphold their shared understandings. Again, we find that the interaction order is recursive. Our belief in norms and in their consequences shapes situated action, but norms are generated and established through that situated activity.

Participants search for established modes of action. The idea of society becomes something of a blind that directs attention away from the local domains in which interpretation occurs. Having directly or vicariously experienced action-scenes, participants evaluate them for their typicality and their relevance as a guide for action. Contexts are stored and sorted to find frames for judging appropriate responses.

We never judge acts or objects as isolated from their surroundings but ask embedded questions such as: What is going on? What should I be doing? What is this thing *here*? We strive for situated, contextual meaning. Past situations—and our interpretations of them—constitute the context by which we make sense of our present activities. Accepting the consequences of time and space links structure to interpretation as the regularities of things, acts, and settings are incorporated into our information processing (Giddens 1984).

We comprehend *things-in-context.* Because agents alter or reshape meanings through interpretive challenges, perceive through diverse perspectives, and have acquired this knowledge in other social contexts, any individual agent's understandings will differ from the understandings of others. Structures, being mediated, do not affect everyone identically, although the effects are often sufficiently similar for smooth interaction. Consensus is the default condition, even if often enough conflicts great and small challenge that harmonious ideal.

One technique to make contexts consistent is collective definition: either reshaping the past or defining the present. If one concludes that a situation requires different action from that suggested by the interpretation of previous situations, one may retrospectively redefine the past, reconstructing it as a guide for action (Maines, Sugrue, and Katovich 1983; Flaherty and Fine 2001). Alterations in historical memory are common, both for communities and for persons. For example, learning that someone engages in sexual acts with a same-sex partner not only may redefine the actions of the person in past situations (occasions that had previously not been defined as gay or lesbian in character) but also may redefine retrospectively the *character* or *frame* of that situation. A wink or a smile may acquire additional laminations of meanings.

The process by which individuals generalize, achieving some measure of cognitive consistency, depends on the belief that, although contexts vary, the object that is their focus has a nearly immutable meaning for all participants. The claim that norms direct action serves as a means by which consistent behavior can be explained: expectations, grounded in the strictures of group culture rather than given by society, are the engine that produces uniformity. As a result, individuals frame situations based on their assumption that social facts matter in directing behavior, even if it is the interaction arena that is responsible.

Acting appropriately depends on determining the type of situation that one confronts and the standards of action that are appropriate—a framing challenge that is evident especially for children. With each new situation, we gain another instance by which to interpret future occasions. When a context differs from what we expect based on past contexts, we review previous, relevant situations and revise our conceptions about them or further differentiate their meaning (perhaps specifying differences in time, place, personnel, or forms of social control).

Although situations are never identical, they can be abstracted and typified. Further, they are perceived as being controlled by and constitutive of organizations, groups, institutions, and societies. The ability to refer to norms proves to be an essential means by which framing occurs. Although behavior may result from situated demands, our interpretations of the behaviors of others are connected to enduring features of a group, organization, or community (Lawler, Thye, and Yoon 2009).

Following Goffman, understanding which actions are appropriate constitutes the situational frame. Fortunately for the existence of easy interaction and the continuation of the interaction order, these understandings are usually readily comprehensible. Although the ease of interaction is occasionally breached and notable and dramatic ambiguities and misunderstandings arise, framing justifies norms through these understandings about appropriate actions. Such behaviors are not demanded by an overarching society but make sense as rules of order within an interaction domain.

## Framing Mushrooming

Mushroomers need strategies to justify their activities, which apparently violate their collective belief that the wild should be protected from human intrusion. Framing allows them to justify their activities as normatively acceptable and to think of their behaviors as moral. In sponsoring ideas of the "ought," mushroomers engage in claims-making that is tied to local practices and group authority. Norms are not hidden in the woods but uncovered by these amateur mycologists, who bolster their community by building rhetorics of virtue.

Despite the linkage of mushroom collecting and environmentalism, in practice mushroomers are engaged in an extractive activity that affects the microecology of forests and fields, an integral part of mushrooming. Some hobbyists speak of "harvesting mushrooms," borrowing an image from agricultural cultivation. Common terms used to describe mushroomers recognize their impact: "collectors," "pickers," and "hunters" (but not "fungus watchers"). In their talk, the tension between picking mushrooms and preserving the environment was evident:

> Andy recounts how he found several Hen of the Woods mushrooms in a local nature reserve. Molly notes that it is illegal to pick there, commenting, "If they catch you, you'll be one sorry person." Andy responds: "I told them [the rangers] that there were kids picking flowers and when they went down there, I picked the mushrooms." [*Loud laughter*] Someone jokes: "You're evil." Molly adds: "That's the height of ingenuity."[1]

Such ingenious mushroomers are esteemed, but with ambivalence. As is often the case, values conflict and groups must establish practices that mediate the conflict.

Mushroomers tell each other repeatedly and heatedly that they treat the woods with respect. They are devoted to this belief—any suggestion that this is not so is met with indignation—but they are equally devoted to gaining natural treasures. Humor is useful in their attempts to frame their activities so as to avoid the conflict, as when a group forayed for treasured morel mushrooms in a nature area where mushrooms should only have been picked for study. One informant joked: "We might study them as they're cooking in the pan. We have to have a certain amount of respect for things."

How can mushroomers frame their activities to justify what might seem to be behaviors that other naturalists would reject? In their framing, they provide excuses and justifications. First, they minimize the extent of the harm, and second, avowing moral identities, they differentiate themselves from and stigmatize those who do *real* damage, preserving their moral stature through boundary work. In this they are similar to other groups that want to gain rewards at the cost of others who are less committed.

*Minimization*    Minimizing potential damage is common among mushroomers. Collectors frame their activity as foraging, similar to the behavior of animals. Since we must all eat something, the somewhat implausible claim is that there is "no difference between the man who buys the mushrooms at the store and the person who picks the mush-rooms out of the woods." Mushroomers argue that there are sufficiently few of them that damage is limited.

Further, some mushroomers claim that picking fungi does not harm the environment because of fungal biology. A mushroom appears to be a plant, rooted in the soil, but in fact a mushroom is the plant's fruiting body, and so these mushroomers define their activity as *mere* fruit-picking. This definition comforts individuals doing what they would otherwise not be likely to do by suggesting that they are contributing to a natural and ecologically sound process:

> Since the mushroom we eat is only the fruiting body of the hidden plant, I have no more qualms about my harvest interrupting a valuable natural process. . . . Anybody who likes oysters (and many who do not) will like oyster mushrooms. So will anyone who likes to contemplate the recycling of nutrients in a forest. When I began eating oyster mushrooms from wasted logs, I became a part of that useful cycle. (quoted in Kaufman 1983, 8–9)

This claim is something of a fiction, since the fruiting body contains the seeds (spores) for additional mushrooms, but it is a comforting fic-tion that preserves the normative legitimacy of mushrooming by sug-gesting that damage is avoided in the name of environmentalism.

*Differentiation*    A second technique is to differentiate oneself from stig-matized others, drawing sturdy normative boundaries. At one extreme are those who pick mushrooms only for study and avoid picking "for the pot." John Schaaf (1983, 37), a former editor of the *Mycena News*, the newsletter of the San Francisco Mycological Society, expressed this position:

> Just as the joy of birdwatching is enhanced by investigating the subject while disturbing it the least, so the mycologist can derive pleasure from the study of any fungus, edible or not, by observing it in its habitat over a time, watching its growth and succession patterns, discovering its higher purpose. A few specimens are sometimes taken, any one of which may provide the makings of a hundred microscope slides. . . . Some of our Council members don't even eat mushrooms; but then you wouldn't expect the head of the local Audubon chapter to go around biting cassowaries.

Schaaf's position is uncommon: almost all mushroomers eat wild mushrooms, and for many it is their main interest. But by violating the norm, he underlines it. Typically mushroomers condemn their "greedy" colleagues who scour the woods. A mushroomer named Joyce told me "that she is angered by how some people pick all the mushrooms they can, and then drop the ones that are inedible by the side of the road. She gives the example of 'Latvians' who go through the woods kicking those mushrooms that they can't dry for eating."

Groups share an implicit belief as to one's proper share. Deviants violate local justice norms, which are linked to assumptions about the carrying capacity of the environment. Such examples frame the activity as moral action: the character of the woods is undermined by human remains. It is bad enough to pick all the mushrooms, but to leave broken mushrooms offends the mycological sensibility. As in all domains, novices must be socialized to normative expectations.

As these mycological examples suggest, framing is critical to the performance of norms and to the politics of identity, just as the existence and knowledge of norms is crucial for framing. Frameworks of meaning permit situations to be interpreted. Our behavior is always potentially meaningful to our colleagues, as well as to those who have had similar experiences. Using similar experiences to bolster community life requires that we treat our common historical past as moral endeavors, making norms real.

## Negotiating Norms

Constraints limit action choices. As I argued in chapter 3, a macrofoundation provides a platform for microanalysis. Norms are never simply personal choices, nor are they captured from the air; their effects are consequential, lasting, and grounded in history.

Yet, recognizing that stable structures exist and actors strive to incorporate consistency and continuity into their worlds, propriety varies because of different experiences, interests, and local cultures. Given this diversity, how do participants adjust their behavior so that situations can operate smoothly? The answer is embedded in interaction itself. Following from the work of Anselm Strauss (1978), I argue that interactants *negotiate* with each other, a process by which individual perspectives are merged to create a social world.

Within the interactionist tradition, few images have had a more profound and enduring impact over the past half-century than that of negotiation, a metaphor derived from the research that Strauss and his colleagues (1964) conducted in two psychiatric hospitals. Focusing on emerging differences in psychiatric ideologies, norms of practice, and competing occupational cultures, they analyzed how these differences affected the interaction order.

Several aspects of the negotiation perspective are similar to normative analysis. First, Strauss suggested that all social order is negotiated order; organization is essential, but it is impossible without some measure of negotiation. Second, negotiations are contingent on the structural conditions of the organization. As patterned creations of meaning, negotiations follow lines of communication. Third, negotiations have temporal limits, and like norms, they may be renewed, revised, and reconstituted. Fourth, changes in the organizational structure require a revision of the negotiated order. External features of life worlds are linked to the micropolitics of the negotiated order. Individuals and society, reflected in the normative order, constantly generate each other through negotiation, and that negotiation occurs within the arena of group life.

Three assumptions are central to the negotiated order perspective. First, negotiated order is based on how group members perceive the rules of the structure in which they are embedded (thus, rules are contextual). Second, change is continuous. Third, individuals and groups continually adjust the situations in which they are embedded, assuming that individuals are conscious of their own positions within the group and that they act to control others' impressions of them. This has the potential to shift the expectations for actions in the group; norms are in dynamic tension.

Face-to-face contact introduces the possibility of multiple meanings and also the possibility of a solution. In situations where the shared understanding of norms is perfect and agreement on the desirability of these rules is universal, no negotiation is necessary. Yet, this perfect understanding is impossible, even when a legitimate authority sets the rules; diversity of perspectives must be coordinated for social order to be achieved. The belief in the reality of norms limits potential meanings by establishing shared interpretations: modes of action that become ritualized and tacit. Although a group may strive to maintain consistent meaning, this consistency is imperfect, given the need to incorporate multiple perspectives. Ultimately, group life is based on adjusting lines of action to achieve collective ends.

Negotiation takes several forms. The *what* that is being negotiated is not always straightforward. For instance, groups must determine whether a norm is desirable. Another issue is whether a given action constitutes an instance of a norm. Both the scope of a norm and its relevance are subject to negotiation. Fortunately, a range of interpretations is often possible if a group does not hold to explicit rules, as long as it still holds to the belief that consensus exists. A measure of ambiguity provides a cushion for internal disagreement. However, once disagreement is recognized, negotiation is necessary if group rupture is to be avoided. Since most individuals are strongly motivated to permit interaction to proceed smoothly, negotiation often proves successful. When individuals place priority on "getting along," negotiation will be the preferred method of agreeing on behavioral proprieties. However, when the establishment of formal and explicit rules is necessary, more formal mechanisms will be invoked that are less subject to negotiation.

## Negotiating Mushrooming

In most activities, even those that might be done alone, participants treasure the presence of others. Yet, having others share one's experiences requires coordination, especially when group members are in competition or do not share the same goals. Group members usually want to coordinate values and expectations and will adjust their actions to encourage harmonious interaction. Although conflict can occur, low-level dissent is camouflaged as much as possible to avoid an explicit clash, which could undercut the idioculture and even threaten the group's existence.

Sharing the woods builds community, but a danger exists. Searching for mushrooms can breed competition. In the zero-sum game of finding mushrooms, the mushroom that I pick, you can not. In each domain norms are necessary for the allocation of social goods. Activities that involve shared space and competition for limited resources require that participants adhere to norms that attempt to preserve harmony. Demonstrating that one has the largest pile of fungus carries status. This is particularly evident among morel hunters, who compare the number or weight of the morels they have gathered. Although this competition is treated as friendly, under the surface the rivalry is real and potential ill will must be masked.

A joking culture legitimates bragging rights but simultaneously exerts social control. Since mushroomers like to demonstrate their prowess, a group needs strategies to mitigate status envy. Ms. Mushroom (1984, 28), the author of a "mushroom etiquette" column, advises:

> One should not overstate one's good fortune. No matter that one has an entire pickup load of Morels to process, one is permitted only to allude to having found a few, and to state that knowing one's friend might be wanting some, one would like to share. Not only does this induce in every acquaintance a warm feeling of friendship, but one appears beneficent while simultaneously retaining a goodly number of mushrooms for oneself.

To be sure, this advice is designed to be humorous, but as with much joking, it captures something fundamental about the strain between collegiality and competition. Both are widely held values that must be negotiated in practice. Bragging rights are legitimate, as participants enjoy narrating stories, but limits exist. These hobbyists assert that they themselves do not engage in extreme forms of status display—*they* do not count or weigh their finds—while defending themselves against the accusation that they treat the activity as mercenary. Stories, if they are to work, require a supportive community of listeners. Jealousy is a natural response, but one that must be tamed in the name of good fellowship and the preservation of group harmony.

The need to curb competition is even more evident in the woods. Here the zero-sum quality of the hunt is clear. Either I pick the mushroom or she does. It goes in my basket or his. A normative ethic of "finders keepers" operates:

> Suddenly one person stopped, exclaiming, and turned to collect two obscure brownish morels in the shade of a rounded white granite rock. I stopped, too, and saw a morel almost under one of her feet. . . . In mushrooming . . . it was all right for me to collect that morel, and so I did. (Geary 1982, 72)

Despite this norm's seemingly universal quality, in practice it is negotiated. That the author was a novice and the other mushroomer had just found a pair of morels bolstered this politeness. To pick a mushroom in another's personal space is a matter of delicacy; to find too many when searching with others without sharing is also questionable. One must balance one's own success with the need for harmonious relations:

> Should one encounter what is termed a "mushroom garden" while at a fellow mushroomer's side, it is considered ill form to sweep the entire contents of the garden into one's own basket. However, should one be confronted by a garden of 100 or so Morels while momentarily alone, one is permitted to gather the first 80 or so specimens before alerting one's bosom companion to the situation. It is wise to leave at least one or two fresh, non-rotten Morels among the remaining 20. (Ms. Mushroom 1984, 28)

Once again, the jocular tone mediates the conflict between the instrumental goals of the hunt and the expressive needs of the community. The existence of a norm (or several competing ones) does not eliminate or erase conflict but rather provides strategies for resolving it through the negotiation of action based on common values.

The danger of competition straining cohesion was evident when a group of which I was a part found an oyster mushroom with a reddish stain. A mushroomer named Jerry immediately joked that it was blood from rival mushroomers. More serious were instances in which collectors raced through the woods gathering all that they could without regard to the primary virtue of sociability. As in any social world, examples warn against improper behavior. In the following accounts from my interviews, conflict is recognized, but humor is used to suggest that it can be managed:

> I'm thinking in particular of the morel pickers who are going out with the idea that it's not just a hunt, it's a race. Fill a basket as quickly as possible. . . . There's an awful lot of greed involved in this. . . . You've got grown-ups acting like children in the woods. . . . If you grab all the mushrooms, that is in many places considered good form. . . . Some people go out of their way to share; they find a patch of mushrooms, and they call their friends in; they share. And other people would never say a word; they would pick every bloody mushroom. And they'll come back with a basket full of mushrooms, and, if on the way back home, they got a full basket and everybody else has little bits, too bad for those people.

> I took some people out to this area that I had picked earlier, and I had left some puffballs to grow. And I had found them, and since I was bringing them to my puffballs, I had expected them to share them. They grabbed them and put them in their bags. And I thought, "I'm never taking you out again!" So, one of the etiquette things is to determine in advance how you are going to divide up the spoils.

Actual instances of storied greed are rare and perhaps are exaggerated for the sake of a compelling narrative. Yet, references to norms manage the strain, as is evident in the tension over the degree to which one should trade personal interests in order to build group relations. This strain is evident in any situation (business, sexual intimacy, parenting) in which the maximization of one's own desires conflicts with local values.

Negotiation ultimately depends on identification: imagining the perspective of the other and adjusting to it (Couch 1989; Mead 1934). Society is built on mutual role-taking, a process that depends on real or imagined relations. Identification and role-taking require understanding the perspective of the other, a skill that is grounded in knowledge of the social categories to which the other belongs. Norms—coupled with routinized behaviors—can serve as an easy solution in otherwise ambiguous circumstances. Whether or not norms maximize rewards for individuals, the recognition of their existence smooths the flow of interaction. If norms are not real, they are as good as real in providing for collective identification.

## Narrating Norms

Although I treat norms as actions that are performed, as *doings*, equally importantly they can be narrated. They are *tellings*. Norms are a resource in the rhetorical construction of social relations and in avowing moral identities. Sharing events permits participants to have their perspective ratified by an audience, and of course, telling itself is a performance: talk as action (White 1987; Austin 1975).

To speak of norms as told can be understood in at least three ways. First, socialization is often achieved through talk. Individuals are not merely shown what they should and should not do, but frequently they are *exhorted* to select certain actions in contrast to others. The cliché "do as I say, not as I do," is an efficient, if not always effective, pedagogic technique. Individuals enter social worlds without a firm sense of propriety; talk presents appropriate models.

Linked to teaching is a second form of normative narrative: warnings in which individuals are hectored to behave in a socially ratified way. These warnings are often backed by threats as to what might happen if one violates core behavioral prescriptions, including the possibility of institutional action, which reminds actors of the potency of organized social control. Such warnings may or may not be effective in interactional arenas where authorities lack routine surveillance. Just because a claim is made for a formal norm does not mean that actors reject their preferred practices.

The third and most interesting example of talking about norms is the process through which norms are transformed into stories: moral messages embedded in narrative. Social actors are continually depicting the world around them through stories that encourage or discourage action. It is this that I focus on in my observations of mushroom collectors.

### Narrating Mushrooming

As in other realms, the narration of norms is evident among mushroomers. While various forms of discourse could be selected for analysis, I have chosen humor because jokes explicitly emphasize the moral boundaries of a community (Fine and DeSoucey 2005). Boundary work—separating proper and improper behavior—is central to amusement. Typically both teller and audience recognize the point of the remark, even when the talk is couched as "fun." The bundle of stories that participants share in their idiocultures transforms individuals into a group. The "formulas of self" produced by these narratives provide the building blocks necessary for an identity to be tied to an interaction order. But within a group, several normative orders may exist, and to preserve the group each must be given deference.

An essential issue for mushroomers is the management of risk, since some mushrooms are toxic if consumed. How do collectors select their hazard level? Humor is one means through which groups collectively transform the dangerous into the manageable (Fry 1963; Davis 1993). The ability of humor to deflect unpleasant thoughts is not merely a technique of individual psychology but a strategic property of self-reflexive groups, organizations, and communities. Disagreements can be made agreeable through the claim that the differences do not rend the fabric of group life.

Concern over the expertise of group members is central for mushroomers. The joking about competence centers on risk norms: coping with personal and communal danger. Risk is not an objective reality (Short 1984; Clarke 2005); rather, it is a construct on which communities may disagree (Douglas and Wildavsky 1982, 186–98). Further, risk is not inherently undesirable when we are confident that we can manage it; it can provide a challenge that leads to active engagement (Csikszentmihalyi 1975), a form of edgework (Lyng 2004). Individuals and groups shape their attitudes toward risk by processing it through talk. Humor is one technique by which actors confront their generalized anxiety and specific responses to that anxiety. Despite different individual judgments, groups persuade themselves that risk is manageable because they can joke about it: how can it be serious if they are laughing?

Central to understanding how communities respond is the variability of risk tolerance, evident in the different normative cultures of mushroomers. These cultures differ in their judgments of the likelihood of danger and of how much unpleasantness is tolerable. Some collectors are cautious in their choices, while others are more daring and are willing to endure diarrhea for a novel experience. For both the conservative and the liberal the possibility of poisoning is real, however close to or away from the boundary of toxicity their explorations take them. Humor provides a basis by which different "oughts" are inserted into interaction realms without producing offense.

*Conservative Norms*    Mushroomers who express fear of poisonous mushrooms reveal what others consider excessive alarm. Some collectors prefer not to touch lethal mushrooms for fear that contact might be toxic; spores might seep through their skin or be ingested unintentionally. Although the amount of toxins consumed in this way is clinically insignificant and fears about these dangers relate more to cultural traditions of mycophobia and beliefs in sympathetic magic than to any real danger, these fears affect action. One mushroomer I observed, named Mark, worried "about touching *Amanitas* and *Galerinas* [both deadly poisonous]. He only touches the *Amanita* with the edge of his knife, and then wipes the knife carefully. I touch a

*Galerina* on a foray, and Mark warns me: 'Now you can't pick any mushrooms for the table.' "

Given that the cautious spurn eating mushrooms, one of the main pleasures of the activity, they must defend their position. They do this by teasing the daring over appropriate norms of consumption:

> Beth says of cooking Honey Caps: "Bring the water to a boil, then throw out the water" [because the poison found in the mushrooms might remain in the water].
> Dave, more liberal, responds: "I never did that and I never got sick."
> Beth retorts, rejecting his rashness: "You're crazy anyhow, Dave."

Through humor, liberals and conservatives spar over the rules for group activity. The existence of a norm does not suggest there are no rival norms: the challenge is to permit each subgroup to feel that the group shows deference to its beliefs and permits space for its behavior. The problem for conservatives is that if they are wrong they have missed out on a treasure. That others consume these mushrooms and survive is a challenge that humor must diffuse. As a result, conservatives present themselves as rational actors who, after weighing the dangers, have made a considered judgment, even while recognizing that their rationality is contested by others. The presentation of their stance results not in measured discourse but in amusing banter. Persuasion is rarely at issue. Normative beliefs have been addressed, but shared affiliation has not been breached because the remarks are not to be taken seriously, permitting rival normative systems to coexist.

*Liberal Humor*   Some daring mushroomers argue that so long as one avoids deadly mushrooms, the experience will be worth the discomfort. Life is filled with adversity, they note, and one learns from distress: no pain, no gain. An aesthetic experience need not be pleasant. For these individuals, the norms of mushrooming include a greater measure of risk and discomfort.

A mushroomer named Howard described his desire to try numerous species, even some allegedly dangerous: "I eat mushrooms every year that I haven't eaten before, and the rule is that you don't eat a mushroom unless you are 100 percent sure. Yet, I question 100 percent." When asked why he would want to try a possibly dangerous mushroom, Howard replied: "To see what it was like. To *tell* someone that this is what it was like, so they don't have to read it out of a book, because books aren't necessarily true. . . . I've put up with a lot of unpleasantness for the sake of the experience."

To defend themselves against the charge that they are suicidal or masochistic, these mushroomers direct humor toward those who publicly avoid any mushroom that might be judged risky. Although most of them are confident in their abilities and do not consume mushrooms whose toxicity they are not *reasonably* certain about, this attitude involves a measure of bravado. Inserting an embrace of threat into group culture (Lyng 2004), they are making a status claim that they have experienced a corner of the mycological world that others have avoided.

Some liberals explicitly counter the belief that they should avoid anything that might be unpleasant or that they cannot exactly identify by brazenly claiming that the effects of poisoning are not so bad. Don, one of the mushroomers I observed, "tells the club that eating *Verpa bohemica* makes some people temporarily lose coordination in their arms and legs. Kristi jokes: 'You just get a little spastic, so what?' (laughter). Don jokes back, 'I was there before I started' (laughter)."

Attributing illness to the mere touch of mushrooms is scorned by those who feel that such fastidiousness is unnecessary or even neurotic:

> Sam jokes to Jerry, the club president, about showing mushrooms to the club: "Be sure you can handle the *Amanitas* first. It sparks conversation." He refers to the time the previous year when the then-president was criticized by some for holding an Amanita, and then touching edible mushrooms.

This joker adopted a transitory persona while he was playing the role of others. Sam was recognized as not speaking in his own voice when making this remark. Yet, his perspective was reflected in the self portrayed in his humor. The selves that are projected or implied are a joking transformation of the real attitudes in the community, but because they do not reflect real persons, the jokes do not undermine friendships. Speakers are joking while expressing normative orientations. While joking, they are not "just joking."

Groups may face a normative battle, but community is preserved when the battle is sheathed in humorous talk, which enables members to realize that alternative standards can coexist so long as deference to the legitimacy of each standard is shown. Humor reveals local ambivalence over proper behavior. Since few participants define *themselves* as embracing an extreme position, they laugh at jabs that exaggerate the attitudes toward danger of those whose desire for certainty is too great as well as those whose desire is not great enough. Jokers satirize excess and inflexibility, and so humorous talk, which constructs the boundaries of appropriate group behavior, can be enjoyed by all members.

Although jokes provide a warning or a lesson, they also make sense in the context of a smooth and enjoyable conversation among colleagues. By conveying shared moral values, at least for the duration of the conversation, they affirm the legitimacy of the normative perspectives that underlie the reality of a group culture. Humorous talk may have the express purpose of entertainment, but it is effective through its ability to bolster belief. Social order can be seen, in this sense, as consisting of shared discourse. Conversation transforms social propriety into sticky rhetoric.

## Norms as Local Production

Norms and behavioral expectations must not be separated from the meaning systems of the groups that enact them or from the interaction that occurs in the local arenas in which they are enacted. The embrace of norms constitutes a commitment to local culture and an obligation to the group. The embedding of norms in group life involves the framing of context, the negotiation of the interests of social actors, and the narrative depiction of behavioral rules. Although I emphasize the agency of sets of actors to create and shape meaning within local contexts, their agency depends on their preference for cohesion. The desire for comity motivates individuals to relinquish their material interests for the sake of others. This does not mean that disagreement is absent, but interacting groups do have a strong desire to adjust. Conflict may be present, but groups strive to transform conflict into accord. Deference and negotiation are crucial in this regard. In many domains, group members prefer not to win at the expense of others but to find common ground. When winners and losers emerge, rituals are needed to smooth the divide. Actors share a powerful desire to cause interaction to proceed without strain, and they adjust their behavior to ensure this result, satisficing outcomes for the sake of harmony. Participants accept violations of their own standards for the sake of comity.

In any system, normative violations are occasions for addressing the validity of previously accepted standards. They become the grounds for talk. The performance of stories may be taken as the reality that stands behind the narrative. In this, narratives provide accounts of what is and what should be. A violation of social standards is the kind of notable event that interactional partners may reasonably share, and it is one that they must address to defend the moral basis of social life.

A normative structure presumes interpretive and behavioral options linked to the existence of a cultural tool-kit. Actors select from among a set of possibilities in responding to a local context. Only rarely is a single behavior judged to be the only appropriate alternative.

Norms are often sponsored by individuals, who become, in effect, normative entrepreneurs who help norms and expectations emerge or change. In endorsing or opposing this normative emergence, actors may shape the social order and take responsibility for encouraging the group to be related to the interaction order. Norms are always potentially in play, being created, altered, or negated.

Ultimately, a model of social life based on local context rejects the view of norms as real, material, and unchanging regularities that exist separate from group culture. By conceiving norms as a part of an interaction order, we embrace the vitality of norms as they are lived.

# Chapter 5

## The Performance of Ideology

One remembers the story, probably *ben trovato*, to the effect that when Churchill had finished his famous rally of isolated England, "We shall fight on the beaches, we shall fight on the landing grounds, we shall fight in the fields and in the streets, we shall fight in the hills . . . ," he turned to an aide and whispered, "and we shall hit them over the head with soda-water bottles, because we haven't any guns." The quality of social rhetoric in ideology is thus not proof that the vision of sociopsychological reality upon which it is based is false and that it draws its persuasive power from any discrepancy between what is believed and what can, now or someday, be established as scientifically correct. . . . Although fortunately it never had to be tested, it seems most likely that the British would have indeed fought on the beaches, landing grounds, streets, and hills—with soda-water bottles too, if it came to that—for Churchill formulated accurately the mood of his countrymen and, formulating it, mobilized it by making it a public possession, a social fact, rather than a set of disconnected, unrealized private emotions.
—Clifford Geertz, "Ideology as a Cultural System" (1973, 231–32)

GROUPS CAN be self-contained, focused on their expressive culture, but their potential goes much deeper: small groups serve as the very basis of political life when they establish the conditions for political action and the foundations of civil society and the public sphere. We see this in social movements (Fine and Stoecker 1985) and in open gatherings, such as town meetings (Bryan 2004). As agents of change, groups are spaces in which a moral order and societal commitment are generated. In this I embrace the motto that all politics is local— not just because politics addresses concerns of bounded relevance, but because politics is performed in interaction scenes that shape civic talk when it becomes legitimate and when it does not (Eliasoph 1998; Walsh 2003). The embrace of political ideas depends on the expectations generated through local affiliation.

In this chapter, I describe how ideology—the intellectual cement of political order and an intellectual construction designed to make persuasive the claim that actions fit together in an overarching frame-work—is based in relations and communities. Where appropriate, I draw again on my research on mushroomers. The group effects on politics are both ideational and behavioral, just as political decisions shape group life.

## Ideology and Its Groups

In analyzing ideology, scholars have noted that it integrates beliefs and resolves social *strains* (Johnson 1968; Parsons 1951, 1967; White 1961) or advances the political and economic interests of social segments, status groups, or economic classes (Mannheim 1936; Marx and Engels 1846/1976). This traditional perspective on ideology has stood at considerable distance from the analysis of interaction. In reaction to this structural approach, some analysts, such as Clifford Geertz (1973) and Thomas Gieryn (1983), propose that greater attention needs to be directed toward examining rhetorical strategies—how and why ideologists use discursive resources as they present ideological beliefs. Fewer stress the need to connect ideology to action spaces or to examine how groups use ideologies as they pursue their everyday activities and recognize their lived experience (Eliasoph 1998; Purvis and Hunt 1993, 479). Yet, it is the connection of ideology with collective action that demonstrates how ideology affects the local level—how ideology shapes groups and how groups shape ideology (Lizardo 2008). Recognizing the salience of local context, we see that social change depends on group culture and that contentious politics emerges from the dynamics of interaction.

Often left undefined in practice, ideology is a nebulous and slippery concept. For Antonio Gramsci (1992), ideology is part of the process of cultural hegemony: it maintains power relations without explicit reference to those relations. As David McLellan (1986, 1) suggests, ideology is perhaps "the most elusive concept in the whole of social science." As such, it has become a "contested" concept, one for which any definition provokes intense controversy. One reason why the construct of ideology has become so controversial is that it is intertwined with related and similarly ambiguous constructs such as myth, belief system, creed, worldview, and value orientation. Ideology consequentially has become a "cluster concept" (Sartori 1969, 398).

The term "ideology" was first coined in 1797 by Destutt de Tracy, a member of a group of philosophers known as the French materialists. These thinkers used the label to refer to a science of ideas that examines the connections among ideas and explores the relations of ideas to sensory reality, a form of Lockean philosophy as imported to France (Mead 1936, 430–31). This approach was proposed as a method for developing ideas that might provide a natural or secular foundation for postrevolutionary society. In its origins, "ideology represented a philosophical attempt to develop scientific ideas as the basis of political order" (Kinloch 1981, 5). The original meaning, interests, and social conditions associated with the construct of ideology highlight themes that are still found in contemporary analyses. Graham Kinloch (1981) suggested that ideologies consist of sets of beliefs formulated in an attempt to develop "rational" or "scientific" solutions to social and political problems. These are diagnoses of the social world that depend on both rational and empirical support. In this standard view, ideologies differ from religious or mythical belief systems in that they attempt to base their truth claims in empirical evidence or in logic rather than through faith, revelation, or the authority of the speaker. This rationalist view of ideology perhaps gives too much credit to cognition, ignoring the role of social factors and group cultures in generating ideological affiliation.

Yet, this view of ideology as linked to rationality or self-reflection is surprisingly common. Alvin Gouldner (1976, 30) proposed that ideologies are a distinctively modern form of belief system and represent a historically novel mode of discourse "predicated on the idea of grounding political action in secular and rational theory." Jürgen Habermas (1970) posited that ideologies imply a self-reflective view of ideas connected to the rise of the modern bourgeois mentality. He further suggested that ideologies require the existence of a state system that is dependent on the persuasion of masses of people and in which alternative sets of ideas are possible and publicly available. Most importantly, theorists such as Gouldner and Habermas argue that ideologies are publicly disseminated forms of modern *discourse* that attempt to base political action in "rational" premises. Discourse becomes part of how ideology is made relevant to actors in their lived experience through what Louis Althusser (1971, 171) spoke of as "interpellation" (or "hailing"—recruiting and transforming its subjects; see also Purvis and Hunt 1993, 482–83).

However, problems emerge with this conception of ideology. It unnecessarily limits the concept of ideology to modern and "rational" sets of beliefs. In contrast, by treating ideology as a field of action, we can make the concept theoretically agnostic in terms of its connection to modernity and rationality. I treat ideology as a linked set of beliefs about the social or political order that is used within a community, whatever the content of the linkage and the beliefs. This stance permits the examination of a wider variety of linked beliefs, not only those that have been defined by elites as ideological, often because of their connection to an established political party or social movement. My approach suggests that ideologies can be produced within a wide variety of social spheres and may include religious ideologies, scientific ideologies, and artistic ideologies as well as political ideologies. Further, the forms that ideology takes are shaped by its local context. Its practice is found within group culture.

Although I broaden the referents of ideology, the concept does not lack boundaries. The ideas that constitute ideology imply shared beliefs about an empirical reality, but not all beliefs should be classed as part of an ideology. Some beliefs lack an evaluative component and are presented as facts. These truth claims are apparently empirical and dispassionate statements about the world. If I claim that today is Thursday, this is my belief, but one that makes no central claim to morality or judgment; it could not be contested, other than empirically, and, thus, is not ideological. Likewise, beliefs that are unconnected to other beliefs would not qualify as ideological. To believe that some foodstuff is harmful or healthy would not by itself be ideological, unless this belief connected to a set of beliefs about the material basis of food production or to a theory about nutrition.

Ideological beliefs are a subset of all beliefs that are connected to attitudes (Brown 1973). In referring to "attitude"—itself a contested concept—I emphasize its evaluative component: the connection of depictions of the world to judgments about that depiction. This collectively held link between *is* and *ought,* as applied to a sphere of action, is at the heart of ideology.

Attitudes, as routinely defined within the social-psychology literature, contain elements of cognition, behavior, and affect (Zimbardo, Ebbesen, and Maslach 1977, 20–21; Schuman 1994). Attitudes provide a way of looking at objects or realities, a guide for evaluating them emotionally, and an incipient program for action. Attitudes are moral statements (*ought* statements) that are associated with truth claims, evaluative sentiments, and dispositions to action. But more crucially, attitudes are not owned by individuals but are part of an epistemic community (Haas 1992) or community of knowledge. Attitudes are situated in an interactional arena. An ideology consists of a bundle of interconnected attitudes (Ashley 1984) that reflects a pattern of beliefs within an interactional order.

Another component of a definition of ideology is that these bundles of attitudes reveal an interpretation of a cultural or political order. Pragmatists posit that individuals and collectivities are driven by problematic situations to make sense of the world and to select behavioral proprieties. Ideologies diagnose what is and is not problematic. They also offer guidelines for how group members should negotiate or resolve those phenomena that they define as problematic.

In essence, ideologies present shared judgments about action, ideas, and organization, implying a critique based on the support of local groups. Fascism, communism, and classical liberalism are quintessential examples of belief systems that explicitly present a social judgment and a proposed solution: they are self-conscious ideologies, but each depends on the support provided to belief-holders by institutions and smaller groups; people do not accept these perspectives or act on them without social support. Even though the labels suggest that the ideologies are generalized systems of knowledge, they are known through the actions that endow them with significance and are tied as much to interacting groups as to the distant groups that shape larger social systems.

Thus, ideology consists of *a set of interconnected beliefs and their associated attitudes that are shared and utilized by members of a group or population and that relate to disputes or disagreements about social and political issues. These beliefs have an explicit evaluative and implicit behavioral component.* Like most definitions, this one has a studied ambiguity, but it focuses attention on two key points: (1) the linkages between beliefs and attitudes indicate that ideology is part of a system by which groups interpret the world in an evaluative fashion; and (2) ideological beliefs guide action in the social and political realm. This definition locates ideology squarely within a group or network of groups. Ideology is social and involves action.

Sadly, much writing divorces broad ideological perspectives from local, clearly definable ideologies. Many analysts fail to specify what, *in practice,* constitutes an ideology. Perhaps we should not be surprised that this task has been avoided: ideology, like culture, is a panoramic concept, a mist swirling above fields of action (Ghaziani 2009). To provide an empirical basis for this analysis of ideology, I draw from literature and research about environmental ideologies, building on my ethnographic observations of mushroomers.

## Ideology as Group Discourse

The traditional model of ideology asserts that ideas are conditioned by social structure, economic organizations, state apparatuses, and the means of production (Wuthnow 1985; Williams 1988). Whether rooted in the intellectual lineage of Marx, Durkheim, or Mannheim, the fundamental argument is similar: ideas are dependent variables that are shaped and even determined by independent societal forces.

However, theorists have challenged this orthodox approach to ideology. Several have either highlighted the cultural autonomy of ideology—a *strong program* of ideology (Alexander 2004)—or stressed the intersecting effects of ideology and social structure (Geertz 1973; Sewell 1985; Wuthnow 1987). Even within the materialist paradigm, greater emphasis has been placed on the independent importance and relative autonomy of ideology and ideological practices (Glaeser 2003; Hall 1986;

Therborn 1982; Althusser 1971). Sociologists now accord greater weight to the effects of ideology in the structuring of social phenomenology and even personal identity (Warren 1990). Still, most analysts ignore how ideology shapes and is shaped through social interactions (but see Gieryn 1983; Lachmann 1988).

A local sociology provides concepts that contribute to such a goal, particularly any effort to determine how collective meaning is constructed and embedded in social interaction. While cultural and materialist approaches illustrate how ideological symbols are not simply reducible to social-structural forms, an interactionist approach can offer distinctive insight and added value by exploring how ideology helps actors cope with their lived reality and facilitates communication.

By integrating meaning and interaction, we reach the nub of pragmatism: how people use ideas to realize their interests and purposes (Thayer 1981). In addressing this concern, I focus on how individuals and groups *do ideology* within local contexts and the connections among ideology, folk ideas, and moral order. This analysis includes the emotional context of ideology, framing conventions in the public presentation of ideology, and the connection of ideology to small groups and the activation of networks and social movements. Following chapter 3, I treat ideology as heeding the obdurate reality of the structures in which individuals are enmeshed while linking it to lived experience and interaction orders.

## Ideology, Images, and Moral Order

Defining ideology as constituted by attitudes and beliefs situated in a local context highlights the connection between ideological beliefs and social structures, but the practical process by which ideas are enacted and connected to topically relevant experience must be theoretically explicated (Rogers 1981, 155). Thus, ideology is effective only when three conditions are met: the context must be dramatically framed to link it to widely held moral concerns or the *ought* beliefs of a community (Gamson, Fireman, and Rytina 1982), there must be a set of images connected to these *ought* beliefs, and the situation must be made locally relevant to participants. Although ideology can be conceptualized as a set of moral concerns activated when they are perceived as relevant, ideology cannot have an impact without being *enacted*. This group-based model of ideology is distinctly different from the traditional macropolitical perspective. Ideology becomes a sphere of action created by groups with their own interests and resources.

Groups share images about what is good, just, and proper, and from these master images they spin analyses, make decisions, and take action, including forms of political engagement if they are sufficiently motivated and have access to the options provided by political parties and social movements. Alan Dundes (1972, 95) refers to these images as "folk ideas," or "traditional notions that a group of people have about the nature of man, of the world, and of man's life in the world." Folk ideas operate like domain assumptions (Gouldner 1970) or presuppositions (Alexander 1982) and are fundamentally prereflective (Rogers 1981, 157). They guide sense-making activities as people interact with the world around them. They proffer "a description of the nature of reality" (Dundes 1972, 102), a description that is *communal* in character.

Ideologies are shared by groups or publics that have collectively shared experiences. These experiences become typified into folk ideas that in turn affect how experiences are understood and judged. Folk ideas frame the situational definitions sedimented into the social order (Busch 1980). Thus, they are not simply derived from an amorphous, collective mentality but are emergent by means of common histories (Sawyer 2005).

Folk ideas are dramatic images that permit individuals to make sense of their world. Dundes (1972), for instance, argues that the idea of "unlimited good" is a central image for many American publics and can be used rhetorically as a form of framing. Unlimited good is a metaphor that can be applied as a rule of thumb in addressing numerous problems. For example, until quite recently, many Americans believed that they could freely use natural resources without limitation; they imagined that they lived amid a "bounty of nature." This theme was evident in my research with mushroom collectors: most collectors resented limits on picking mushrooms because they claimed that there would always be a new crop. They resented the state or city parks that prevented them from picking mushrooms and often violated those rules. They also told stories and jokes about evading detection, pretending to look at flowers or birds, or about picking every last mushroom in sight, leaving only one to prop-agate a future crop. The idea of "overpicking" did not fit the images that groups of mushroomers held. Mushrooms were treated as a renewable resource,[1] and collectors mobilized this image to legitimate their self-interest. Picking the fruiting bodies of mushrooms, like picking berries, did not, according to their claims, affect the plant itself, and this claim was linked to the core folk idea that nature is bountiful.

Social-psychological research finds that people see their world not through a prism of complex formulations but through simple slogans, images, and metaphors as depicted within group surrounds.[2] Labels or categories combine experience into understandable and repeatable chunks (Rosch 1978), creating typifications of lived experience (Rogers 1981), but do so in arenas in which the typifications are explained and validated by others. Cognition must be supported through group action (Lichterman 2005). Although ideology depends on this mental clumping and chunking, the activation and organization of consciousness occurs within shared contexts. As Gouldner (1976, 82) wrote, ideology "activates certain [attitudes and] affects . . . and permits these to be communicated via reflexive, articulate and shared ideas."

Benedict Anderson (1991) argued in his examination of *imagined communities* that modern ideologies are uniquely reliant on shared language for obtaining social support and then on printed discourse for transmitting them to a larger public. For the idea of a nation to exist, a bounded set of communication channels must constitute the community. Yet, one should not privilege the text too firmly: the subtlety and detailed content that characterize written texts are lost on most of those who share ideology. We are predisposed to accept ideology without thinking, because the labels or categories are accepted as natural or inevitable (Berger and Luckmann 1967; Gramsci 1992).

Ideology does not belong only to intellectuals, nor, as Mannheim hoped, can it be avoided by them. Communist and fascist publics had "ideology," but this was vastly different from the finely spun interpretations of their leaders. There is ideology accessible to most and ideology debated by the few. Indeed, many adherents embraced only fragments of the larger ideology. These fragments were often condensed and dramatically mobilized in resonant images, as one especially ardent Nazi demonstrated when he declared, "What the Fuhrer appeals to . . . what carries us along is not rational argument, but the image" (Lifton 1987, 99).

With respect to the environment, images such as unlimited good, earth as a lifeboat, Mother Nature, the land ethic, the temple of nature, climate change, stewardship, and renewable resources shape how people approach nature and how they expect social institutions to respond. These common public images also become linked to imperial or Arcadian views of nature (Worster 1985), and they are used by supporters of competing ideologies (Lichterman 1996). My analysis of mushroomers, for instance, revealed three distinct groups of collectors: those who embraced a protectionist ethic (giving nature rights), those whose vision was organic (being at one with the environment), and those who took a humanist perspective (humans are just another species and have no fewer rights than other species; Fine 1998, 7–12). Each group's orientation suggests a certain political attitude as well as specific arguments and practices of collecting. The broad question revolves around the rights and privileges of human beings in their natural surroundings: do humans have dominion over "nature," or does "nature" have a voice?

It is not environmentalists as such, however, who have an ideology. Environmentalism is a label that is too broadly encompassing for meso-level analysis. Rather, we find groups with interests and resources. Thus, mushroomers, rock hounds, bird-watchers, and butterfly collectors may develop variant ideologies that address the local concerns of each public. Likewise, groups like Greenpeace, the Audubon Society, and Earth First! present variant views. Of course, as noted in chapter 2, groups rarely develop culture by themselves but rather borrow from the cultures of other groups, applying them as appropriate.

To speak of ideology as fixed is misleading, given the diversity of meso-level perspectives; what we find instead is a neighborhood of compatible ideologies, each spiraling from its interactional home into sympathetic groups that hope to build alliances by emphasizing what they treat as shared beliefs (Lichterman 2005). Groups may become linked into institutional networks through those who are brokers (Burt 1992). At the same time, relations within and among groups are in dynamic tension. Should the ideological formulations within a group seem too dissimilar, it may split or separate, as nearly happened in the Minnesota Mycological Society in a dispute over the best location for meetings between those who considered themselves scientists and those who "picked for the pot" (Fine 1998, 183–84). Further, groups may join together in the belief of a common worldview and set of interests.

Underlying the belief that ideological formulations are simple, based on moral evaluations, and reliant on dramatic images is the claim that a close connection exists between ideology and rhetoric. Through discourse, ideology is performed and made visual in the mind's eye of the audience. As in a good speech, dramatic images are central to an ideological identity and personal commitment (Billig 1987), and the images that generate responses are those with resonance (Schudson 1989). These images are a lens through which groups can view the world.

Ideology may appear analytical on its surface, but the immediacy of the imagery associated with it is replete with metaphor (Raynor 1980, 103; Mullins 1972, 506). As J. D. Raynor (1980, 104, 107) contended, the linguistic form of ideology "is picturesque and flamboyant; in particular, it abounds with metaphor." He asserts—metaphorically—that "metaphor is an important brush in the ideologist's paintbox, filling in the picture with a broad sweep, creating connections with the range of associations which a well-turned metaphor has at its disposal." Metaphor is a handy tool for the ideologist in presenting "how things are" and "how they ought to be"—images that resonate with lived experience and offer an appealing sense of how life can and should be lived. Through metaphor, the ideologist mobilizes images that enable publics to experience the "moral."

Dundes (1972) and others (Gusfield 1976; Nisbet 1976; Brown 1977; Lakoff and Johnson 1980; McCloskey 1990) have argued that interpretations of the world are inevitably grounded in metaphorical understandings. Thus, metaphor is not a distinctive feature of ideology; instead, it is built into the very structure of discourse and action. Ideologies are characterized by an abundance of metaphor, not only in the conscious tropes of speakers but in their choice of images when they are talking informally.[3] The examples of environmental worldviews presented earlier—different mushroomers thinking about nature as a temple or a refuge or a bounty—reveal this wealth of imagery.

By focusing on metaphor in activating images of what "ought" to be (Hitlin 2008; Lakoff 2006), I point to the centrality of ideology within a moral order (Wuthnow 1987). Typically, *ought* statements characterizing an ideology are most effectively employed by embedding them within an example that highlights their topical relevance. Examples work better than abstractions for framing and mobilizing attitudes. When social movement actors wish to galvanize public support, they offer instances that crystallize the *oughts* held by their audience, extending them to action that can be effective within local domains. By focusing on a recognized danger, environmental activists hope that these local troubles will be generalized to systemic problems (Lichterman 1996) and that a cadre of ideological selves will be created in the process. For instance, the groups of mushroomers I observed were vehemently opposed to a housing project that impinged on one of their collecting sites. On one foray, the discovery of the construction site provoked great anger—unusual for this typically apolitical group—about how the wealthy were destroying the community (Eliasoph 1998). This threat to the preserves of club members was generalized in global statements about limiting human privilege at the expense of nature, always expressed with concern ostensibly rooted in damage to the fungal ecology.

Advocates in the environmental movement continually align action with a symbolic moral order by transforming personal passion and identity work into movement support. Consider the mobilization of public concern over "acid rain" (a frightening image), often noted in my mycological observations in the 1980s and now supplanted by concern over "global warming" and "climate change." For scientists and public policymakers, acid rain may have been a technical matter, but for the public (and mushroomers as a case in point), the controversy was moral and local. The impact of acid rain began with the term itself. The mass media's use of the label "acid rain" was a decision of consequence: it made the term available to be borrowed in local discourse. Both serious and jocular rhetoric were conditioned by the image of droplets of acid pelting down, stoking fears of "dead lakes."[4] The technical extent of the problem was obscure to the mushroomers I observed, but the belief that it could affect them was not. In their discourse the issue was made relevant by discussions of what acid rain might do and had done to mushroom fruitings, by bumper stickers (STOP ACID REAGAN), and by their political discussions. After one poor year of chanterelle fruitings, collectors speculated about a connection between their local concerns and this public policy issue. By making this connection, they activated an environmental ideology grounded in dramatic images and folk ideas: the belief that nature is threatened by human action and must be protected.

These images are not inevitable, and they are subject to change. Although images are often taken for granted, they may be challenged by individuals or subgroups. This problematizing is often a result of a dramatic event (an oil spill or nuclear power plant leak) elaborated by a moral entrepreneur. Suddenly the standing image is challenged by another image that for the moment is more potent. Moral entrepreneurs take dramatic events and shape them to be persuasive (Schneider 1985; Best 1999; Loseke 2003). The image now must be defended or dropped, but either way it is "in play" by the group and no longer taken for granted.

## Ideology and Emotion

Ideologies are deeply and sincerely felt, just as feelings lead to ideological choices. Ideology is linked to emotion recursively: it causes and is caused by affect.[5] Ideology expresses the transformation of shared feelings, known through images and metaphors, into beliefs about the good self and the ethical social system.[6] People understand ideology by means of emotional experiences that help make sense of the world. Through ideology, emotional reactions are generalized beyond their local contexts. This observation does not deny the cognitive or behavioral component of ideology but emphasizes the centrality of emotions. Further, emotional responses cannot be separated from cognitive ones, just as attitudes are linked to both. Logic is metaphoric and grounded in lived experience (Rosental 2003), while emotions can only be meaningfully felt and understood by those with an analytic conception of social settings and interactions—a dual-process model (Vaisey 2008, 2009).

The emotions that people experience sensitize them to beliefs and attitudes that are linked to cognitive choices and behavioral options. Images of the morally proper structure of society influence which solutions they feel are those that "make sense." These images operate viscerally as emotional tools, as effective rhetoric always does, and suggest that conclusions about the moral order must be based in lived experience.

My research with mushroom collectors revealed that environmental ideology derives as much from affect and lived experience as from analysis and represents the interpenetration of the two. These mushroomers loved being in the woods, loved finding specimens, and their beliefs followed. One told me that mushrooming was "looking around for a little gem of beauty. Finding something small and precious in a large [world]." As David Sloan Wilson (1978, 1, 11) noted: "Nature is present to naturalists the way God is to saints or the past is to humanists—not simply as a matter of fact but as an insistent and live reality. . . . Part of the delight [of nature is] the joy of things, things not as poor shadows of some ideal reality but solidly affecting and significant in themselves." The point, found in nature writers from Henry David Thoreau to Annie Dillard, is that our experience of nature is based in sentiment. Emotion translates nature into cognitive categories and policy initiatives. Feelings of love or exhilaration make protecting the natural environment necessary, just as fearing nature leads to a desire to tame it.

Recognizing the power of images of nature need not imply a lyrical naturalism; rather, nature is a socially potent concept with effects that are separate from analytical reflection. Although one's attitude toward nature is conditioned by place, social relations, and shared pasts (Worster 1985), the love of nature is not only learned but felt.[7] Lived experience is not simply generated from teachings of how one should feel under the circumstances but is an authentic reality (Hewitt 1984).

If being in the woods and describing the experience produces a strong emotional response, then beliefs, attitudes, and institutional policies that facilitate this response are likely to arise. Today many believe that an emotional reaction to nature validates one's self. For city and suburban residents, contact with nature is a special occasion, one marked as being "in nature." We expect that these moments will be satisfying, and we are primed to narrate our experiences. Many mushroomers fondly recalled occasions in their childhood when they went hiking or camping, and they claimed that these experiences influenced them. Linked to their warm memories of childhood, their experiences had shaped their attitudes and ideology.

## Ideology and Performance

A pragmatic approach to ideology recognizes that ideologies are not merely held by individuals but, like norms, are presented to others—ideology is a dramaturgical tool (Wuthnow 1987, 147). Ideologies are performed when their presentation contributes to smooth interaction, justifies claims to authority or resources, and benefits the self-presentation of a group or actor. Ideology can be hidden or shaped when doing so seems advantageous. Topics of public controversy are subject to slanting and shaping when it seems that groups or their members would benefit.

But what do we mean by the presentation of an ideology? Given that ideologies are broad and vague bundles of beliefs, communicating an ideology involves teasing out a strand of that bundle. The local context of action channels the behavior and talk that are enacted and the response to them. Situations shape ideologies, just as ideologies shape situations. Following Goffman's (1974, 11) model of framing, actors seek to learn: What kind of situation is this? That is, what interpretive frameworks best define the local context? In this way, beliefs and attitudes are useful tools for interpretation.

Considering ideology as relational deemphasizes ideology as a single set of beliefs and attitudes separate from the situation in which they are presented. Ideological action is socially and situationally contingent. Although in theory beliefs may exist apart from settings, the compelling issue is when and how they become announced and acted upon. As William Gamson, Bruce Fireman, and Steven Rytina (1982) argued, collective behavior frequently depends on the recognition of an injustice frame. Following Goffman (1974, 44), this argument refers to how experiences of reality are defined through events that *key* meanings for groups and thereby provide a new framed reality. The process by which events gain meaning is collective. A set of beliefs by itself is insufficient for action, but experience must be defined so as to suggest that these beliefs should be put into practice. The assumption of a shared history and common future legitimates collective action. Framing a situation through a socially sanctioned experience justifies action (Goffman 1974, 82). To the degree that a community puts beliefs into practice, collective action is enhanced and ideology becomes recognized.

Beyond these collective assumptions and meaning contexts, perhaps what is most compelling are the identity labels associated with the ideologies that communities hold. A change in these labels reflects a change in self. Presenting an ideology is a means of labeling an actor or group. With regard to contemporary ideologies about nature, the self-presentations of individuals are often linked to their belief that they are "environmentalists"—a desired label so vague and vapid that virtually every citizen or corporation can claim membership rights. Over 80 percent of the mushroomers I interviewed described themselves in this way, but the meaning of this label varied considerably, referring to different levels and types of political action and a wide array of beliefs. Liberals and conservatives both claim the label, although they define it differently. A master status such as "environmentalist" covers a vast array of views and encompasses some who profoundly disagree with each other. By associating with this valued but amorphous identity, mushroomers could gain the status benefits of the label while rejecting any undesirable implications. The degree to which they altered the meanings attached to this label depended in part on their ties with mentors and peers (Lachmann 1988).

In their routine interactions, actors continually make adjustments between their beliefs and their understandings of the demands of the interactional and cultural order (Lachmann 1988). They sometimes hide feelings or identities deliberately, and in extreme cases they deny their beliefs in order to maintain relationships, avoid stigma, establish consensus, or sustain joint lines of action.

Mushroomer communities had ideas about how human beings (and communities) should treat nature, such as not leaving trash, not trampling on flowering plants, or avoiding burning fossil fuels. There were *oughts* and *ought nots*. The specific practices stemmed from an underlying, if uncertain, ideological formulation. The mushroomers I observed had to decide whether, when, and how to bring violations of their standards to the attention of others. When did an annoyance become a cause for action? When was it time to confront a moral deviant? How important was it to preserve a relationship by ignoring beliefs? Keeping in mind the trade-off between beliefs and a stable communal future, the potential complainer had to gauge the likely reaction to the complaint, treating the audience as a generalized other through role-taking (Couch and Weiland 1986).

The salience of an ideological performance can also be illustrated on a more collective level. Groups with a complaint based on their *ought* rules have tactical problems. They may confront relatively intractable forces that benefit from maintaining the status quo. Oppositional groups must determine the most effective strategies for raising complaints and framing demands, and they must imagine responses from either supportive or hostile audiences. They must also confront the power of prevailing, if non-activated, ideological outlooks. Environmentalists may find that their complaints are not recognized as sufficiently privileged to enter into dialogue with developers. Under these circumstances, activists opting for confrontation must be highly cohesive, unless they can mobilize other powerful institutional actors such as the mass media to generate that cohesion. Without this support, such a tactic risks breaching the possibility of dialogue and threatens group solidarity. When striving for enhanced power or legitimacy, groups hope to strike a balance that incorporates as large a community as possible while achieving tactically feasible ends.

These conflicts are evident within and between environmental groups in debates between radicals ("deep ecologists") and those who work within the system. Because environmentalism cuts a wide swath across the political spectrum, environmental groups must decide which audience they wish to persuade and through which strategies. This division is evident among both larger interest groups and small social groupings. Among mushroomers, these debates provoked hostility between those who wished to pick edible mushrooms for profit and those who objected to the "massive desecration" of the forests and, not incidentally, to the competition for these scarce resources. I witnessed bitterness linger as one mushroom club debated whether commercial pickers should be licensed and limited by the government. Each group mobilized ideology and *ought* rules to make its point. Such debates can rend the organizational structure of a club, especially if overarching agreement is lost or is treated as secondary to the immediate disagreement. Yet, these debates are important and even necessary for the demarcation of ideological boundaries and for legitimating claims to authority and resources. Groups that survive are those that can merge ideologies or find grounds that cement participants in common cause.

## Group Identity, Networks, and Ideology

Ideology is both personal and shared. It is simultaneously a characteristic of the social actor, enacted in a relationship, and a property of the group or community—what Edward Shils (1968, 70) terms an "ideological primary group." In its cognitive and emotive components, we find the actor enshrined; in its enactment, we see the community as hero.

Ideology is situated in an interactional node, a small-group culture, and through the extensions of small groups it radiates throughout a network, becoming a property of more extensive social formations (see chapter 8). This group focus does not mean that ideologies, or other beliefs, are created within each small group in which they are found. Rather, the small group is an arena of ideological enactment and a place in which values take form and are invested with local meanings. What are the implications of seeing ideologies radiating from small groups? Such a perspective demonstrates that ideological formulations are nurtured in small groups and diffused through social networks and institutional communication channels, including mass media. Groups provide a space for the enactment of the key processes involved in ideological work (Mullins 1972, 509), including identification, ritual, and resource mobilization.

*Identification:* Through its presence in group culture, ideology serves the rhetorical purpose of promoting identification (Shils 1968, 70). As David Manning (1976, 154–55) writes,

> A political ideology is intended, via action, to establish the identity of a body of persons who are thereafter to be understood to be related to one another in a particular way. The relationship is only one amongst many that each of the potential members of this group may, at a given time, have with a number of other persons, but it is the only relationship which ought, according to the ideology, to embrace them all. . . . Without commitment the group cannot hope to transform its circumstances with a view to eliminating or isolating relationships incompatible with the one deemed to be ideologically sound.

Ideology depends on identity and, to be shared, on identification with others (Feuer 1975; Warren 1990). To hold an ideology, one should support a group espousing it (Manning 1980, 82). But groups do more than accept an ideology; they may also attempt to persuade those outside of the group through recruitment or calls for change. Ideology serves an important role in this regard, providing a mechanism that facilitates and controls discourse with outsiders. That is, an ideology offers a means by which the group member can sway or recruit others. Simultaneously, it demarcates the boundaries of acceptable belief, inoculating members from external influence. An ideology "constructs a boundary with a special one-way permeability" (Gouldner 1976, 81). In doing so, ideology provides group members with a "party line" that guides interpretation and action.

*Rituals:* Above all, an ideology is a tool through which a group binds members, legitimating calls for commitment and practical assistance. It is a moral and social connection that helps groups counteract the free-rider problem (Olson 1965). When ideology is activated, group ties based on principled agreement constitute a central feature of attachment.

Talk is generally less effective in cementing loyalty and a sense of community than is action: putting words into deeds. As a consequence, groups bind their members to the group and to each other through rituals (Collins 2004; Turner 1988). Ideology can become ritualized through the meaning of a secret handshake or blood brotherhood. Rituals display in symbolic and behavioral form central elements of an ideology: they provide the basis of common attention and attitudes. For instance, the ritualistic structure of meetings of the Minnesota Mycological Society called for the president to stand before the club, displaying, naming, and describing the mushrooms that had been brought in, and then requesting narratives of discovery or consumption of those specimens. On days when few specimens were shared, the meeting ended early and was considered disappointing. This performance not only had an educative function for new members but demonstrated in concrete form the bounty of nature and the desirability of consumption and species diversity. This ritual enacted the sociopolitical beliefs held by these naturalists. The organization of the meeting connected to the community's ideology.

*Resources:* Beyond the value of community as such, ideologies are linked to resources, which affect and constrain ideological presentation, enactment, and the recruitment of supporters. We should focus not only on the "use value" of resources but on the centrality of resources as symbolic goods. In extending the standard analysis of resources, Louis Zurcher and David Snow (1981, 470) rightly proposed that "ideology is probably the best example of a resource that functions in a symbolic fashion and that is importantly related to a movement's mobilization efforts and organizational viability." Ideological phrases, slogans, and rhetorical images are vital idiocultural resources that symbolize the nature and causes of discontent for movement actors and energize and justify their actions. Following Zurcher and Snow (1981, 471), resources include symbols. Mobilization should include symbolization, the process by which objects acquire meaning.

The enactment of ideologies mobilizes the symbolic and material resources necessary to promote or counter an injustice frame (Gamson, Fireman, and Rytina 1982). A key resource is the recognition that others in one's local world feel similarly or can come to feel that way. However, the recognition of the existence of a like-minded community is a necessary but insufficient condition. In addition, a communications network must coordinate action; a consensual authority system is required to permit social control and routinization; and finally, material resources enable the performance of appropriate actions. Taken together, public support, communications, authority, and material resources facilitate the cementing of ideology.

The resources required depend on whether the ideology is challenging (promoting systemic change) or identificatory (presenting a position that does not demand change). Challenging enactments typically require tighter organization and more powerful resources because of the consequences of the demands and the likely response of those whose privileges are being attacked. As a result, social movements face distinctive organizational hurdles because of the need to mobilize in the face of opposition or inertia.

Each ideological community is built on a network of social relations, and each network has access to a set of resources. Embracing an ideology does not mean that one must be part of a social movement group, but it suggests that those who share those images and metaphors constitute a quasi-group that can be activated when appropriate (Mayer 1966). Groups have a crucial role in ideological formations in terms of how they link up to networks and resources.

Ultimately, networks and ideologies function in a recursive manner in providing the basis for action. As Zurcher and Snow (1981, 458) argued, ideologies provide "the cognitive map articulating the problem, focusing blame and justifying action. However, social networks channel the diffusion of these ideas for action."

## Ideology in Practice

Throughout this chapter, I have connected ideology to a local sociology by emphasizing the importance of groups and action to conceptual formations. I have drawn from a pragmatic perspective, treating ideology as based in an interaction order. Although my focus on environmental ideologies has grounded my discussion of ideologies in an examination of consensual and communal beliefs, further research must describe the presentation of particular ideological structures in light of competing perspectives. Further, I have set aside larger economic structures and state apparatuses in this chapter not to deny that they exist but to stress their dependence on an interaction order. I do not wish to exclude macroconcerns but to see them as building on a meso-level of analysis where groups shape belief.

To conclude: (1) ideologies build on a set of dramatic metaphors and images to which people and groups respond based on their shared experience and expectations; (2) ideologies are not purely cognitive but depend on emotional responses; (3) ideologies are presented at such times and in such a way as to enhance the public reputation of presenters or adherents, ideological enactment being fundamentally performative; and (4) ideologies are linked to groups and to the relationships among groups that depend on resources to enact ideologies. Ideologies are symbolic, affective, behavioral, and relational.

In focusing on these themes, I have tried to avoid an overly abstract conception of ideology, divorced from action. Clifford Geertz's (1973) metaphor was prescient: ideology has been a "muddy river." But treating it as a local achievement within a group culture may clarify what otherwise seems opaque. The pragmatic lens I have used illuminates ideology's links to lived experience and social interaction and highlights its value for meso-analysis.

Ultimately, ideology is not only a set of relations among ideas but a set of relations among social actors. The nub of ideology is its use in practice: the translation of an affective and cognitive domain into collective action. Ideology is not to be found in the air but on the ground.

# ═ Chapter 6 ═

## Wispy Communities

In the beginning, fans organized localized spaces—small clubs and group living arrangements—and purely conceptual space—the communication ties created through the letters to the editor pages of the science fiction magazines and through publication and dissemination of fanzines. . . . While clubs . . . tied fans into geographically proximate communities, science fiction fandom owes its social reality as a worldwide movement in the 1930s to the fanzines. . . . By 1936 fans were traveling from one city to another to gather and gossip and chat, to meet friends made in the fanzines, and to talk about the stories in the pulp magazines. The science fiction convention was born.

—Camille Bacon-Smith, *Science Fiction Culture* (2000, 11–12)

I N A HOTEL in Louisville, men and women from thirty-five states and four countries, many of them strangers at the outset, gather for a long weekend. They intend to pay homage to a cult film that is dearly beloved by each of them. The film, *The Big Lebowski,* is not widely appreciated outside of their community. During the gathering, labeled the Lebowski Fest, participants discuss the details of the production, meet actors, listen to bands, hear academic presentations, consume food and drink mentioned in the film (White Russians), hold a costume party, and reenact favorite scenes.[1] For the occasion, they have left their "mundane" lives and reconstituted themselves as a community, embracing and enacting a mass-mediated identity. They have become, briefly, a wispy community: tight-knit, but quickly unraveling once they exit the parking lot. In their shared interest these fans have created a basis for allegiance. They combine social relations, formulated through a local interaction order, with the solidifying existence of group culture.

The Lebowski Fest reminds us that groups need not be permanent, made to last, but can provide temporary scaffolding, shaping identities even if for brightly intense but brief periods. The commitment of the participants *for the moment* and *to the scene* makes these gatherings a prism through which we can see the effects of local contexts and interaction orders, even when they are not backed by ongoing institutional support.

In previous chapters, I focused on stable groups: groups that expect to continue. However, as the Lebowski Fest indicates, some groups establish identity in limited domains of time and space; these are what I label "wispy communities." Further, in contrast with the small groups I examine in much of this book, these communities can be minute or extensive— ranging from a handful of participants to hundreds of thousands—and thus, some of these gatherings stand outside of the definition of "small group" as I have presented it. Yet, despite standing outside the definition, what makes wispy communities relevant to my argument about the centrality of group culture is that the participants imagine themselves as belonging to the same domain and building a culture tied to the community. In their ability to establish a linkage between culture and identity within the framework of an interaction order, these gatherings can contribute to civil society.

Wispy communities are not necessarily political—many are grounded in esoteric leisure worlds—but they generate a shared past linked to common interests that persuades participants that they belong to a larger community. Although wispy communities may be peripheral to large political debates, they provide social capital. As Robert Putnam (2000, 95) claims: "When philosophers speak in exalted tones of 'civic engagement' and 'democratic deliberation,' we are inclined to think of community associations and public life as the higher form of social involvement, but in everyday life, friendship and other informal types of sociability provide crucial social support." Perhaps science fiction conventions and the Lebowski Fest are not higher forms of social involvement, but the involvement that they do build is real.

Given their lack of institutional solidity, these transitory social worlds can be seen as a form of imagined community. Admittedly, this usage twists the term as employed by Benedict Anderson (1991) to explore nationalism. Few things have a greater institutional solidity and less wispiness than a state. Anderson, a professor of international relations at Cornell and a scholar of Southeast Asian culture, proposed that the idea of an imagined community helps explain how states generate cultural belonging among the populations under their control. Despite the psychological ring of the term "imagined," Anderson was not much concerned with the construction of a shared past as a performance but with the consequences of language and literature bolstering state legitimacy.[2]

In the past quarter-century, Anderson's slogan has become a mantra, reverberating throughout those scholarly domains interested in the formulation of national identities, which are believed to be "real" and "eternal." Over time the term has gained other implications. An imagined community is a form of selfhood based on parasocial ties with authorities and ties among equals, and it is found in communities of many forms. The concept, when broadly used, suggests that shared interests (common likes and dislikes) are a source of collective and personal identity. Emotional ties to all sorts of lived worlds create affiliation (Lawler, Thye, and Yoon 2009). And crucially, these worlds need not have a permanent organization to generate attachment. A wispy community, by establishing connections and a shared culture, allows participants to recognize that they belong to a community of interest even if its salience waxes and wanes.

Participation in events such as the Lebowski Fest, the United States Chess Open, the Gen Con Gaming Convention, the Annual Foray of the North American Mycological Society, the Outsider Art Fair, or the Burning Man Festival depends on the recognition of shared concern. This is like citizenship itself. But these spaces are bounded. For a time, participants embrace a group with common cultural objects. These are communities of limited liability (Janowitz 1952; Hunter and Suttles 1972), voluntary worlds in which a shared interest becomes the basis for a joint, but ephemeral, identity. Both the prevalence of such groups and the possibility of their decline (Putnam 2000; McPherson, Smith-Lovin, and Brashears 2006) are central to debates over the fate of contemporary society.

In this chapter, I discuss how stable groupings constitute communities and then turn to identification and culture within evanescent micropublics, what I call wispy communities, or temporary worlds of action. Extending Michel Maffesoli (1996), I argue that these are cultural tribes, found in voluntary spaces in which individuals and groups perform their identities. In wispy communities the gathering is real, although the embedded identity is neither continuing nor insistent; it resides in latent memory to be activated as appropriate. The communities that are constituted by these evanescent gatherings are near-groups—they appear at moments when they become a scene "where the action is" (Yablonsky 1959; Goffman 1967; Sato 1988). Their transitory quality requires less commitment in that the identity is not always active.

Participants vary in how they conceptualize their relationships with the groups in which they participate. Some groups are crucial to personal identity, whereas others have lower salience and thus the identity is activated only by the presence of others who are similarly motivated (Maffesoli 1996, 148). When no countervailing pressure or external demands exist, participants may accept the proffered identity, but when they must choose among competing identities, those linked to wispy communities are easily set aside. Such communities often create less devotion than ongoing groups. Allegiance to a group can be based on salient and lasting commitments or on temporary and oscillating ones. What characterizes wispy communities is the assumption that the basic form of connection is that of acquaintanceship. Primary or strong ties are more characteristic of ongoing communities.

The archetypal strong-tie group is the family, that solid, sticky, greedy community. The family is a tiny public that is recognized both by those who are inside, shaped by the power of the kinship culture (Zeitlin, Kotkin, and Cutting-Baker 1982), and by those outside who recognize the group from the public identity and institutional legitimation of the participants, bolstered by a ritualized and contractual ceremony of formation, supported by state power.

Although strong groups are imagined, I address more temporally bounded communities of shared but occasional concern. These communities, while treasured by participants, are provisional in character. Unlike the sturdy, sanctioned bonds of family, such voluntary communities are fleeting, justified by the satisfactions that they provide: fun is their guarantor. As Erving Goffman (1961b, 17) writes of games, extending to leisure gatherings, "fun alone is the approved reason for [participating]." In contrast to "serious" activities, one can rightly complain about activities that do not provide pleasure, excusing withdrawal. Ray Oldenburg (1989) stresses the important expressive function of voluntary places when he presents a model of interaction spaces that depicts "third places," in contrast to groups found at home and work. Wispy communities are likely to be domains of entertainment and sociability; the sharing of emotions persuades participants that they are in a caring community (Erickson 2009) and sometimes suggests a sense of "one big family" (Stanley 1982, 20). Although individuals gather in these spaces, they also separate, and few costs are paid by the departed. Such communities provide pleasure and identity, but they can be escaped without blame. Rather than having the features of greedy institutions (Coser 1974; Puddephat 2008), these communities are generous, only requiring interactional loyalty during the period of participation. Yet, during that period, many of these temporary gatherings, perhaps surprisingly, become total institutions: they encompass the individual in activities that leave no space for external engagements.[3] There is insufficient social control or desire for such control to demand adherence, but the understanding is that while the scene is active it commands attention. Its very wispiness is appealing. Temporary groups are common, yet despite their prevalence, they have been little studied by sociologists who focus on groups that are more stable, continuing, and linked to institutions.

Recognizing the variety of wispy communities speaks to a *division of leisure*, in contrast to the division of labor. While one's occupation and technical skills are near the top of the identity hierarchy, affiliation with an imagined community based on a leisure interest is often judged much lower, despite the pleasures it brings (Stebbins 2006).

Most wispy communities are entered into voluntarily. People select both their area of interest and their depth of immersion, although, of course, satisfaction with a local culture shapes loyalty. Those who engage in *serious leisure* (Stebbins 2006) may locate this sense of self higher on the identity hierarchy, yet the commitment required to partake in a related wispy community remains low, and there are few exit costs. Because commitment varies as a function of the material and temporal cost of involvement and a sense of emotional benefit, choices are linked to how a group provisions resources that generate satisfaction (Fine 1989).

Wispy communities are expected to generate a surplus of fun that, embedded in the memories of participants, creates sharable stories. The glasses of participants are rose colored and more than half full as they view their world from within their transitory interactions. Although fun is the approved goal and intended result of these activities, separation from everyday life and routine identities bolsters the emotional release necessary for enjoyment of the organized sociability at hand.

## Wispy Worlds

I differentiate subtypes of wispy communities depending on the extent to which people gather routinely—that is, whether it is a "club" or an "occasion." Within the occasion form, I distinguish the extent to which participants treat their involvement as linked to their identity—whether their community is an "event" or a "gathering"—and then, based on size and institutional control, whether the gathering constitutes a crowd (a "nation") or a group (a "fest").

Sociologists have often treated "community" as the fundamental basis of social order (Nisbet 1966; Etzioni 1993). The term refers to both spatial reality and personal identification (Hillery 1955). First, communities are domains in which individuals reside, work, or play together. Shared space is a convenient shorthand to suggest the frequency of contact. Common venues permit ongoing interaction and a sense of belonging. Traditionally the idea of community depended on the recognition of bounded place that could be seen through the density of actors, the depiction of sociometric relationships, or the mental mapping of locales. In the original formulation, communities were spatial units, but with the development of transportation and communication systems, coupled with the growth of communities of interest to replace or supplement communities of ascription, place as a criterion of belonging has lost its hold, replaced by personal interest or affective commitment. The development of online communities has further weakened the relationship between space and community, as it is now possible to interact with others without being physically co-present (Zhao 2003; Hellekson 2006; Burgess and Green 2009; Hills 2002). Only additional research will reveal the impact of email, Facebook, Twitter, and web forums on the amount and form of wispy communities. Gatherings may increase in number because of the ease of communication; they also may become less fleeting because cyber-communication can transform temporary gatherings into more stable forms as they migrate into active and continuing Internet groups (Ruth Horowitz, personal communication, 2011).

Second, in addition to the frequency of interaction, community also implies commonality based on belief and identification. If people, embedded in groups or networks, believe that they share a common world with linked outcomes, then they recognize the existence of community. Whether based on interaction or activated through identification, a community creates a common space in civil society. This domain of action constitutes a tiny public in which identifiers believe that they have the right and sometimes the obligation to claim allegiance and to draw boundaries. As important as interaction and identification are, they produce community only if participants affirm boundaries with other groups and recognize the local interests that boundaries imply. When individuals see themselves as an interest group or a specialized public, they can address issues that affect their lives within civic culture. While many leisure groups reject direct engagement in the public sphere (Eliasoph 1998), some groups, such as those interested in public issues (environmentalism or social justice), consciously insert their views into civic debates (Lichterman 2005).

## Clubs and Occasions

Although much community research addresses the organization of domains of segmental importance, such as work, neighborhood, or family, freely chosen worlds are valuable sites through which to examine the influence of local culture as a font of affiliation. These worlds may include leisure, civic, or political groups. Voluntary commitment (Goffman 1961b; Stebbins 1979; Mitchell 1983) suggests that identities and cultures are not institutionally demanded but are negotiated. In a world in which people enjoy multiple activities—what Richard Peterson and Roger Kern (1996) speak of as omnivorousness—groups have cross-cutting membership.

Social worlds (Unruh 1980) are organized through two distinct structural forms: the "club" form (organized through "meetings") and the "occasion" form (divided into "events" and "gatherings"). Both are "encounters" (or "focused gatherings"), in Goffman's terms (1961b, 17–18), but they differ in temporal structure, routines, shared pasts, and prospective futures. Many small communities—clubs—establish a regular schedule of meetings as part of their organizational routine, incorporating advance planning to promote ongoing commitments. Set meetings support a vigorous gossip network (Bergmann 1993) as well as a self-referential idioculture. Participants share stories, jokes, and other narratives that reference common experiences (Fine 1995; Polletta 2006; Eliasoph 1998) and create local slang or jargon (Bacon-Smith 1992; Ross 1991). In order to endure, the club form requires strong social ties among a clump of tight-knit actors whose interaction is habitual and expected and whose local culture is elaborate. In a club, self-reflexive roles are ephemeral (Zurcher 1968) and do not necessarily extend beyond the club meeting, even if social relations are intense within. The interactional authority of the club is established through temporal, spatial, and behavioral routines. The weekly poker game (Zurcher 1970) or meetings of the chess club (Puddephat 2005), environmental group (Lichterman 1996), dramatic society (Stebbins 1979), or fantasy-gaming group (Fine 1983) exemplify the type of public that Howard Aldrich (1971) labeled a "sociable organization." Although not linked explicitly to neighborhoods, such clubs draw members from a geographic area, and similar clubs emerge in different areas, inspired by the awareness of like groups.

The first Baker Street Irregulars, the most famous Sherlockian society, served as a model for a hundred similar groups that gathered regularly "to eat, drink, take quizzes, listen to talks, engage in theatrical presentations, sing, play games, and, most importantly, escape into a world where all the inhabitants share a similar passion" (Pearson 2007, 105). The mushroom society that I observed was one of nearly a hundred such clubs that meet regularly in the United States. Attendees display the mushrooms that they have collected, listen to mycological talks or view slides, consume fungal snacks, and plan forays or public displays. As Nina Eliasoph (1998) and Paul Lichterman (1996) point out, groups with political interests develop as well, only occasionally linked to broader movements.

Other, less formalized, groups exist in countless numbers, even if their informality makes them unstable. The fantasy-gaming groups that I observed mattered a great deal to their participants. Players spent long hours together and felt that their shared leisure was a high point of the week. Their Dungeons and Dragons worlds were elaborate, and players had deep affection for their imaginary characters and for each other, but the group dissipated when a few key members were no longer able to attend regularly.

Routines and rituals provide these groups with tensile strength, but they crucially depend on the continuing commitment of a core of individuals to provide services that groups require to satisfy members (Fine 1989). Should these individuals leave without committed replacements, the club may disband. The fact that clubs often lack a means of motivating desire for leadership makes them fragile. Voluntary groups constitute microcommunities that, when stable or enduring, provide members with

personal identity. Participants deliberately fit meetings into their schedules, attending as long as they define the club as satisfying or until other
commitments take priority.

For a club to survive and expand, current participants must not only
remain active but continually recruit new members, often by activating
social networks to draw friends to the group and then socialize them.
Although media may attract additional members to an established club,
networks are the most effective source of recruitment (Snow et al. 1986).

A robust belief exists that interest precedes involvement. For instance,
to facilitate the formation of clubs (for example, Scrabble or political discussion), Yahoo! suggests: "Connect with a world of people who share
your passions." Similarly, atheists advertise a local club on Facebook:
"This meetup is the place where freethinkers, atheists, Brights, skeptics
and seculars come together midweek for a discussion, some food and
maybe a laugh or two." Although typically a kernel of interest exists
prior to recruitment, that interest often extends and deepens through
participation, and recruitment is most effective when interest merges
with friendship. Should friendship not motivate joining, it must develop
shortly thereafter. Interest must be transformed into pleasure.

Despite the rhetoric centered on recovering a latent aspect of one's
identity hierarchy, fun is the basis on which commitment rests. The
social aspect of club life must be highlighted, as is evident in the party-
like features of political volunteering or seminars for art collectors.
These are more than instrumental groups, but work and focused discussion need to be nestled in pleasure. Thus, pizza is often a lubricant and
a glue. The American Atheists website notes that "whether it's our
annual National Convention, Regional Atheist Meets, or local parties,
you can be sure to have a great time [and] help out our common cause."
Perhaps social capital has virtues for the society writ large, but great
times are required for individuals to invest that capital.

With the development of virtual communities (Jenkins 1992), a
shared physical space has become less essential. Pleasure can be found
in cyberspaces. Internet communication may serve as a platform for the
development of a face-to-face group, which, if successful, can feed back
into and strengthen the cybercommunity. Internet discussion boards are
not as tied to place, but if the group decides to meet in face-to-face con-
viviality, a gathering spot is necessary, and thus geography shapes
recruitment and commitment. As a result, the club form privileges local
groups that have an ongoing character: group stability is essential for a
club (Hoggett and Bishop 1986; Fine and Holyfield 1996). Even if attendance oscillates, a core group is required (Zurcher 1970, 174) that pushes
ephemeral roles toward permanent identities, activated in the presence
of the club. It is the fragility of the club form in the face of competing

obligations (reflected in the decline of clubs such as parent-teacher associations and bowling league teams) that Robert Putnam (2000) and other critics decry as revealing the decline of social capital, whose vanishing has allegedly dire consequences.

## A World of Occasions

In an omnivorous world of multiple possibilities, some activities stand outside temporal routine. These represent "occasions." Rather than being tied to a schedule, such activities are constituted as a rare (and hence memorable) assembly. Occasions may have an audience similar to a club audience, but they provide a more expansive moment, with more widely dispersed participants, than the regular meeting of a club.

I divide the occasion form into two subtypes: the event and the gathering. The event is an occasion on which individuals gather with little demand that their presence implies an identity and no expectation of meeting others. The gathering, in contrast, often involves identity and networking. Yet, in both cases the roles of participants are more ephemeral than those found in clubs: both the event and the gathering are temporally bounded and not routinized.

*Events Apart*    The purest form of an occasion of limited investment is the *event*, a brief gathering in which individuals share a space without expecting to develop lasting ties. People often attend events with friends, but these interactional bubbles rarely merge with other bubbles. Typically such events are focused on a performance that generates intense and sustained attention by the audience (Boorstin 1961). The attachment is more likely to be vertical than horizontal. The event does not develop a community with a shared history based on social relations, although it can become a memory marker for individuals or groups, enabling them to refer to the event later in order to share experiences. More common is that attendees purchase or acquire an object (a souvenir) that provides physical commemoration (Stewart 1984), not just for the purpose of private memory but for sharing and narrating (Mitchell 1983). The event itself rarely develops social investment *among* audience members as opposed to investment by the audience in the performance and performers.

*Gathering Together*    Unlike club meetings, gatherings are liminal, untethered to a temporal routine. Perhaps the gathering is regularly held annually or biennially, but when any occasion is organized less frequently than on a monthly or bimonthly basis, its mnemonic form changes: the occasion is no longer built into personal schedules but requires special arrangements to cause participants to break from customary routine (Zerubavel 1979, 1997). Gatherings tend to focus on a shared interest that becomes elaborated. A novel (*Lord of the Rings*), television show (*Star Trek, Buffy the Vampire Slayer*), film (*The Big Lebowski*), type of music (the Deadheads), game (Dungeons and Dragons), or brand of car (Saab) might justify such an occasioned gathering (Muniz and O'Guinn 2001; Bloustien 2004; Bacon-Smith 1992; Hunt 2008). Yet, as Henry Jenkins (1992, 90) observes, the interpersonal satisfactions that derive from the gathering establish bonds that in turn generate the imagined community. The topic justifies the interactions. People assemble because they expect festivals of fun, and then they return to mundane worlds without expecting that long-term relations or commitments will have developed. Unlike at events, connections are made, but unlike in clubs, they are not cemented. The paradox in gatherings is that participants rely on others for their satisfaction, but they do not necessarily want to incorporate these others into their stable networks. For a bounded time, interaction and identification can be intense and desired, but when participants exit, they do not assume continuing contact.

At a gathering, participants strive to commemorate the experience. Here too merchandise may be purchased to make memory material; however, unlike at events, often the object is linked not just to what is planned by organizers but to the memories of other participants. While space and time are relatively minor considerations at events, at gatherings the interaction of attendees reflects attempts to connect the experience to a particular space and time. To demonstrate that they belong at a gathering, fans will not only search for common contacts and acquaintances (Bacon-Smith 1992, 30) but engage at times in name-dropping. This serves a dual purpose. Establishing that the network is dense is a virtue. First, as Camille Bacon-Smith observes, such connections legitimate one's right to participate, revealing one's status in the local culture. For instance, this could result in one participant identifying another as a novice and embracing a mentor-pupil relationship. Second, the recognition of a network situates the experience in preexisting cultural schema. Excitement strengthens a wispy community and encourages enthusiastic participation in the localized code of behavior as attendees are *caught up* in the emotional contours of the event (Stromberg 2009). They come to recognize the virtues of community beyond the boundaries of a tight group of friends.

Festivals, conventions, and tournaments constitute the archetypal form of wispy communities. Their size varies from microscopic to vast, but whatever the size, they generate intense engagement for bounded periods. In contrast to clubs, the nonroutine quality of the occasion generates involvement, coupled with activities that provoke *take-away memories*. The weekly poker game is designed to provide comforting, pleasant routine, whereas it is the extraordinary experience that matters for the success of occasions.

Time transforms events into gatherings. When events stretch over several days, permitting the development of social connections, or when interaction among participants is encouraged in planned activities or is required to achieve superordinate goals, an event can become a gathering, shifting attention from the focal performers to the audience. Gatherings presume the possibility of community, establishing social ties and generating identity. The archetypal form of the gathering is the multi-day festival, such as, famously, Woodstock in 1969. At Woodstock, an event, extended temporally, was transformed into a socially significant gathering of like-minded others in which horizontal, peer-to-peer connections mattered as much as vertical relations between performers and audience. The fact that attendees at this mega-concert, sponsored by entrepreneurs, became known as the "Woodstock Nation" signified that this occasion went *beyond* an event—a concert—but was an imagined community with its own norms, culture, and, importantly, politics. Under the right circumstances, cultural events can generate tiny publics that impact civil society through the creation of new identities. Even if these identities are not continually salient, they can rise to salience on occasion. Contributing to what makes these communities dramatically imagined is their evanescence: the sprinkling of the magic powder of immediacy transforms routine selves into "citizens." The idea of the gathering encourages participants to develop affective ties and to see themselves reflected in the newly established community. As Freud (1922) noted of the development of group ties, primary cathexis is shifted from the event leader (the performer) to the gathered community (the other attendees): the brothers replace the father.

As noted earlier, crowds typically do not consist of monads (Aveni 1977; McPhail 1991) but of groups. The challenge is to take a crowd composed of isolated clusters and transform it into a focus of identification. When networking is facilitated, small groups can become incorporated into a larger, occasion-based mass. For the duration of the occasion, participants may establish intense relationships, even if no expectation exists that the relationships will last.

For the sake of parsimony, I divide gatherings into mass macrogatherings ("nations") and focused microgatherings ("fests"), recognizing that wispy communities fall on continua of size and intensity.

## The Organizational Challenge of Macrogatherings: Creating a Nation from Air

A macrogathering is analogous to an evanescent city-state, as in the case of the Woodstock Nation. In its purest form, it creates an imagined community. This "hypercommunity" (Kozinets 2002, 21) is intense, extensive, and transitory (Dowd, Liddle, and Nelson 2004). Woodstock, held in August 1969 in Bethel, New York, brought together some half-million young concertgoers (often derided as "hippies," a term that proved a communal affirmation for some) for "An Aquarian Exposition: Three Days of Peace and Music." What made the gathering more than a concert was the power of co-presence (the "be-in") to create a powerful and distinctive social identity, one that would be recognized by participants and outsiders alike (Costello 1972, 188). An activated identity can shape civil society if the identity is linked to causes and beliefs.

Similar to Woodstock, the Burning Man Festival held in the empty Black Rock Desert in the Nevada backcountry, now institutionalized as an annual event, has received extensive attention as a macroform of wispy community. For its duration (eight days in 2011, August 29 to September 5), participants ("Burners") establish what they describe as "Black Rock City," a community with a self-generated ideology, norms, values, and techniques of social order (Kozinets 2002). More than just a gathering, Burning Man holds (imperfectly) to an anticonsumerist ideology. Even if the gathering has now developed, for both legal and pragmatic reasons, a sophisticated structure and an extensive organization (Chen 2009), the community continues to be seen as having been established from the bottom up and as challenging corporatist ideologies. This perception enables Burners to address issues in the public sphere. The gathering's collegial quality provides meaning as a *group* with a single perspective rather than as an inchoate mass. A short-lived nation is formed in which attendees are temporary citizens, complete with local rhetoric, preferred behaviors, and moral order.

In some other gatherings, there are even boundaries of participation. At the Michigan Womyn's Music Festival, for example, not only are men excluded (including boys over age ten), but so are male-to-female transsexuals (Dowd, Liddle, and Nelson 2004, 157). Gatherings of motorcyclists in Sturgis, South Dakota; New Age enthusiasts in Glastonbury, England; recreational vehicle (RV) owners in national rallies; techno dancers at Berlin's "Love Parade" (Borneman and Senders 2000); fantasy-gamers at Gen Con (Fine 1983); and science fiction fans at Worldcons (Bacon-Smith 2000, 11–29) evince a similar desire to establish a differentiated community from the merging of individuals and microgroups. Each of these, while ostensibly a leisure gathering, produces identities that address public issues, such as sexuality, energy, environment, or space exploration.

But what is perhaps most critical is a desire on the part of these groups to control their own spaces—to gain authority to set the rules for action in the face of external control. Participants crave a "temporary autonomous zone," to borrow the anarchic phrase of Hakim Bey (2008). These gatherings require more than a physical landscape—they need to develop what Bacon-Smith (2000, 11) terms a "conceptual landscape": a landscape of local authority. While the scene is tied to its location, it gains power from the meanings that participants share and from their ability to enforce those norms and that ideology. The mega-gathering is a scene where smaller groups intersect and where, given shared activities, identifications bloom (Lawler, Thye, and Yoon 2009). Small groups in large gatherings begin by being mutually unaware, but identification spreads to encompass all those present. This identification may start when small groups first plan to attend the event (with identification generated from previous groups and gatherings), but it becomes more powerful as the gathering unfolds.

The challenge in such an extended, complex, multi-day event is to create social order while avoiding explicit control. The iron fist of power must be gloved in wispy silk. Participants commit to the idea of the gathering but may resent the organizational structure (Chen 2009), as the presence of an organizational elite appears to violate the gathering's egalitarian philosophy. Despite communal rhetoric, hierarchies from which attendees seek to escape are extended into the venue; the rejection of hierarchy is itself rejected (Gray, Sandvoss, and Harrington 2007, 6).

Given that leisure worlds are dependent on consumption, such gatherings are prone to become what Michael Brake (1985) refers to as "manufactured subcultures" (see also Dayan 1986): they develop a structure that may charge for the privilege of attending and relying on corporate sponsors, despite the existence of countervailing ideologies. Recognizing a desire to break free from materialist chains for the duration of the gathering, organizers must adjust to governmental, capitalist, and consumption structures to provide food and water, location, and safety. Collective identity ignores how the gathering links to an awkward and contradictory reality.

The Burning Man Festival struggles with the economics of consumption (Kozinets 2002), largely avoiding monetary transactions on site (there are no boutiques or restaurants), but the gathering does require capital. Having grown from modest beginnings on a San Francisco beach in 1986 to an elaborately choreographed week in Nevada, this autonomous zone has undergone a transformation that longtime participants find dramatic and often disconcerting. In 2011 a ticket for Burning Man was a steep $320 for each of the approximately fifty thousand participants. (In a bow to lower-income Burners, "scholarship" tickets were also available.). Every macrogathering needs some structure to provide the goods, services, and security necessary for participants. A division of labor is required, even if it is imagined that undesirable forms of civilization are being jettisoned.

The challenge for a culture within an autonomous zone is recognizing that, while acquiring resources and providing goods and services is crucial for the organizers, these concerns stand in the cognitive background for participants. For participants, establishing emotional affiliation is crucial. In such wispy communities, what is essential is not what is being staged (or not *only* what is being staged) but the orgasmic power of "coming together," even if that reaction depends on transitory identification. At the event, participants are impelled to venerate the community (Chen 2009), even if they return to more mundane lives afterward. The challenge lies in reigniting the identification.

As significant as Woodstock or Burning Man is for participants while these events last, participants cannot escape *identity closure*. Perhaps identity reverberates in an *affective afterlife*, but the features that make this identity insistent become latent. Identity is salient within the framework of the gathering, but its impact swiftly dissipates into a comfortable—perhaps nostalgic—latency. These events are integrated into an autobiographical self (Hewitt 1989; Vinitzky-Seroussi 1998) that needs to be activated to become relevant. Without activation, the experience becomes the basis for a retrospective narrative, a cognitive souvenir of an otherwise fleeting experience.

## Microgatherings as Cultural Referents: Creating Fests from the Ground Up

Not all temporary gatherings have the same expanse; most are far smaller than a "nation." In these cases, organizational challenges, while inevitable, are less salient. To be sure, no numerical boundary separates nations or macrocommunities from fests or microgatherings, but there remains a qualitative difference between throngs of tens of thousands and encounters of hundreds.

My research has examined conferences of folk art collectors, tournaments of chess players, political conventions, and forays of mushroomers, all of which reveal the fest structure. These events are sufficiently compact that participants can meet or recognize other attendees during the event and also renew relations. At such fests, acquaintanceships are the basis of community. As happens after macrogatherings, microgathering participants often do not maintain ongoing connections with those they have met; if they attend another gathering, however, the previously established associations are reignited as they share *identity-salient* narratives about happenings deemed relevant to common interests (Yerkovich 1977).

It is not that individuals cannot escape the gathering should they wish to but that their commitment, coupled with their sunk costs, has made escape undesirable. Organizers create interactional opportunities to extend that allegiance. For example, chess tournament organizers establish other gaming or sports opportunities, termed "side events" (such as a golf or poker tournament). Some side events still involve chess, such as lectures, "simuls" (a celebrity grandmaster playing dozens of lesser-ranked players simultaneously), and minitournaments of alternative forms of chess (such as blitz or bullet [speed chess], bug-house, or chess 960 [Fischer random chess with pieces randomly placed on the back rows]). In addition, tournament directors often set aside a "skittles" room in which players can play informal games while not being held to a norm of silence.

Participants arrive at a designated location (typically a hotel or resort) to sojourn for several days. During this time, they participate in activities that establish the conditions for community and identification. Major chess tournaments may last as long as two weeks (world championship matches extend even longer), or they may be as short as three days (with smaller tournaments limited to one day).

Games are the heart and soul of any chess tournament, and before the rounds the players meet their opponents. Although talk is considered inappropriate during the game itself, prior to the game and afterwards strangers become acquaintances, demonstrating that their allegiance is to the community and not simply to their own record. The activities surrounding games, less formally structured than the competition itself, permit players to get to know each other and to develop feelings of belonging to the chess subculture. As participants question each other as to whether they are having "fun," it can be seen that fun is both the generator and the guarantor of community and self-image. Fun is the underlying trope for the success of voluntary community.

The focal power of these gatherings encourages identity salience. The gatherings capture the attention of the participants, making the community more than imagined, if less than institutional. As noted, participants attend because they see the gathering as consistent with a self they have previously embraced. Although in contemporary society people belong to multiple communities—even if some communities lack salience when latent (Jindra 1994; Mitchell 1983)—these identities are embraced only as long as they generate sufficient engagement to justify their costs, as Goffman (1961b) noted in his examination of the microsociological dynamics of "fun in games." Fun is their justification, but fun arises from a supportive structure. For a gathering to be successful, participants must feel that they have received their "money's worth" and their "time's worth," including the pleasures of meeting others who—for the moment of communion—share their interests and passions. As revealed by wispy communities, identity oscillates from manifest to latent—and sometimes back again.

## Wispy Imaginings

How do individuals define themselves as connected to social worlds? Identity is not predetermined but rather is claimed, desired, and shaped. In this fundamental sense, all identities, and not only national identities, are imagined. We can be citizens of the Woodstock Nation or art world enthusiasts or environmental activists or political volunteers or chess players or fantasy-gamers. There is a world of selves that we can embrace should we choose and should there be structures to help us. Some identities claim permanence and salience, while others are explicitly transient and temporally bounded, linked to the groups and occasions that appear and vanish. But each shapes how we conceive of ourselves and how we fit into a larger social order, giving us possibilities for engagement and imposing constraints as well. Each matters in the creation of the shifting sands of tiny publics. Temporary identities provide for the belief that we need not be limited to permanent, narrow, assigned selves. I speak of these latter identities, evanescent as they are, as belonging to wispy communities.

Although some activities are routine and backed by forces of institutional control, others are locally organized, tied to the preferences of participants and shaped by the context in which action unfolds. And yet they are more than unstable interaction scenes in that they have both a shared past and an imagined future (Katovich and Couch 1992). These pasts and futures are what permit them to fit into civil society, even if politics may not be their explicit purpose. In this they differ from routine, institutionalized transactions among strangers or inhabitants of instrumental roles that do not treat these limited connections as having the continuity of pasts and futures.

Through the examination of a range of evanescent gatherings—fan cultures, brand communities, leisure gatherings, tournaments, conferences, reunions, festivals, rallies, or even weddings—we can recognize how groups contribute to the establishment of identities and cultures.[4] These communities are simultaneously imagined and material, even if they are explicitly temporary. The gatherings make latent identities manifest and powerful for the moment, underlining the commonalities that bind groups together, as exemplified in the momentary solidity of their social relations. In this way, wispy communities may offer an answer to those, such as Robert Putnam (2000), who worry about the decline of solidified groups but seem unaware of the social forms that have replaced them. The power of group dynamics makes these wispy relations real as the group pushes participants to establish a fleeting but real social structure and culture, which can become reactivated at a later time. The gathering provides moments and memories to which participants refer with the understanding that others recognize the reference— a criterion for a group culture.

The concept of wispy communities as a distinctive form of local affiliation underscores both the communal features of occasions and their evanescent quality. During the gathering both identities and relations are real and usually intense, but they fade into memory after the conclusion of the gathering. An insistent present becomes a shared past. This quality of remembrance suggests that these occasions constitute imagined communities: they are lodged in imagination, they delineate the dimensions that connect us to those with whom we share experience, and they differentiate us from those beyond our social boundaries. These tiny publics can reveal that we belong together and that we can build multiple worlds—some of them transitory, some enduring, but all of them building on the reality of local cultures to provide an opening on how our worlds might be.

# Chapter 7

## Tiny Publics in Civil Society

> If some obstacle blocks the public road halting the circulation of traffic,
> the neighbors at once form a deliberative body; this improvised assem-
> bly produces an executive authority which remedies the trouble before
> anyone has thought of the possibility of some previously constituted
> authority beyond that of those concerned.
> —Alexis de Tocqueville, *Democracy in America* (1835/1966, 232)

I TURN FROM the constellation of groups as building blocks within the
cultural order to the analysis of groups as fostering a politics built on
the local: How do groups constitute and organize political life within
the public sphere? How can one take the discourse on civil society and
connect it to group dynamics? This turn moves the groups approach
to the central circle of sociology. The argument is applicable to all
Western society (Warren 2001), but nowhere is it more applicable than
in the United States, given the competing ideologies of the individual
and the association. We readily recognize the rhetorical trope that suggests the United States is not only a nation of individuals but a nation
of individualists. The image of the solo actor, it is claimed, defines us as a
people and is often taken to explain how America is distinctive from other
nations—a perspective labeled "American exceptionalism" (Lipset 1996).
The image of the defiant self, the proud outcast, or the lone cowboy is
pervasive in our national culture (Wright 1975; Bellah et al. 1985, 142–63;
Arieli 1964; Lears 1981, 19).

Simultaneously, this individualism has been characterized as a threat
to civil society, ranging from the psychological (Slater 1970; Lasch 1978)
to the economic (Hartz 1955, 211–19) to the social (Putnam 2000). Robert
Putnam portrays contemporary Americans as anomic and given to highly
individualized activities, such as "bowling alone," at the expense of civic
engagement or communal life, but his perspective, while insightful, is also
cramped: it ignores the full range of tiny publics, many outside of organizations. The image of the isolated actor belongs to a tradition as venerable as sociology itself, and it has resurfaced periodically throughout the

past century (Wellman, Carrington, and Hall 1988). The "decline of community" thesis (Paxton 1999) is rooted in studies of the transition to urban life (Simmel 1950) and the passage from Gemeinschaft to Gesellschaft (Tönnies 1887/1957). For Robert Nisbet (1966, 7), this thesis represents the animating force behind the development of the discipline of sociology in the nineteenth century, what he labels a "revolt against individualism."

This concern challenges another common view of the United States, borrowed from a reading of Alexis de Tocqueville, as "the association-land *par excellence*" (Weber 1911, 53). For every commentator who has remarked on American individualism, another has portrayed the United States as a nation of joiners who are tied to an organizational establishment of community. As early as 1835, de Tocqueville (1835/1966) remarked that Americans "constantly form associations"—an observation reiterated 150 years later by Seymour Martin Lipset (1985, 141), who noted that, compared to other nationalities, "Americans are more likely to take part in voluntary efforts to achieve goals." Edward Banfield (1958, 17), too, portrays American communities as constituted by a dense web of communal organizations and notes that "Americans are used to a buzz of activity having as its purpose, at least in part, the advancement of community welfare." David Riesman's famed "other-directed man" suggests a similar striving for community participation (or at least conformity) through associational involvement (Riesman, Glazer, and Denney 1950), as does William H. Whyte's (1956) "organization man." The image of Americans-as-joiners is widely held, and such associational participation has been taken as central to civic republicanism (Warren 2001, 9) and democratic theory (Dewey 1927, 148; Sandel 1996, 208).

## Civil Society as a World of Groups

These two venerable traditions, the loner versus the joiner, jockeying for intellectual dominance, have proven difficult to reconcile. An emphasis on one seems to discount the other—either one is alone or one belongs to an associational society (Bellah et al. 1991; Lichterman 1996, 9).

Yet, this dichotomy neglects an alternative model of civic engagement; significantly, this alternative has been featured in studies that examine the birth of the public sphere from the late seventeenth century to the early nineteenth century: the centrality of the small group as a means of connecting individuals to civil society.[1] If civil society relies on the self-organization of social relations (Calhoun 2001a, 2001b), then the formation of the socially embedded small group is central, whether politically self-conscious or not.[2] Theorists of civil society point to the crucial formative role of small-group settings such as the coffeehouse

(Habermas 1991, 32; Back and Polisar 1983), the lodge (Koselleck 1988, 70–92), the club (Agulhon 1982, 124–50; Amann 1975, 33–77), the salon (Giesen 2001, 223–24), and the literary society (Habermas 1991, 34).[3] Mario Small (2009, v), describing the empowerment provided by urban day care centers, suggests that these small institutions provide clients with the resources to achieve ends that their own limited resources do not permit. Even de Tocqueville (1835/1966, 662–66), often perceived as an associational theorist who examined larger organizational forms, recognized that associations can be "very minute" and "carry out [a] vast multitude of lesser undertakings"—functioning more as a committee than as a large movement. In effect, de Tocqueville envisioned a small group of like-minded others.

Some theorists posit that the ability of the public small group to generate an alternative to state and family is central to civil society, even though these theorists typically lack a social psychology by which to interpret their historical claims.[4] Thus, the elements of group dynamics have been largely ignored in prior works on the public sphere, but at the cost of overlooking the linkage between individual and society. Democratic theory requires the small group in order to make sense of how persons become embedded in communities and institutions. Groups, movements, and minute associations are essential tools, both for purposes of recruitment and for training citizens in those civic skills that are required to be successful and self-validated (Verba, Schlozman, and Brady 1995). Despite the fact that the meso-level of analysis (the group level) has often been ignored, its importance is genuine. Michael Walzer (1992, 107) argues: "Civil society itself is sustained by groups much smaller than the *demos* or the working class or the mass of consumers or the nation. All these are necessarily pluralized as they are incorporated. They become part of the fabric of family, friends, comrades, and colleagues, where people are connected to one another and made responsible for one another." Walzer's view provides the grounding for an understanding of society as a web of groups, "establishing small publics" (Cohen and Arato 1992, 252).[5] The group, in providing the basis of and public space for social attachment (Arendt 1972; Back and Polisar 1983), creates an alternative to a dichotomous model of individualism versus associationism.

In some sense, this perspective is implicit in the literature on civic engagement. Putnam's (1995, 67) definition of civic engagement—"trust, norms, and networks that can improve the efficiency of society by facilitating coordinated action"—describes well what small groups do, and not just associations. Indeed, the very idea of associationism, with all it implies for democracy and civil society (Kaufman 1999), affirms the value of group interaction in a polity.

This approach highlights the importance of local interaction contexts—the microfoundations of civic society. Small groups are cause, context, and consequence of civic engagement. The attachments of individuals to those small groups in which they participate explain how public identities develop and how individuals use these identities. Focusing on small groups allows us to understand how civil society can thrive *even if* formal and institutional associations have declined. Rather than suggesting a decline in civil society, a proliferation of small groups without formal affiliations represents a healthy development in democratic societies, in that intersecting webs of allegiance are thus established, a point noted by Nicolas Lemann (1996) in his *Atlantic Monthly* article "Kicking in Groups," where he discusses the value of youth soccer leagues for the integration of suburban communities.

Drawing on *sociological miniaturism* (Stolte, Fine, and Cook 2001)—seeing large-scale sociological issues embedded in microdynamics—I identify a set of interactional processes through which small groups create the foundations of civil society. By examining microlevel phenomena, I uncover the bases of large-scale social forces (Collins 1981), just as these microlevel phenomena are structured through macrolevel constraints (see chapter 3). I hope to extend previous work by moving the locus of analysis from idiosyncratic, personal choice to the opportunity structures and constraints created by group settings (Harrington and Fine 2000; Harrington 2001). This approach focuses on meso-level contextual factors that receive little attention (Strauss 1982; Maines 1982; Hallett 2003).

Groups are ubiquitous. Families, friendship cliques, work units, athletic teams, gangs, and leisure clubs form the basis of any contemporary social system. The irony of Putnam's memorable slogan is that it is nearly impossible to find anyone bowling alone (Fine, Hallett, and Sauder 2004). Whether or not Americans bowl in leagues as frequently as they once did, observation at local lanes reveals that they are bowling with friends, families, and coworkers.

The small group provides a communal space that tames asocial individualism as well as the oppressive conformity of associational control. Even crowds, while appearing disorganized, are organized through the presence of numerous dense groups (Aveni 1977; McPhail 1991, 2008), just as subcultures consist of networks of groups (see chapter 8). Through the power of small groups, individuals find arenas in which to enact their "autonomous" selves and demonstrate allegiance to communities and institutions. They create social order without recourse to legal institutions (Ellickson 1991).[6]

Ultimately, small groups constitute a performance space in which civil society is enacted. First, groups are the crucible for the development of civil society. Groups define the terms of civic engagement, provide essential resources, and link movements to larger political and cultural domains. Second, small groups serve as a locale for the distribution and maintenance of collective goods. Finally, small groups are an outcome of civic engagement, and the proliferation of groups reveals social and political health.

## Small Groups as Causal Structures in Civic Engagement

Small groups are incubators of civil society. In the course of interaction, participants define a set of social problems as deserving a collective response. As a result, groups become the vehicle through which people and resources are mobilized. These are the *framing* and *mobilization* functions of small groups. Each is necessary—although not sufficient—for civic engagement. Finally, through the acts of framing and mobilizing, small groups create *citizens*—that is, they produce identities that embed individuals in larger entities, such as the nation.

### The Framing Function

Framing, as originally postulated (Goffman 1974; Bateson 1972; Gonos 1977), extended to the analysis of social movement cultures (Gamson, Fireman, and Rytina 1982; Snow et al. 1986); applied to norms and ideology (see chapters 4 and 5), framing attempts to address the question: how do participants in group activity determine what is happening? Frame analysis asks how group participants create interpretive tools to unpack local meanings. Put another way, framing refers to how groups develop schemas to explain reality and determine the appropriate response.

From the universe of potential civic engagement opportunities, members of small groups evaluate which issues will receive a collective response; in other words, groups are arenas where individuals determine what constitutes a social problem. For example, observation of urban neighborhoods in the United States reveals that some small groups—such as residents on a block or in a cluster of homes—define trash on the streets as a civic problem, whereas others do not. Neighborhoods have an important structuring effect in civil life (Grannis 2009; Brown-Saracino 2009). This not only results in neighborhoods that come to look very different from one another due to local cultures but also reveals fundamentally different construals of citizenship and civic engagement.

Group interaction makes some frameworks probable and others unlikely. If, as John McCarthy and Mayer Zald (1977, 1215) postulate, "grievances and discontent may be defined, created and manipulated by issue entrepreneurs," those entrepreneurs require an attentive audience to complete the social construction of civic reality. No civic issue is possible without local groups to provide sponsorship and endorsement.

Seen in this light, framing involves the creation of culture—a core function of all groups, and one not limited to the public arena. As described in chapter 2, any group in which participants interact regularly and recognize their relationships as meaningful develops symbols and references that can be drawn upon with the expectation that fellow members will appreciate their significance. Whether church groups, political volunteers, or mushroom clubs, each develops a meaningful culture that leads to commitment and sometimes to the desire to reach beyond the boundary of the group.

Small groups situate local frames of reference within a larger context, aligning them with ideologies, symbols, and movements. For example, group cohesion justifies sharing experiences through personal narratives (Mitchell 1983). These local stories, bolstered by their claimed truth, justify the embrace of broader cultural themes. This is evident in the stories that mushroomers tell when they return from forays—the hunt is not over until the story has been told (Fine 1987a). As discussed in chapter 5, these stories provide the basis for commitment to certain types of environmentalism and may also lead to collective action. Through narration, events radiate outward from the point of interaction. Conversely, through narration small groups translate general issues into local concerns. For instance, constructs of far-reaching significance, such as "citizenship" or "sacrifice," are defined locally as well as nationally. This localism constitutes a major source of variation in civic engagement: the expression of patriotism in a New England college town might take the form of a demonstration, while in a neighboring rural town it might take the form of a bake sale. Both activist groups may rally around a nationally recognized symbol, such as the flag, but define patriotism through local norms of participation. Small groups facilitate microlevel variations but also provide for linkages at the macro level through shared frames of reference.

This accounting for variation in the qualitative, *locally constituted*, and interactional aspects of civil society represents a major benefit of the groups approach. David Snow and his colleagues (1986) found that goals are framed in social movements through a predictable four-step process. Issue definition occurs first. The movement then progresses to alignment with other groups, moves on to amplification and extension—linking a local scene to larger structural domains—and culminates in social transformation. In the right circumstances, a local concern can thus become an access point for national or global civic engagement. Phil Brown's (1997) discussion of "popular epidemiology" documents how a small local movement—citizen mobilization to resist toxic waste contamination in Woburn, Massachusetts—spread beyond the original group, linked with others, eventually reached the media, and resulted in extended awareness and response. In turn, groups are vehicles by which national issues are linked to localities, as in the mantra to "think globally, act locally."

By bridging local and national cultures, small groups define and validate situations so as to make action possible. This includes not only defining what constitutes an issue worth civic engagement but also creating a collective response. Groups have long been a source of tactical innovation in civic activism. Strategies that became hallmarks of the civil rights movement, such as the sit-in and the bus boycott, were developed by specific small groups responding to local conditions. Their size and the opportunity they provided for democratic involvement made these movement groups incubators of innovation in both policy and tactics (Polletta 2002). Such innovations have often been hailed as critical in determining whether movements thrive or die (Morris 1981; McAdam 1986).

The framing of group culture posits—explicitly or implicitly—a relationship to the state, the public sphere, and other civic institutions. How the group defines the boundaries of legitimate action shapes the concerns of each participant (Eliasoph 1998), and civic involvement thus becomes validated through the frameworks embedded within group traditions.

### The Mobilization Function

Beyond defining the territory of civic engagement, groups acquire the resources necessary for collective action. These tiny publics serve as the gravitational centers of civic life, drawing individuals into participation not only through compelling ideas but through material resources and the commitment of others.[7] As Mark Granovetter (1977) demonstrated in his work on threshold models of collective action, the likelihood of an individual engaging in a civic movement depends on the number of others already involved. The ability to draw a crowd signals a movement's viability, legitimacy, and potential impact—what Paul Hirsch (1986) speaks of as the "bandwagon effect."

Groups provide the basis for involvement. Each participant is a node in a social network—a link to other persons and resources that can be utilized in collective action. As John McCarthy and Mayer Zald (1977) document, personal networks are conduits for money, publicity, and the materials essential to the survival of civic movements: activities are provisioned through ongoing social connections (Fine 1989). First and foremost, movements must draw people. The groups perspective points to the crucial role of face-to-face interaction. Micromobilization is essential for civic action (Whittier 1997). Empirical evidence supports this claim, demonstrating that strangers are rarely recruited to participate in social movements. Rather, recruits are drawn from active networks of family, friends, and associates of movement participants (McAdam 1986; Snow, Zurcher, and Ekland-Olsen 1980). Civic engagement is rarely a forum in which citizens forge social bonds but rather a place in which existing social ties are leveraged for collective action (McPhail 1991; Fine and Stoecker 1985). The rapid growth since 2008 of the Tea Party movement, truly a political force based on a reticulated network of loosely connected groups lacking a central organization, demonstrates the power of local action spaces, perhaps emerging from churches, neighborhoods, or parents' associations. To be sure, external sources provide resources, but without local energy, the movement would have died aborning. Although it is common to speak of the Tea Party as a solidified force, this is a classic wispy community that expands and contracts depending on its appeal at the moment. It will continue to influence politics only when sympathizers find action spaces that engage them.

## Creating Citizens

The small group not only is instrumental in the creation of collective action but also shapes how individuals conceive of their own identities. As I discussed in examining temporary communities in chapter 6, this extends Benedict Anderson's concept of a nation as an imagined community. For Anderson (1991, 7), the idea of the community is central; he argues that "regardless of the actual inequality and exploitation that may prevail in each, the nation is always conceived as a deep, horizontal comradeship." Anderson treats nationalism and civic engagement as cultural artifacts—vehicles through which individuals identify themselves and their siblings (Brubaker and Cooper 2000; Greenfeld 1992; Koselleck 1988). But this perspective, valuable though it is, largely ignores the interactional process that generates identity.

It is through interaction and affiliation radiating outward from small groups that civic identity is created. Small groups can represent the state and the nation in microcosm, serving, as Hank Johnston (1991) notes of Catalonia, as repositories of civic memory and as sites for the retelling of national identity narratives. The emotions, cognitions, and cultural artifacts generated within small groups (Scheff 1994) connect individuals with nationalist projects, sometimes explicitly—as with groups that define themselves as reflecting national identity, such as Boy Scout troops (Mechling 2001)—and sometimes implicitly, as when nationalist culture is exemplified in food preparation, clothing choices, or holiday celebrations (DeSoucey 2010). As Michael Billig (1995, 6) observes, it is the taken-for-granted, banal quality of civic identity that makes it so powerful. Although my argument is not fundamentally about the construction of nationalism, small groups establish the identity and the socialization processes involved in identifying as a citizen.

## Small Groups as Context for the Enactment of Civil Society

In addition to mobilizing the interests, resources, and tactics necessary for civic engagement, tiny publics offer a social soil in which movements grow. At its most basic, civil society consists of individuals acting in concert to pursue shared goals in the public arena. Small groups supply the context for concerted action. The group enacts civil society and civic virtue through an array of structural properties that induce individuals to forgo immediate self-interest in favor of collective goods. These structural properties, such as repeated and reciprocal interactions among members, allow groups to perform the monitoring, sanctioning, and provisioning of selective incentives that civic engagement requires (Kaufman 1999).

As Mancur Olson (1965) argues, collective action does not occur naturally. Neither shared interests nor the presence of resources is sufficient to produce civic engagement. Self-interest, opportunism, and the diffusion of responsibility create obstacles to collective action. The issue is encapsulated in the "free-rider problem": self-interest leading individuals to strive to reap the benefits produced by groups without contributing to the production or maintenance of those benefits (Hechter 1987). Individuals may enjoy the fruits of others' civic engagement, such as mobilizing for clean air or water, without contributing to those efforts. As Aristotle recognized, "What is common to the greatest number has the least care bestowed upon it" (*Politics*, book II, chapter 3). Or in a later formulation, "Everybody's property is nobody's property. Wealth that is free for all is valued by none" (Gordon 1954, 124).

Rational individuals place the collective interest ahead of their own interest only under specific conditions, and these conditions are often found in group interaction. In small groups, individuals can interact in ways that are not possible either in larger institutional settings or in the atomistic free market. Group settings provide a face-to-face context in which individuals develop reciprocal, trusting relationships based on repeated interaction and fine-grained information sharing (Geertz 1978; Uzzi 1997). They also provide contacts in which these interactions lead to the construction of an identity invested in group participation.

Small groups promote civic engagement by placing individuals in a position where they have more to gain or less to lose by cooperating with the group than by acting as free agents. The incentives are reinforced within small groups through regimes of monitoring and sanctioning (Hechter 1987). The interaction that is characteristic of small groups permits individuals to monitor one another's behavior for the amount and quality of contribution to group goals. When individual participation is found wanting, face-to-face interaction provides immediate and powerful sanctioning mechanisms. Tactics such as ridicule or ostracism discourage individuals from behaving outside the normative boundaries of group behavior (Dentler and Erickson 1959; Seckman and Couch 1989).

Through their microstructures—opportunity structures as well as mechanisms of accountability and sanctions—small groups make a unique contribution to civil society. Macrolevel entities such as states, complex organizations, and large associations cannot reproduce these structures effectively. When they attempt to do so, the costs are prohibitive and the results are often perceived as illegitimate or inappropriate (Ostrom 1990). In a similar form, markets do not fully support the costs of monitoring and sanctioning. Few neighborhoods would choose to post a security officer on each corner to ensure that no one is robbed, but many form volunteer associations through which residents patrol their own block.

Central to solving this dilemma is Robert Ellickson's (1991) proposition that groups provide "order without law." The informal power of the group—the strong motivation to go along, preserve reputation, and reap other benefits of community affiliations—constitutes order. Group members do not always maximize their individual interests (the rational choice assumption of amoral individualism), but when they recognize the value of participating in group life explicitly or tacitly personal interests are satisfied.

Roger Gould's (1993) analysis of nineteenth-century French working-class protests demonstrates that participants were mobilized not by class or occupation, as previously imagined, but by neighborhood networks, the intersection of small groups. Gould's evidence, including transcripts from the trials of insurgents, reveals that participants in the protests were motivated by neighborly pressure: "Failure to participate in the insurgent effort was construed as a betrayal of loyalty to the neighborhood and sanctioned accordingly" (Gould 1993, 739; see also Calhoun 1982). Other studies have echoed the finding that small face-to-face groups, rather than more abstract relations—such as shared position in economic or political structures—underlie some of the most powerful instances of civic engagement. Research on the East Germans who tore down the Berlin Wall (Opp and Gern 1993; Pfaff 1996) as well as on American civil rights activists (Chong 1990; Robnett 1996) indicates that local affiliations were decisive in motivating individuals to participate in these democracy movements.

These findings attest to the power of groups to monitor, sanction, and offer selective incentives efficiently. Such functions flow from a structure of interdependence and repeated, face-to-face interactions rather than from a particular expenditure of resources. Small groups provide an informal, yet powerful, control mechanism that prompts individuals to moderate their egocentrism without resorting to the social control that is often characteristic of organizational life. Small groups permit individuals to collaborate flexibly to achieve common interests without the infrastructure and resources that more formalized organizations entail.

Underlying the effectiveness of groups is the reality that participants know each other and shape their behavior and self-image in light of expected responses (Gecas and Schwalbe 1983; Holstein and Gubrium 2000). As discussed earlier, local cultures are the source of norms and behavioral expectations; members in good standing accept these standards as legitimate.

To the extent that individuals treat the group as providing a behavioral standard by which they judge themselves (Burke and Stets 2009), the necessity for external control is diminished. What might otherwise be conflict among individuals is mediated by the urge to participate in group life so as to achieve both instrumental goals and expressive fulfillment. As a result, small groups serve an important function that is often associated with formal organizations—the development of enforceable trust. Given that individuals often participate in social life in the context of their groups, civil society reaps the benefits of group surveillance. We are particularly likely to trust those whom we can observe.

Status and reputation, both important selective incentives, are enacted within small groups and shaped by cultural norms and expectations. Small groups depend on recognized placements of others within a meaningful social field. Each member is situated within a network of power, influence, and action (Bales 1970).

This system of incentives, grounded in reputational politics, is important not only in directing members' behavior within the group but in socializing individuals to civic life and legitimizing the status systems of larger public domains. Thus, the family, the first small group in which people participate and of which they are aware, serves (for better and for worse) as a model for how status, rewards, and power should be distributed within public life. The groups in which individuals are socialized (both as youths and as adults) model civic engagement. The ideas of justice, inequality, and respect found in small groups are translated into members' conceptions of the good society. Status becomes enacted within the group, modeling status in larger social systems as well.

## Small Groups as a Consequence of Civil Society

The proliferation of small groups is a suitable gauge of the health of civil society. In this sense, Robert Putnam (2000) is correct, even if he limits his focus to the more established associations. Societies characterized by extensive civic engagement require a high density of small groups to facilitate the debate, advocacy, and commitment that promotes collective action. As Elinor Ostrom's (1990) work on cross-national patterns of civic action reveals, the capacity to generate group activity to solve public problems is not a given in social structure but is variable. Some societies are more successful than others in this regard. Empirical studies indicate that the United States remains near the top globally in generating small-group membership (Curtis, Grabb, and Baer 1992; Curtis, Baer, and Grabb 2001).

Although large and formal associations have declined, there is evidence that the profusion of unaffiliated small groups offers significant benefits to civil society. The presence of many independent small groups provides individuals with multiple, and often cross-cutting, opportunities for affiliation. Although we do not have data on the friendship nodes online—some of which have many of the features of face-to-face groups—these linkages provide another basis of close-knit cohesion. Such groups aid civil society in several ways, not least by exposing individuals to varied experiences and perspectives. Such exposure is crucial to the democratic process (Sunstein 2000, 2001) and works against the balkanizing pull of "amoral familism" as well as that of highly concentrated associations (Portes and Sensenbrenner 1993; Banfield 1958).

Despite evidence that groups benefit civil society, the benefits lie not in any capacity to produce agreement among groups but in members' commitment to the group. It is dangerous to hypothesize that the more groups, the more pastoral the society. The policies that individual groups propose need not be benign. Pollyannas cannot halt a local militia. Although groups contribute to civic engagement and civic engagement is indispensable in democratic societies, civic engagement does not necessarily produce harmony, nor is conflict inherently destructive to democratic theory (Mouffe 2005). In societies in which value divisions are sharp and policy prescriptions diverge, civic engagement may lead to conflict, which, while democratic, may also prevent elites from enforcing their will in "solving" problems (McLean, Schultz, and Steger 2002; Kaufman 2003). With their heated passions and firm ideologies, groups may divide as well as bridge. As Robert Putnam (2000) argues, bridging relations among associations generally strengthens liberal democracy, while bonding relations that emphasize insiders and outsiders creates sharper internal boundaries that are sometimes harder to bridge. Some groups have beliefs that, while indigenous to the group, are harmful or conflictual to a diverse and mutually respectful society. Put another way, the flowering of groups can create either networks of shared affiliation or islands of discord. We must avoid utopian proclamations that groups necessarily end conflict or that all groups propose solutions that are democratic or enlightened. What groups do is to establish places in which debates can be held, multiply experiences, and create tiny publics in which individuals feel invested because of their knowledge of others.

Still, recognizing that the presence of groups does not erase disagreements, the small-groups approach to civic engagement is distinct from that of social capital theory (Woolcock 1998) in emphasizing the intrinsic value of groups. In contrast, those working in the "decline of community" paradigm appear most concerned with the formal linkages *among* small groups. Thus, when it comes to bowling, the real issue for Putnam and others is not that individuals go to the lanes alone, but that there has been decline in the bowling leagues that once connected citizens who might not have otherwise known each other because of their different social networks.

The capacity of a society to generate small-group activity suggests civic health since small-group membership breeds additional small-group membership. That is, groups are not only precursors to civic engagement but also consequences of that engagement. To the extent that group members define their activity as satisfying, group involvement justifies further involvement in communal ventures. The enjoyment of group activity frames additional participation. The idioculture of the group postulates, explicitly or implicitly, a relationship to the state and other civic venues (Koselleck 1988, 91; Habermas 1991, 36–37). How a group defines proper action in its traditions, beliefs, and actions shapes the concerns of each participant, setting the stage for continuing involvement.

If an idioculture promotes group membership and civic engagement by creating citizens and civic-mindedness, the emotions generated by belonging to a small group also provide an incentive for further engagement. They remind participants of the affective rewards of forgoing personal interest to work cooperatively. By providing a structure for affiliation and cohesion, groups offer both a model and a reason for participation in larger social domains. What one learns within the group context can be generalized to other domains; it becomes a resource that can be harnessed for public participation.

The ability of a social system to generate affiliation with microcommunities indicates the health of that system. Within the context of a civil religion, people construct shared meanings, strengthening the community.

At times these groups may be linked together in wispy communities that build on smaller, more solid ones (as with fantasy-gaming communities that consist of numerous individual groups that meet on occasion at conventions, or local groups of political volunteers gathering at party conventions). Even unaffiliated groups spending time together provide a basis for social allegiance, such as individual mushroomers traveling to a national foray where they reignite long-standing social ties. Just as the group represents the civic assembly in microcosm, the civic assembly motivates individuals to create microcommunities of trust. The power of networks of groups (described in chapter 8) does not erase the value of group diversity and decentralization. Whether or not associations *among* groups are declining, there is reason for optimism in the rapid expansion in the types and missions of independent small groups, fueled partially by the establishment of discursive worlds based on electronic communication (Putnam 1995).[8]

The expansion of small groups confers benefits on civil society. Research on civic life suggests that the concentration of power in a handful of associations is linked to a decline in civic engagement. For example, Victor Nee and Brett de Bary Nee (1973) document the stranglehold that large family associations and the Chinese Six Companies—the "tongs"—held over the residents of San Francisco's Chinatown. With the concentration of networks and resources in a few associations and the unavailability of alternative affiliations for individuals, the tongs could enforce conformity to a rigid and limited social, political, and economic agenda. This strategy benefited the community, but it also contributed to the isolation of Chinatown's residents from the larger civil society for generations.

Concentration of power can also be destructive for civil society by creating free-rider problems: decreasing the willingness of smaller or less powerful groups and individuals to engage in the civic arena. The perceived benefits of community participation decline dramatically when actors believe that their efforts will be relatively ineffectual compared to those of larger, well-entrenched groups. Civic engagement is low in areas dominated by what Edward Banfield (1958) called "amoral familism": the tendency of individuals to cluster into large and powerful family associations that exclude the broader community or more diffuse social units. Southern Italy, long associated with lawlessness and the cosa nostra, is often cited as a vivid example of this problem. However, when new groups enter an entrenched community and the potential for new affiliations emerges, the result can be a revival of civic health. This is suggested by Alejandro Portes and Julia Sensenbrenner's (1993) research on Ecuadorian businessmen, who attained success by breaking with the Catholic Church and its onerous cultural requirements for male family heads to become Protestant evangelicals. Conversion did not lead these men to break ties with their families but rather to reformulate their relationships by adding cross-cutting small-group affiliations that counterbalanced the balkanizing effects of familism.

A benefit of pluralism is increasing the diversity of small groups, and this is one reason why future research on civic engagement must highlight the small group. Rather than focusing on intergroup linkages to gauge the health of civil society, we may find that a better measure is the proliferation of small assemblies, clubs, and cliques that are not necessarily formally affiliated with one another. This proliferation does not automatically create consensus on those issues that society faces or necessarily persuade participants that they should take an active role in the public sphere. Some groups reveal schisms and disputes. By creating a home space, however, the local context for allegiance to society, small groups—de Tocqueville's "minute associations"—establish a supportive domain for active consideration and for collective engagement.

## Small Groups and Civil Society

The lack of analysis of small groups in civil society theory is distressing given their ubiquity in everyday life. Citizens are continually embedded in small groups; groups link the individual and the organization, community, and state. Civic life in any diversified society would be impossible without them. The dynamics of collective affiliation are reflected within small groups, creating social order.

Groups provide an interactional arena in which concepts of the good and proper society are explored and negotiated. Groups also shape civic identity and affiliation by allowing members to communicate within a context where both trust and social influence are vital social forces (Fine and Holyfield 1996). Although some groups are explicitly tied to political, national, and civic issues, this need not be the case for a group to have an impact on civic life. As Nina Eliasoph (1998) demonstrates, group life creates expectations that govern the amount of direct and active civic involvement, and regardless of whether civic involvement is encouraged, a group connection legitimates civic belonging, providing a latent basis for activism.

Groups work hard to create civil society. They serve as the creative nexus, the context, and the consequence of civic engagement. First, group dynamics create the desire and the means for public action, shaping the institutional identity of participants as well as mobilizing resources. The outcome of group interaction is a culture in which volunteerism, citizenship, and collective action are alive and well. With their shared histories, participants can build off these collective experiences to act in more extensive ways. Second, small groups provide arenas in which various forms of civic engagement are played out. Groups provide a discursive space where ideas of patriotism, nationalism, civic politics, and the public sphere can be explored and enacted, whether or not policy prescriptions are proposed. Finally, in a healthy civil society affiliative opportunities proliferate, counterbalancing the balkanizing tendencies of large associations. Cliques, clubs, congregations, and teams are not spontaneously generated but born of other groups. Given that individuals belong to multiple small groups, each one presents them with an alternative model from which they can choose their level of desired engagement in other venues. A multitude of groups and cross-cutting affiliations promotes civil society and is the product of that society.

Isolation in civic life is rare—a matter of deviance, not normalcy. Despite the compelling resonance of the image of "bowling alone," a society in which people actually bowled alone would be dramatically different from the environment we inhabit today with our relatives, friends, and colleagues. We should not make the mistake of assuming that outside of association there is silent solitude, just as we must not forget that sovereign selves require help from friends. Groups provide autonomy and audience, generating the freedom and the connections through which citizenship is animated.

# = Chapter 8 =

## The Extension of the Local

Culture areas are coterminous with communication channels.
—Tamotsu Shibutani, "Reference Groups as Perspectives" (1955, 566)

A SOCIOLOGY THAT focuses exclusively on small, interacting groups is a limited discipline. Apart from a few microscopic "tribal" societies, most groups connect with other groups. This recognizes the presence and power of networks in creating and extending social control, shared perspectives, and normative order and, at times, in generating divisions, inequalities, conflicts, and resistance. Culture extends from local scenes through processes of domain extension. Scenes build on each other to create a more extensive and robust social system. Local domains of knowledge are expanded when groups come into contact through the linkages of members, the deliberate diffusion of information, or the use of resource power to force others to heed the choices of those more dominant. Just as groups vary in their authority, control, and resources, they vary in their effect on the choices of communities, large and small.

Networks are never simply linkages among individuals but rather linkages among individuals embedded in groups; as such, they lead to advantages for those who are widely known and have extensive ties (Burt 2010). Mark Granovetter's (1973) influential distinction between strong and weak ties showed that an associational network constitutes clumps of strong ties linked by weaker acquaintanceship ties. As Craig Calhoun (1993, 37–38) phrases it, in "nearly any imaginable case there will be clusters of relatively greater density of communication within the looser overall field." Since most individuals participate in multiple groups or shift their group affiliations (Ikegami 2000, 1002; Mische 2007), the pattern of linkages is complex. Brokers who are tied into several groups and who can link groups are particularly influential (Burt 2005; Hillmann 2008); agents of control can bring demands from one group (a police unit or legislative assembly) to another (a gang or small business). As Harrison White (1995) argues, those sites at which groups (or, more precisely, group members) gather become points of connection and diffusion, permitting the coordination of a society composed of many sites (Omar Lizardo, personal communication, 2009). The bridging and brokerage function of salient group members helps establish interstitial networks (Emirbayer and Sheller 1999).

Moments of group activation are crucial to the expansion of a cultural context. In this light, Lewis Yablonsky (1959) spoke of the activation of "near-groups" in describing how groups (in his case gangs) extend the local culture by involving those who belong to the penumbra of the group. The same can be said of political parties when dramatic occurrences—such as legislative campaigns and, more particularly, elections—generate excitement and participation among partisans. In my research with political volunteers, I found that for most of the year these men and women were engaged in other activities—the mundane activities of their own lives—and only occasionally did they come together in emotion-drenched solidarity. Their world changed as I observed them in the thrill of political gatherings. At these times and places, they truly felt that they were political actors. Wearing buttons and chanting rhythmically as orators assailed their opponents, they believed that they mattered in creating an engaged civil society. Such quasi-groups recognize that boundaries are flexible and can be expanded under conditions in which the scene is defined as "where the action is" (Goffman 1967; Sato 1988).

Those who have detailed the cultural components of subcultures emphasize the salience of linkages that connect groups (Barnes 1969). These ties capture the reality that, within a social system, institutions knit communities and spread culture because they are organized through small groups that, while often spatially and temporally bounded, are also intersecting. Small groups are specialized publics in an institutional division of labor, and thus people participate in groups in several life-world domains (work, family, religion, education, leisure). Involvement in multiple groups raises the possibility of boundary spanning. Wispy occasions that bring sequestered groups together (movement rallies, Boy Scout jamborees, gaming convocations, political conventions, scholastic chess tournaments) extend and integrate networks.

These linkages are evident in the ethnographic examination of group cultures. For instance, many political tasks are organized on the local level. The political activists I studied volunteered in a state representative district, and the participants knew each other from being neighbors and working on the same local campaigns. However, they could be recruited for congressional, gubernatorial, or national campaigns, and when these similar-minded participants from numerous local districts met, their local cultures mixed. Conventions and rallies as ritual moments have the same effect. Small groups are incorporated into larger ones. Restaurants have a different linkage structure. Since the job market for cooks is fluid, workers frequently change position, moving from one restaurant to another. However, the close ties at the previous restaurant do not evaporate, and on several occasions I observed cooks revisiting their former workplace or meeting former coworkers after hours, extending groups and sharing ideas about cuisine, customers, and employers. These gatherings were filled with stories about notable events and common acquaintances. Cooks see themselves both as working for a particular establishment and also as participants in a distinctive occupational culture. In youth sports, the participants' extra-group connections—through family networks, parental migration, or participation in schools, churches, or leisure worlds—allowed for rapid cultural transmission (Opie and Opie 1959). These children had an intense curiosity about the culture of their peers. Meteorologists who had to coordinate with neighboring offices to forecast severe weather developed friendships across geographical boundaries, even though they sometimes made fun of different office cultures. Internet social networking creates tight-knit virtual groups that reveal many characteristics of group dynamics, although of course they lack face-to-face communication and acquaintanceships tend to be less intense. As these cyberworlds develop, they increasingly supplement the centrality of face-to-face worlds. People are coming to feel that they know their cyberpartners as well as their physical ones.

A similar process operates within elite social fields. Government and institutional decisions are rarely made by individuals in isolation but through the advice or vote of working groups situated in interactional webs (Hart 1994; Jackall 1988). Through connections among groups, with the authority structure that this implies, the decision is spread to other micropublics.

At the core of all associational networks are tight relations through which local cultural elements are produced, retained, and disseminated. When participants extend their group identification to a larger subsociety or network, the local context provides the basis for an extended civil society. This constitutes a "network of publicity" (Emirbayer and Sheller 1999, 145) through which what is known locally is incorporated into a larger and more comprehensive network. As Mario Small (2009, 9) explains with regard to urban day care centers, parents become linked to more extensive forms of social capital through the culture of the local center and the connections that result from participation.[1] Even if we treat media as a primary basis of cultural extension, media are constituted by work groups, just as their audiences often are groups as well.

Developing a theory of *group extension* is crucial for treating the local interaction scene as a means through which wider cultural relations and behavioral commonalities are built. Ethnographic corners provide a site for the intense investigation that field researchers hold so dear, but they are never so bounded that they do not have ties to other corners blanketing the city and beyond. Those found at corners have resources to shape what happens in other spots. The question for further meso-level research is: how extensive and in what patterns do we find translocal connectivity?[2]

The recognition of group extensions challenges us to extend beyond the local, develop mechanisms that "link up" from groups, and incorporate group cultures within larger social systems. To this end, I suggest that groups are linked in associative networks through *interlocks*. These are sites of communication that connect groups to larger publics (White 1995, 1053), often through places where groups can communicate in *free spaces* (Evans and Boyte 1986). Through the iterations of microcultures, groups provide larger systems with tensile strength based on communal affiliation.

## Subcultures as Extensions

In this volume, I have described the culture of an interacting group, but how does that culture spread beyond the group? What bridges permit the diffusion of cultural content? Society is composed of multiple interaction arenas, reticulated but not isolated. In between the group and the culture (or the nation) are cultural communities that are not necessarily based on routine interaction but rather are linked through common interests or background. These are *subcultures*, or what I call *networks of groups*.

Of the dimensions on which we divide ourselves, none are more central than those classic sociological variables of age, gender, race, and class. We confidently place individuals in such categories, reading bodies and other indicators of belonging (Goffman 1983, 14). Through a set of *identity marks*, we categorize individuals. Added to these primary distinctions are secondary, though still consequential, ones such as religion, occupation, region, ethnicity, and creed. The array of identity marks establishing boundaries is extensive. Even if some marks are not always easily read from bodies, they typecast a person, suggesting which identities should be assigned, who belongs together, and what responses are appropriate. These divisions correspond to partitions in the corpus of knowledge. Just as we speak of racialized pools of knowledge (Maines 1999; Fine and Turner 2001; Robinson 2008), knowledge can be gendered, classed, and further divided according to one's social placement.

The underlying recognition is that culture is capital that is not uniformly distributed throughout a social system, particularly in societies, such as contemporary Western ones, that depend on an extensive division of labor (Bourdieu 1984). Societies are built on tiny publics, both those grounded in personal interaction, as described earlier, and those that I describe as subcultures, a bounded network of groups with a shared, if diffuse, culture. It is here that the life worlds—and the culture worlds—of groups intersect; at this intersection local cultures are extended outward, while individuals borrow the cultural themes of others to shape their own.

The concept of subculture, although not the term itself, can be traced to the research and writing of Frederic Thrasher (1927/1963) on the ecology of 1,313 Chicago gangs. Thrasher argued that delinquent gangs have traditions that emerge from their responses to the environment and that, as local traditions are shared through the intersection of gangs, distinguish participants from those outside the gang milieu. The shared cultural traditions aid socialization and recruitment: first to a local group and then to a larger domain of identification. A model of culture that recognized that the traditions of related groups could be integrated proved compelling, especially for those who examined the group-based traditions of delinquents (Matza 1964, 19; Jenks 2004). That a world of identification exists outside of the local gang helped solve the puzzle of why delinquents in different gangs act much the same. Yet the boundaries of subculture too often seemed imprecise. At first researchers (Green 1946; Gordon 1947) equated subculture with society, erasing what is cultural about subculture by conflating the structure of social relations with the cultural content of interaction, only integrating culture through the recognition of shared value orientations (Miller 1958; Cohen 1955; Sherif and Sherif 1964). Recently, scholars, drawing on cultural studies, have analyzed subcultures in light of larger cultural themes. They downplay the role of local groups (Muggleton 2000; Hebdige 1981), although they recognize the existence of multiple and competing subcultural groups, differentiated by style but often characterized by a shared desire to resist hegemonic cultural institutions (Bennett and Kahn-Harris 2004; Hall and Jefferson 1976). Despite the recognition of diverse subcultures based on stylistic choices (Chaney 2004), each subculture has been pictured as internally homogeneous and tied to values and collective representations; these representations erase the reality of the subculture as an interaction order. By contrast, a model of subculture as building on the shared meaning of a network of groups, expressed in action, permits an understanding of the relationship between the group and the larger community in which the group is embedded.

To address how group extensions shape the interaction order, it is essential to distinguish between culture and social structure. As David Arnold (1970, 114) notes, "While subcultures grow out of the interaction of groups of people, they are not themselves those groups" (see also Yinger 1977). Subcultures are cultures, and they are linked to communities with pools of knowledge. Knowledge pools come to characterize the habitus of group members, just as one's social location affects the knowledge pools to which one has access (Bourdieu 1977; Bourdieu and Wacquant 1992); the relationship between community and culture is recursive. Demography does not determine cultural awareness by itself, but only as those features are connected to domains of action. For example, not all teenagers are aware of the traditions of a given contemporary youth culture, although demographic boundaries might place them within this imagined group (Hebdige 1981). With the flowering of youth styles, the homogenizing tendency of a societal youth culture proves inadequate. Groups extend only so far.

What might a group-based model of subculture look like? Given that much of my ethnographic research has been on youth subcultures (baseball teams, fantasy-gaming groups, high school debaters, chess clubs), I focus on the diverse cultures of adolescence (not "youth culture" as a single categorical field). Although I have observed face-to-face interaction, an emphasis on interaction raises the question of diffusion: How does cultural material get spread throughout a subsociety in which most individuals are not in routine contact? How do some cultural elements become widely known throughout an extended population? These linkages share "known culture" beyond a group's boundary (see chapter 2). This knowledge then becomes a resource that is part of a group's tool-kit and can be drawn upon to solve problems, create divisions, or justify conflict.

## Groups and Interlocks

A groups model locates culture within interaction arenas. Such a stance seems at first to preclude widespread understanding. If culture can be localized, it can also be borrowed. Fads and fashions are examples. Although fads might be local at first, they need not remain so. People are open to ideas and behaviors that they can incorporate into their cultural repertoire and possibly gain status by sharing with colleagues. This was dramatically evident in the rarefied world of high school debate. Debaters on a high school team continually listened for arguments that they could use in other contests. Hearing an effective claim from a rival team, they would share it with their teammates, possibly incorporating it into their arsenal of argumentation. Over the season, novel arguments spread through the debate community, locally and nationally. Since the world of debate maintained Internet discussion boards, ideas could spread rapidly, and an argument that was effective at the start of the year would be easily defeated by the end. Perhaps the idea was a product of a school team, but if it was judged worthy, the idea—a cultural meme (Heath and Heath 2007)—caught on. Innovations can be incorporated when they solve problems or create pleasure, but they must be shared for that to happen.

Although culture enters group history when activated in interaction, cultural elements constitute a subculture through diffusion among groups. A group can be studied as a closed system, as in the world of high school debate, but group members rarely interact exclusively with one another. Groups are connected to other microcommunities through a tangle of social connections or *interlocks*. Individuals may identify with several groups simultaneously or sequentially. Groups connect through various mechanisms, including intergroup communication (communication from one group to another), multi-group communication (communication from one group to a number of groups, as in the case of the mass media), or communication among groups by nonmembers who have a position that demands or facilitates such communication. Through these interlocks, group boundaries are bridged and cultural options extended, resulting in common discourse throughout the network by means of the performance of shared knowledge. Once spread, cultural content may be localized within groups and the diffused material marked as their own. Each group develops a variant form of the culture of the larger network.

Cultural extension emerges from multiple group cultures and then, when shared through media, digital communication, or face-to-face communication, shapes those idiocultures. The transmission of culture results from interaction, as groups are characterized by *knowing in common*. The diffusion of a cultural item may remain limited as it spreads slowly or not at all, unless sponsored by a *cultural entrepreneur* with access to the mass media or an extended social media network. Reaching a wider audience, such an entrepreneur can achieve wholesale transmission rather than retail. After circulating through media (mass and social), a cultural item may be further diffused through interpersonal channels (Rogers 2003). While media diffusion broadens the reach of knowledge, the extent of diffusion should not be equated with the method of transmission. Sometimes the mass media have a small audience, and sometimes interpersonal communication can spread widely.

The cultures of adolescence epitomize subcultures that build communication channels apart from the reach of traditional media. Although established media are influential in shaping adolescent society, it is also formed through other channels, including various electronic communication formats. Facebook and Twitter are rivaling broadcast television in their impact. Much material that is widely known among groups of young people—dirty jokes, sexual beliefs, aggressive humor, drug lore, and pranks—is not spread by adult-dominated, corporate media. In contrast, this diffusion is highly dependent on technology, as mail (now sneeringly referred to as "snail mail"), automotive transportation, telephone, fax, texting, discussion boards, and tweets affect the speed and direction of information spread. Researchers such as Iona Opie and Peter Opie (1959) once marveled at how swiftly children's folklore traveled, but with social media diffusion is virtually instantaneous, a result of web browsing, email, and instant messaging. The Internet promotes specialized transmission, and anyone lacking interest remains unaware of the content. Although I made my observations of fantasy gaming prior to the development of email and websites, gaming (Multi-User Dungeons, or MUDs) was one of the first electronic locations where participants could form their own cybergroups, and what they learned in those groups affected their choices in tabletop gaming. In theory, anyone could gain entrée to these targeted sites, but in practice they were focused information conduits that defined the boundaries of a subsociety.

The claim that subcultural traditions derive from the diffusion of group cultures is consistent with Karl Mannheim's (1952, 307) explanation of the formation of youth cultures. Mannheim argued that youth cultures originate in groups ("generational units") that create interpretive frameworks and develop and share distinctive cultural patterns. Subculture is a gloss for knowledge and behaviors that spread within interlocking groups, extending and then shaping the local. This occurs through multiple group memberships, weak ties, structural roles, and media diffusion. The extent of the subculture consists of the boundaries within the social network. To reiterate Tamotsu Shibutani's (1955, 566) sage remark, the epigraph for this chapter, "Culture areas are coterminous with communication channels."

## Multiple Group Membership

An individual may participate in several groups simultaneously; traditions that are embraced in one group can easily be introduced into others through overlapping membership. James Patrick (1973), describing a violent Glasgow gang, found that elements in the gang culture were shared in reform school by boys who used their weekend passes to acquire the latest street lore. This pattern is also found in prison, where, because the institution assembles those of a similar background into a shared space, diffusion of culture is rapid (Giallombardo 1974; Cardozo-Freeman 1984). A more mundane example is the preadolescent boy who participates on a sports team with teammates from other neighborhoods. Hockey camps, scout jamborees, church youth groups, extracurricular lessons, and summer camps reveal the range of groups that preadolescents belong to in addition to their school peers. These multiple connections characterized the Little League baseball teams I studied; these groups served as a nexus point for boys who attended different elementary schools. On one occasion the team was a central vector by which a rumor that a boy had suffocated from ingesting Pop Rocks candy spread throughout the suburb (Fine 1979a). From the team as node, the rumor diffused widely. Salient concerns of a peer group can be transmitted readily if they are appropriate for sharing and self-enhancing for the sharer. A shared past is established within the weave of communication channels. In turn, cultural items are brought to local peer groups by returning youngsters. The youth who belongs to several groups with few common members performs a crucial brokerage role for the spread and adaptation of cultural traditions over social gaps and holes.

## Weak Ties

However dense their social networks, individuals often maintain acquaintanceships outside the core groups with which they affiliate. As a result, a network that is based on an interacting group is neither totally bounded nor finite (Barnes 1969). As Mark Granovetter (1973) famously noted, external contacts or weak ties are of crucial importance for disseminating information throughout a social system.

A series of influential studies by Stanley Milgram and his colleagues (Milgram 1967; Travers and Milgram 1969; Korte and Milgram 1970), based on an idea from the inventor of the radio, Guglielmo Marconi, and the Hungarian mathematician Frigyes Karinthy, reveals the extent and robustness of these network strands: six degrees of separation connects us all (Watts 2003). In one variation—known as the Small World Experiment (Schnettler 2009)—Milgram asked randomly chosen subjects in Omaha, Nebraska, and Wichita, Kansas, if they personally knew a target person in the Boston area. If so, they would have been asked to forward a letter directly to that individual (no one did). If not, they were asked to forward the letter to a contact who they thought would be most likely to know that individual and to send Milgram a postcard so that he could trace the skein of connections. The same request was made of the second person, and the next, until at last the letter reached the target. Although the lengths of the chain varied as a function of the techniques used, most successful chains reached the target in five to six linkages (most chains were not completed). The phrase "six degrees of separation" was born. Milgram discovered that certain individuals, because of the breadth of their networks, their motivations, and their structural positions, often serve to knit networks. These individuals are similar to those "connectors" whom Malcolm Gladwell (2000) describes in *The Tipping Point* as constituting the means through which disparate groups are linked. Similarly, Ron Burt (1992, 2010) describes techniques by which structural holes in a social system are bridged by brokers.

Because of the social, occupational, and geographical mobility characteristics of contemporary American society, we maintain social ties with others at great physical distances and across social and demographic divides. These connectors are crucial for building trust among groups that might otherwise define themselves as distinct or even in opposition. Such ties provide opportunities for the spread of information if suitable motivation exists. Studies of rumor diffusion, hysterical contagion, and the flow of news reveal that information and behavior spread rapidly under favorable conditions—that is, if the information is regarded as important and structural conditions are conducive for dissemination (Smelser 1962; DiFonzo 2008).

Cultural diffusion among children can be rapid because of established weak ties, based on membership in strong groups. In addition to the school peer group, children who have moved across the country or across town may maintain distant friendships. The onetime childhood pastime of having pen pals exemplified this phenomenon. Likewise, spatially or genetically distant cousins who populate extended families provide children with peers with whom to compare their life situations and cultures. Since children's culture has both regional and local variations, these kin ties provide a mechanism by which cultural traditions bridge geographical or cultural divides.

Conversations with infrequently met acquaintances are structured to facilitate rapid dissemination of large chunks of new information, a process that anthropologist Sally Yerkovich (1977) labels "updating." Conversants cover many topics briefly. Through extended questioning, participants may choose to delve into relevant topics in greater detail. The spread of culture from a participant in one local network to an acquaintance in another is crucial for creating a culture that transcends any single group. But, as noted in the discussion on the creation of idiocultures, not all channels are created equal; different communication conduits disseminate specific cultural genres, following patterns that depend on the topic and the perceived interests of audiences (Dégh and Vazsonyi 1975). The usability of particular forms of culture results from local norms. As I studied Little League baseball teams, I saw that some boys specialized in transmitting sexual lore, racist jokes, sports information, or entertainment gossip.

Perhaps the archetypal weak tie involves information spread through social media. Although this has some features of mass media communication, electronic communication allows like-minded individuals to converse, even if the parties are barely acquainted. Chat rooms, discussion boards, networking sites, and email lists enshrine the weak tie as the essential connection of the digital age. On occasion, ties can shift from weak to strong, as with Internet dating sites. Technology reduces the need for geographical propinquity, favoring interest-based publics, even while such online communities are backed by interaction scenes where embodied connections bolster imagined connections online.

## Structural Roles

Cultural information can also be spread by individuals who perform specialized structural roles in intergroup relations. These role inhabitants link groups through their positions and responsibilities, even when they are peripheral to any of the groups with which they have contact. The traditional form of this brokerage role was that of the traveling salesman (Spears 1997), who moved from location to location with a collection of anecdotes, gossip, and jokes along with whatever products he had to sell. Itinerant preachers and motivational speakers have a similar role. Even drug dealers—traveling salesmen of an alternative age—spread cultural traditions (Partridge 1973). Publishing representatives perform an analogous role on college campuses, keeping faculty members abreast of intellectual trends among their distant colleagues. I observed the same process when I studied self-taught art. Dealers at art shows or in their galleries shared happenings in the art world with potential customers, although not without a whiff of self-promotion. The list of such transgroup communicators is long, and it includes comedians, lecturers, auctioneers, presidential candidates, after-dinner speakers, and medicine-show hawkers. Talkers who speak to multiple audiences expand cultural knowledge. Although the primary task of these speakers is not to diffuse cultural traditions, this is an ancillary and unintended result of their multi-group contacts. Through their roles, these workers connect groups that lack other points of contact.

## Media Diffusion

Although mass media may be an unlikely source for intergroup diffusion, they link groups in addition to transmitting background knowledge to a mass public. Cultural information is shared when a communicator touches many groups simultaneously. What is learned from the mass media can be borrowed and shaped within tiny publics with shared interests. As Omar Lizardo (2006) demonstrates, mediated popular culture can connect actors in weak-tie networks; popular culture works best in this regard, in contrast to more specialized highbrow culture. In my ethnography of Little League baseball teams, conducted in the mid-1970s, moments from the then-current film *The Bad News Bears* were reenacted by several teams, and that popular film helped define social relations. In an earlier decade, the films of James Dean had a significant impact on youth styles, convincing adolescents that they shared social capital. More recently *Star Trek, The Matrix, The*

*Blair Witch Project, Harry Potter,* and even *The Social Network* have shaped youth culture and interpersonal relations. Over the decades, influential entertainers such as Lady Gaga, Michael Jackson, Madonna, the Beatles, Elvis Presley, the Grateful Dead, Frank Sinatra, and Bing Crosby have influenced waves of young people, convincing them that because of shared tastes they belong together: these *known strangers* resonate through waves of parasocial interaction (Caughey 1984; Horton and Wohl 1956), affirming horizontal affiliation as well as vertical connections with the performer.

A selection process occurs as well as what we might label "treatment effects" of media knowledge. Cultural productions, like concerts or plays, are not viewed by a random sample of the population. Instead, attendance is shaped by cultural and social selection and in turn builds cultural and social capital. The shared interests that create media audiences establish subcultural boundaries; given that cultural interests depend on socialization, these preferences may mirror demography (Peterson and Kern 1996). In other words, content produces social relations, and social relations shape exposure to culture.

Media diffusion must never be abstracted from interaction (Friedson 1953; Bacon-Smith 1992). Popular culture is typically created not by isolated artists but through group interaction; the facilitation of other groups is required for its transmission, and it must then be viewed by groups that incorporate the messages. At each point of creation and diffusion, groups are influential. Audience members take raw, cultural "stuff" and fashion it to fit the needs and interests of the groups to which they belong; the fan cultures thus built (Jenkins 1992; Hills 2002; Gray, Sandvoss, and Harrington 2007; Long 2003) are subcultures that depend on connecting a community with forms of media. Even a communication form seemingly far removed from face-to-face interaction—the mass media—builds on an interaction order.

Together these four interlocks illustrate possible transmission vectors. Because the messages of the mass media do not reach everyone, do not cover all content, and do not provide critique, interpersonal diffusion is essential for the cementing of subcultural traditions. Yet, mere knowledge does not ensure that content will be incorporated into a cultural system. Group identification or affiliation is required for the acceptance and preservation of a cultural form.

## Identification

Sociologists are properly skeptical of any approach that examines traditions without recognizing that traditions shape the identities of individuals and communities. We define ourselves by the cultures that we share. Shared symbols create our sense of self. Put another way, identities are acquired through boundary work as individuals view themselves as members of a group, as marginal to the group, or as outsiders (Lamont 1992).

Through participating in diverse groups, individuals find alternative identities (Zurcher 1977; Gergen 1991). Culture is not a blueprint for socialization; instead, local cultures are a part of the tool-kit that creates identities (Smith 2008). This is evident when we consider voluntary socialization—an individual having to decide whether to espouse an alternative culture. The embrace of cultural models requires identification with like-minded others. Values, traditions, and artifacts affect identity only insofar as individuals define themselves as belonging to a community whose members share meanings *and* recognize this sharing.

Recognizing the identity of another involves assigning that person to a position (Berger and Luckmann 1967, 132). Conversely, social worlds exist to the extent that individuals define themselves as members of the group (Unruh 1982). Gregory Stone's (1970, 399) conception of identity as a "coincidence of placements and announcements" properly recognizes the interrelationship between the individual and the group. Subculture and identification are dialectic processes, each implicated in the construction of the other.

Although identification with a social segment is crucial to the establishment of a subculture, identification need not be total or all encompassing. Such a view falsely assumes a binary conception of identity as present or absent. In contrast, subcultural identification varies along two dimensions, centrality and salience. *Centrality* refers to the *depth* of a member's commitment to the population segment, while *salience* refers to the *frequency* of the activation of that identification. Both dimensions acknowledge the situational character of identity (Gecas 1994): an identity may be latent (Becker and Geer 1960) most of the time, or it may become activated (manifest) in many contexts. An individual may identify with a number of segments of society, some of which demand or facilitate strong commitment to norms and behaviors. Similarly, an individual may identify more strongly with a local group to which he or she belongs, while in other circumstances the larger population segment will be more prominent. Most teens interested in fantasy gaming first join because it is a group of friends engaging in enjoyable play. Only later do they think of role-play games as providing an identity. A boy who joins an adolescent gang hangs out with members of that group and not with "gang members" in general. The group constitutes the basis of identification. In his work on Chicago gangs, Sudhir Venkatesh (1997, 2008) finds that affiliation involves both emotional and rational choices but always is based on social relationships. However, both the centrality and salience of the identification with the group may vary with the occasion, as evident in

Lewis Yablonsky's (1959) characterization of New York gangs as near-groups that oscillate in the extent to which they can energize peripheral participants, or as in Ruth Horowitz's (1983) recognition that Hispanic gang members oscillate between conventional and rebellious values. Groups swell in size when they become sites of action (Sato 1988), a finding evident in the mushroom society that I observed: attendance waxed and waned according to the season and the weather.

Sometimes group members identify strongly with both the interacting group and the subcultural population. Adolescents identify with numerous groups—a sports team, friendship clique, chess club, or debate squad—as well as with teenagers in general. When the identification involves emotional energy, I speak of the identification as *hot*, in contrast to the *cool* judgments of rational, economic actors. Hot identification is typically more closely linked than cool identification to qualities of self and to shared traditions.

When identification with the larger population segment is cool, the culture of the group is localized, and few significant interlocks are found with demographically or behaviorally similar groups. Identification is provisional and strategic, and the network is weakly formulated. If hot identification—identification that shapes a self-image—extends beyond the interacting group, members are more receptive to the incorporation of translocal cultural traditions.

Characteristics of individuals and of subcultures may predispose individuals to emphasize the centrality of a group. Group or subcultural identification may result from individual differences, background characteristics, or latent culture. Further, identification with a community or interacting group may be facilitated by structural conditions. It is a mundane, if consequential, point that subcultural identification is likely only if an individual has the opportunity to interact with others who similarly identify with the population segment and shared culture. Groups vary in the degree to which they are embedded in a centralized organizational network (affiliated with nonlocal organizations, such as Young Democrats or Students Against Drunk Driving) or a horizontal network (affiliated with comparable local organizations, such as high school debate teams that belong to the same state scholastic debate association and compete in the same tournaments). These extra-organizational ties promote identification with the population domain and the subculture in which the interacting group belongs. Participants in social fields characterized by constricted vertical and horizontal connections, such as gangs and friendship cliques, are likely to identify more strongly with the local group than with a more diffuse population. This hot identification must be balanced with the cool identification generated through the interlocks discussed earlier.

### Community Response

Subcultures operate in dynamic tension. Treating subculture as static ignores the reality that cultural content and identification change through the explicit or indirect responses of those outside the group boundaries. Although group members choose behaviors, hold expectations, and select forms of identification, the public treatment of subcultural segments also affects an interlocking network. Artifacts that are salient to outsiders, for instance, may become central to a group's identity. Groups can borrow media catchphrases and twist them to their own ends, such as the Hells Angels' positive use of the term "one percenter" after being labeled the 1 percent who cause trouble (Thompson 1967). Media emphasis on the hairstyle of the Beatles aided its adoption by friends during the mid-sixties, and the bare midriff look of Britney Spears became popular in similar fashion more recently.

Although the acceptance of media portrayals is not readily predictable, media can produce changes in subcultural content or in identification. But at the same time groups may challenge, reject, or embrace the public definition by which others characterize them. Widespread media portrayals are likely to be reacted to *in some way* by those labeled. For groups that reject established cultural models, messages of the mainstream media condemning the behavior may hasten its spread in a process of deviance amplification (Wilkins 1965). Stanley Cohen (1964) demonstrated that British television and newspaper reports on the disturbances of the Mods may have led some nonmembers to adopt the behavior and artifacts of those who had been condemned in order to gain a sense of belonging. Something similar, although milder in form, occurred when fantasy games, such as Dungeons and Dragons, were condemned by moral entrepreneurs as satanic. The condemnation spread knowledge of the game to those who had been unaware of it (Martin and Fine 1991), and thus a small social world soon became a fad.

Community response supports the extension of idiocultures by bringing groups with similar interests into contact. Outsiders may exclude deviants from conventional spaces, forcing them to socialize, a process of differential association (Sutherland 1947). In the case of juvenile gangs in Glasgow (Armstrong and Wilson 1973), media portrayals of Easterhouse as having the "toughest" gangs led gangs throughout the city to challenge them. Although some of the boys felt that they were not as tough as others described them, the publicity created group encounters and established a context in which performance and identification became necessary.

An analogous situation is seen with adolescents generally. Through both mass and social media, teens learn of the cultural styles of peers who, through their prominence, become role models. Adults expect young people to share interests and, whether or not they do, to be an age-based subculture. These portrayals of youth, coupled with the age segregation of adults and youth (Fine and Mechling 1991), increase the likelihood of peer identification and acceptance of subcultural prescriptions.

Encounters with agents of social control may create or strengthen identification among a broader population segment, whereas the existence of factions and local traditions might otherwise militate against it. While conflict among groups heightens within-group identification, creating an intensely local perspective, outside intervention amplifies subcultural identification. Rival gangs may spontaneously form a coalition against law enforcement (Yablonsky 1962), as happened when fear of the Los Angeles police spread in the aftermath of the 1992 trial of police officers in the beating of Rodney King. Likewise, public housing officials' disregard for rival gang boundaries when providing homes after urban renewal dismissed real dangers to adolescents, strengthening the salience of gang membership (Rymond-Richmond 2007).

When subcultural identification exists, the responses of outsiders affect its centrality. Outsiders may give excessive attention to those who participate in targeted groups, such as those who associate with individuals whom the government considers to be terrorists, militants, or racists. Even if these individuals are only acquaintances, the surveillance under which they are placed may cause them to define themselves as belonging together. Whether the attention is positive or (more often) negative, identification becomes activated. In contrast, when a subsociety is ignored by the larger society, members may either lose interest in the group or no longer be ashamed to reveal their membership, normalizing their identity.

By shaping an individual's definition of belonging, community reactions to subcultural traditions and to the groups that display them affect the centrality and salience of identification and the embrace of cultural traditions. In addition, because community responses to local cultures are fluid, subcultural themes and identification shift over time.

## Linked Worlds

Building on the platform of tiny publics, with their array of idiocultures, a network of linked groups, a subculture, or even a national culture emerges. Approaches that ignore interaction are challenged to analyze culture because of an unwillingness to examine meaning in situ. Still, avoiding how culture is extended and spread has dangers as well. Small groups are locations where culture, subsequently spread to larger social units, is nurtured, borrowed, and preserved, but nurturing, borrowing, and preserving is often only the start of the creation of a meaningful world.

As I near the end of this volume, my claim is that the previous chapters are insufficient. By being fully local, bathed in groupy sociology, they are cramped and partial. To understand why groups matter, we must specify the conditions under which they are tied together, and we must understand the power of the culture that emerges from their connections. People do not belong to a single group. We are never just clansmen in remote microtribes. Rather, our groups are deeply varied and richly diverse. They exist simultaneously and sequentially. They are horizontal and vertical. As a result, our friendships do not dissipate when we shift groups or when we select a group in which to participate. The multiple group memberships, the weak ties, and the brokers who have feet in many camps all create a robust cultural world that depends on an inter-action order but is not limited to one. Further, as media continue to evolve, our understanding of how these distant—and not so distant— voices matter must be incorporated into our understanding. My research has concentrated on the face-to-face, but it has become increasingly evi-dent that the virtual realms of social media are an essential supplement to the appreciation of group extensions. This is a task for the future.

This recognition of the significance of group extensions emphasizes the vital and compelling pull of small groups. Groups are never content-free gatherings but are embedded within systems of meaning and hives of relations that swell through copious linkage. The analysis of culture must begin in those local scenes where culture is formulated, but to understand the impact of culture on social segments and society itself, a local analysis must be only a start: a tiny spore from which a mighty mushroom grows.

# — Chapter 9 —

## Action and Its Publics

For myself, I always write about Dublin, because if I can get to the heart
of Dublin, I can get to the heart of all cities of the world. In the particular
is contained the universal.
                            —James Joyce, letter to Arthur Power, 1922

I N HIS PROVOCATIVE, transformative fashion, emphasizing the power
of the local, James Joyce posed a challenge for thinking about society.
For insights to be universal, they must be local first. This is, of course,
the novelist's creed. Each story describes a scene, but each must brim with
insight, convincing audiences that the act of reading is not voyeurism but
education. The places, the actions, and the persons depicted stand for
more than themselves.

Throughout this volume, I have presented a sociology of the local
and described the role of group culture and shared pasts. Now, in
attempting to bring the themes together, I present a theoretical approach
to understanding local context that incorporates idiocultures, tiny
publics, meso-level analysis, and the interaction order. My argument
embraces the Joycean challenge: how does a sustained focus on the
local allow us to understand social order? As I began by suggesting,
this question confronts much of sociology, a discipline committed to
examining how broad and unseen structural realities ("social facts")
overwhelm or even erase the specific characteristics of place and identity and the apparent idiosyncrasies of group life. In this final chapter, I describe what it means to adopt an approach that takes local
context seriously.

Although this argument might seem fully microsociological, it is not
microsociology as often presented. Too often microsociologists, just as
macrosociologists do, search for transcendent forces or generic processes
(Prus 1987; Couch 1984), relying on methodological individualism. In
contrast, I contend that the group represents a distinctive meso-level of
analysis. Order cannot be explained by erasing the mechanisms of its
production and its persistence.

157

## Conceptualizing Localism

The particular circumstances of action provide *opportunity structures* that allow for developing meanings and structures, and these meanings and structures reverberate beyond group boundaries. Commitment to a group and its local culture produces standards for action, which then shape the group and radiate outward (Lawler 1992). By local culture I refer to meaning that is tied to a recognizable interaction scene and its participants. In the strong case, affiliation shapes the actor's identity and generates motivation for either change or adherence to accepted standards. In the weak case, it creates a desire to follow tacit understandings of propriety. In either case, individuals do not negotiate their relationships afresh every time they meet; instead, as described in chapter 4, they rely on expectations that have developed over the course of their relationship.

Since every act constitutes and is constituted by a local context, particularity is universal. If everything is situated, that situated quality becomes a feature of social organization. But simultaneously, a situated context shapes the evaluation and interpretation of action. Put another way, the local provides a *stage* for action and creates a *lens* through which participants typify groups or gatherings, establishing boundaries. Thus, the local is both a material reality and a form of collective representation. Action is always generated in response to other actions within a local scene, as well as to the local meaning of that scene.

The tension that Joyce refers to between universalism and particularism has long been evident in social theory, although we might alter his wording to make a distinction between generalism and localism. This strain is not the division between theory and empiricism, or between generalization and description, or even between macro- and microsociology. Rather, it reflects a division over the extent to which action is responsive to the conditions of those settings in which it emerges as opposed to seeing action as a result of general forces separate from *embedded practices*. Meaning-making is an ongoing process that is achieved through shared histories. Although meanings are negotiated, they are never negotiated anew but are based on established understandings (Strauss 1978). The groups model does not deny the obdurate reality of structures but treats them as developing from and cemented in action. Consistent with Anthony Giddens's (1984) structuration theory, structure emerges from repeated action and local practices—what Keith Sawyer (2005) labels "emergentist" theory.

Although this approach challenges standard views that ignored the cultural contexts of action, there has recently been an upsurge of interest in contextual forces. Researchers have given increased attention to localism in several domains, including the "neighborhood effects" literature in criminology and inequality (Sampson, Morenoff, and Gannon-Rowley 2002; Quillian and Pager 2001), the analysis of mechanisms of cause and effect (Gross 2009; Hedström and Swedberg 1998), socially embedded and networked political and economic transactions (DiMaggio and Louch 1998; Hillmann 2008), the importance of emotional attachments to nested groups (Lawler 1992), the centrality of local orientation to identity (Bearman 1991), and the impact of the conditions of scientific production on discovery (Knorr-Cetina 1999; Collins 1992; Henke and Gieryn 2008). The diversity of such efforts suggests that an ontology of the local is not tied to any epistemological strategy but relies on a conception of the locus of social causation.

Although they have provided a valuable start, these streams often ignore the specifics of group interpretations; thus, they do not grant sufficient weight to the effects of local context on action. Even an ethnographic approach, such as the extended case method (Burawoy 2009), is often more concerned with structural effects than with the contours of group life. The influential neighborhood effects literature is valuable in suggesting that structural forces alone do not shape outcomes and that variables such as collective efficacy (Sampson, Morenoff, and Earls 1999; Sampson and Raudenbush 1999) depend on local conditions. This research domain is insightful in questioning the view that all poor neighborhoods are alike and recognizing that community can buffer external threats, providing for distinctive cultures (Fischer 1982). Yet, it does not examine the historical processes (Brown-Saracino 2009) and the spatial features (Grannis 2009) that contribute to community identity and through which neighborhood cultures are developed. Valuable as these microstructural perspectives are in recognizing local diversity, the outcome of many of these research traditions has been to downplay the contextual processes of local effects.

We need to go further, however, than merely situating a localism argument in contrast to a microstructural view; we also need to differentiate this approach from one that on its surface seems a good deal closer to it, in both its methodological and theoretical traditions. Specifically, the model of group culture that I have put forth challenges those dramaturgical and social-constructionist traditions in sociology that have downplayed the importance of history and collective understandings in favor of the idea that order is routinely constructed anew. To analyze how systems form and survive without recognizing that they depend on microcommunities that have common pasts and joint imagined futures, that exist in space (physical or, increasingly, virtual), and that have social relations generated through emotional energy is to miss the process by which an interactional order develops (Harrington and Fine 2000). I do not suggest that all action is *interaction* or that humans do not act outside of the presence of others. Such a claim is self-evidently false. Actions beyond the reflexive or the biological—such as voting, jogging, praying, or writing—have been learned, involve our imagination of others, and depend on implicit standards for performance and on beliefs or practices that are assumed to be widely held. Even private acts result from the embrace of group-based values. Although I argue that interaction is consequential in generating social order, private acts, too, are shaped by being affiliated with groups and are also resources for shaping those groups.

## Localism and Negotiation

A local sociology illuminates several critical theoretical concerns. Localism uncovers the processes through which innovation, socialization, and change are constituted in practice—that is, how they are revealed in action tied to social commitments. Through the dynamics of community affiliation, localism stands at the junction of the interactional and the institutional, escaping the traditional black box that links micro- and macro-interpretations. The challenge for actors within ongoing, unscripted interaction is to organize social relations that have been shaped by stochastic and external forces, interpreting them in light of shared pasts and local histories (Katovich and Couch 1992) and always responding through established systems of interpretations.

A focus on local context extends the negotiated order approach pioneered by Anselm Strauss and his colleagues (Strauss et al. 1964; Strauss 1978, 1982; Kling and Gerson 1977), which recognizes that negotiations never occur anew but are based on sedimented understandings. This approach challenges constructionist, interactionist, phenomenological, and dramaturgical models that treat meanings as continually being formed and re-formed given the needs of the moment (Blumer 1969, 2; Denzin 1985). Although not the only variety of dramatism (Brissett and Edgley 2005; Burke 1984; Evreinoff 1927), Erving Goffman's *Presentation of Self in Everyday Life* (1959) has been taken as providing the charter for the belief that it is the "moment of action" that creates expectations within fleeting gatherings. It is not that dramatism denies order, but rather that it makes order "fully situational," continually establishing relations within the realm of encounters. Ephemeral micropublics (what have been labeled "Goffman publics"; Ikegami 2000, 997; White 1995), found in public spaces, suggest that interaction lacks tradition; in contrast, ongoing groups can overcome the problem through shared ritual and common expectations (Collins 1981).

Dramaturgical theorists, borrowing implicitly or explicitly from Georg Simmel (Zerubavel 1980), properly uncover regularities in the formal contours of interaction in anonymous domains, treating scenes as invitations for choosing among situational definitions. These domains of anonymity and spontaneity do exist. Using the heuristic of life as theater, some adopt a model that is more improvisation than script, a world in which we do not know in advance what direction the scene will take. These scholars construct *a model man in a modal scene* whose motivations—such as preserving social order or bolstering the primacy of interaction— are characteristic of "natural" human desires, and they suggest that it is these motivations to cope with immediate uncertainty, rather than shared and confident understandings, that determine the course of action. These processes are treated as generic, ignoring history and social relations. Meaning is treated as epiphenomenal, drawing on the standard reading of W. I. Thomas and Dorothy Thomas's (1928) dictum that all that is needed is a new, emergent definition and situations can change radically. If challenged, few deny that embedded, stable meanings matter (Goffman 1974, 1), but the interactionist approach has frequently promulgated a fluid model of behavioral preferences that rapidly alter social arrangements—a view that privileges immediacy over established understandings.[1]

Despite a mutual concern with interaction ritual, *dramatism*, which emphasizes the ongoing shaping of untethered interaction routines, contrasts with *localism*, the claim that action is shaped by and responsive to group belonging. Thus, practices—actions understood by reference to local cultures—are central. The response to situations is a grounded performance shaped by a self-referential group that shares (albeit imperfectly) an interpretation of norms, values, beliefs, and rituals (Eliasoph and Lichterman 2003). These cultural elements develop from an awareness of a larger social system organized through membership in multiple groups, media representations, and institutions of socialization (see chapter 8). Even if actions reverberate beyond the interacting group, it is the group that establishes their legitimacy. No matter how much we focus on the here and now, a self-referential history sets the terms for negotiations.

A sociology that emphasizes localism asserts that interaction is the basis of culture but also that local culture is the basis of interaction. Because they are bounded and segmented, groups provide diverse opportunity structures for organizing society: not only are they outposts of society, but they are models for how society should be. That local settings, by maintaining boundaries, become the site for exclusion or segregation suggests why members of social categories have differential access to knowledge, resources, or relations. Local settings are where processes of stratification are generated, reproduced, and transformed, as a result of both the "selection" effects as to who participates and the "treatment" effects of participating in the group (Omar Lizardo, personal communication, 2009). What happens in the group does not always stay in the group.

Global phenomena are constituted by local processes, but simultaneously the group, by limiting participation, establishes and reaffirms status divisions. Examining widespread (and sometimes hidden) connections is not easy, but studies of both Brazilian youth activist networks (Mische 2007) and Muslim terror networks (Sageman 2008) reveal that the intersection of small groups of friends and colleagues can affect global social change. These groups are influenced by media and networks (including social media). As groups form and solidify they provide the infrastructure for dramatic change and even political violence. Both Brazilian leftists and Palestinian jihadists reveal that in groups of intimates people are willing to take risks and engage in actions that they would not willingly participate in by themselves or as members of larger, amorphous movements. It is the tight-knit group—the tiny public—that provides motivation for social engagement. The linkages of these tiny publics present models that are diffused by media, spawning many such groups.

## A Puny Program? The Significance of Context

How is context brought into the theoretical armature of sociology to explain agentic choices? People make choices, self-consciously or not, but are these choices externally determined, are they outgrowths of the psychic underbrush, or are they shaped by forces *within* gatherings and groups (Sewell 1992)? Culture is located within groups and shaped by the shared experiences or background knowledge of participants. Instead of presenting a *strong program* of cultural sociology (Alexander 2003), in which culture in itself is a determining, exogenous force, I suggest a program that is deliberately and unabashedly puny. I make this claim playfully, but also with a vital purpose: to move culture from an autonomous force to a marker whose recognition and use reveal *social relations*. The issue is metaphorical, but also real. It is not that believers in a strong program deny that actors matter but that their analytic strategy downplays the role of actors' choices in shaping culture and accentuates the importance of structures and institutions (Alexander 2006, 4–5). In contrast, building on Ann Swidler's (1986) metaphor, I suggest that culture is a *resource* for agentic action. It is a tool used by those with interests to create moral order and behavioral routine. Treating local scenes as fields of action underlines the centrality of groups and gatherings. In contrast, we must examine how groups with local microcultures are linked in associative networks (Ikegami 2000, 998; Emirbayer and Sheller 1999, 145) and build structures that transcend the local. We should not lay every-thing at the door of the institutional or a discursive regime that lacks speakers. Put another way, the sociology of local effects *is* a strong pro-gram, but of a different sort: it recognizes that actors respond to their surroundings even as they shape their surroundings. In his analysis of interaction orders, Erving Goffman (1983, 4) suggested that scenes are isomorphic, a result of shared socialization and cross-group communi-cation. Although such outcomes might suggest that culture is operating autonomously, his suggestion points to similar paths to group history.

For a local sociology, culture is a form of group practice that is linked to the meso-level of analysis and used by members to achieve personal and collective ends. It occupies the space that links individual action and the structural constraints of institutions, a space that is often evident within bounded social worlds (Unruh 1980; Becker 1982).[2] Interaction provides a dynamic for social life, but it often does not recognize that shared references constitute an essential way in which actors transform their interaction into routine, ritual, and tradition, setting boundaries and expectations. Local worlds, and not interaction alone, provide action with meaning, establish tightly held values, and in this sense incor-porate cultural continuity. As Ann Mische and Harrison White (1998, 695) explain, "Social action is interaction that induces interpretations and thus builds continuing relations."

By building shared pasts and prospective futures, group culture creates an ongoing social order (Katovich and Couch 1992; Heimer and Stinchcombe 1980). Local action systems thus become the guarantors of societal order by providing a platform for civic commitments (Mische and White 1998, 696); individual groups may or may not encourage such opportunities. This approach stresses the importance of ongoing gatherings—willed communities and socializing microinstitutions (Emirbayer and Sheller 1999, 152)—organized through loosely linked networks. Since shared meaning contributes to the establishment of cohesion and communal identity, I extend local sociology beyond the interaction scene and into the realm of belonging and shared affect (Lawler 1992), where locally produced meanings (rules-in-use) are trans-formed into moral imperatives (*ought* rules). Affiliation with ongoing groups is a means through which actors select a frame to determine what is valued (Gamson, Fireman, and Rytina 1982; Snow and Benford 1988).

## Toward a Sociology of the Local

No one doubts that context shapes behavior, but is context theoretically crucial? Does it only constitute error variance, hiding the larger effects of institutions and structures? Claiming that social order is generated through routines, habits, and rituals, supported by emotional energy, Randall Collins (2004, xiii) argues that collective awareness and attention provide a basis for social order: "The aggregate of situations can be regarded as a market for interaction rituals." This approach, building on local cultures and conditions, is consistent with the process that political scientist James Scott (1998, 6) refers to as "mētis"—the knowledge that derives from everyday experience. "Mētis resists simplification into deductive principles which can successfully be transmitted through book learning, because the environments in which it is exercised are so complex and nonrepeatable that formal procedures of rational decision making are impossible to apply." Scott refers to this as "the art of the locality" (316).

To borrow from Jeffrey Goldfarb's (2006) resonant image, we must focus on the *sociology of small things,* a phrase that captures the *place* of action more than its inherent importance. Small things matter to big processes. Goldfarb begins by theorizing the kitchen table. His point is not simply that mundane events must be theorized but that it is the conditions of the place in which they occur that create allegiance, shared perspectives, and the possibility of collective action. "When friends and relatives met in their kitchens, they presented themselves to each other in such a way that they defined the situation in terms of an independent frame rather than that of officialdom" (Goldfarb 2006, 15). Those sitting at a kitchen table constitute a tiny public that motivates action. The hearth became a central symbol in the resistance to Eastern European authoritarianism, but kitchens and porches are also found in democratic polities. These tiny publics become the basis of forms of deliberative democracy, whether in New England town meetings (Bryan 2004) or Brazilian community forums (Baiocchi 2003). As I noted in chapter 7, similar discourse can be found in bookstores, salons, clubs, and even public meetings and gatherings (Habermas 1991; Emirbayer and Sheller 1999, 150; Mische and White 1998, 706). In a related vein, Angela McRobbie speaks of "bedroom culture": the development of an oppositional, feminist stance by teenage girls who establish their bedrooms as private zones in which they gather in small groups to discuss those cultural (and, implicitly, political) issues that concern them (McRobbie and Garber 1976; Lincoln 2004). For these adolescents, the bedroom is the hearth. In such spaces, participants assume that others share history, emotional concern, and a sense of belonging. Being the place where politics is discussed and enacted, tiny publics provide the basis of civil society (Fraser 1992).

Crucially to a theory of local culture, I examine arenas, relations, and shared pasts as building blocks for developing a local sociology, each having been woven in through previous chapters. I then argue that it is through action that meaning is treated as consequential within a group.

# Practices of the Local

I return to the Joycean challenge: translating the particular into the general. As I discussed in chapter 2, every group with which we identify creates a culture from its opening moments (Fine 1979b; McFeat 1974; Sherif and Sherif 1964). These cultures are the means by which identification occurs and groups have consequences. Local culture generates emotional energy, cohesion, and action routines that promote order by investing participants in group outcomes. In the process, these local arenas produce knowledge regimes that generate stratification, building a hierarchy of groups. In this, Randall Collins's (2004) account of interaction ritual chains is particularly insightful: social relations, he notes, are embedded in tradition and in prospective futures. Further, because the linkage of groups extends the influence of any interaction scene, local cultures are more than transient scenes: through their connections they serve as the basis of a broader social order.

The local is simultaneously a stage on which social order is produced and a lens that allows actors to typify scenes. It is both an opportunity structure that generates action and a nexus point through which action has consequences. Examining the local as a stage, I focus on features that motivate participation, using *arenas, relations,* and *shared pasts* as theoretical concepts and as sites for analysis. The metaphor of the local as a lens treats *action* as an interpretive mechanism. From the creation of boundaries and bridges, based in the extension of cultures, actors create associational networks, using interlocks among groups.

## The Local as a Stage

*Arenas*    Every local scene is shaped by the constraints, opportunities, and understandings made possible through the physical (or virtual) space in which it unfolds: an arena of action. Responsibility to and reliance on the space, by building trust and developing obligations, becomes in effect a form of social capital (Small 2009). Although resources must be mobilized for group life, finding a place to gather is among the most essential things necessary for group satisfaction. A vibrant public sphere requires numerous corners, salons, and niches, and obtaining material resources cascades from that choice.

Behaviors, thoughts, and emotions are performed as a consequence of the symbolic meaning of space. People believe that churches demand quiet attentiveness, that schoolrooms promote ordered participation, and that taverns encourage sociable involvement. As Helena Wulff (1988, 25) argues from her study of a microculture of adolescent girls, a routine meeting point becomes imbued with particular experiences in the minds of members. An ongoing interaction scene requires locales where individuals regularly congregate with their expectations intact. Formal meetings or routine schedules are not required, but the need for a place to gather suggests that the availability of spaces characterizes the group. In some spaces—Little League baseball fields, restaurant kitchens, school classes—the presence of group members may be required, but other places function as magnets for voluntary groups, such as fantasy-gamers, mushroomers, and political activists. Although some groups are spontaneous, many groups with adult members, tied to a tyranny of scheduling, establish timetables. The fantasy-gamers I observed, for instance, knew that a group would form each Friday evening at the start of the weekend in the community room of a police station, and the mushroomers I studied attended a regular Monday gathering at a community center to display specimens they had found that weekend.

Although facilitators supply these locations, once present the group colonizes the space by rearranging furniture, setting displays on tables, or, if the location is "owned" by the group, decorating the walls. For the period of use, the group transforms the space into a home field (Oldenburg 1989) or a free space (Evans and Boyte 1986). As described in chapter 3, each space has an obdurate quality, but the power of a group culture permits physical locations to acquire meaning. For instance, in their borrowed space amateur mushroomers changed the arrangement of chairs and later returned them to the original configuration. In contrast, the meteorologists had lengthy discussions within their union and with their supervisor about how the office space should be arranged. The staff debated the location of the printer because that choice would advantage some employees and disadvantage others; they also discussed the height of partitions in the office, a decision that influenced sociability and private concentration. These groups recognized that how they shaped their space contributed to the quality of their social interaction.

Established and self-referential groups require spaces for scheduled meetings: time and space must be coordinated. In a world in which spontaneous neighborhood groups have diminished in salience, replaced by affinity groups, the planned and announced use of space as a local outpost of action has become more common. Yet, in established neighborhoods—whether gritty corners or leafy cul-de-sacs—gatherings can be spontaneous. A mix of the scheduled and the impromptu is evident in arenas where people know that acquaintances are likely to be found—the parks of preadolescents, white box gallery openings, or welcoming cafés.

Often, to identify the locale is to recognize the group. This centrality of place is crucial in the case of ensemble comedies in which the locales of action define the show. The sports bar Cheers on the eponymous situation comedy was emblematic of the relationship of the characters, and the physical space, in turn, shaped beliefs about what actions could and should be performed and provided response cues to audiences. While television sitcoms use place as an access point for viewers, unscripted groups likewise depend on the ability to read place. Gallery openings or forest forays have expectations that shape dress codes and behaviors.

The first analytic challenge is to understand the culture of place. A Little League baseball field is a stage set for performances that encourages the belief that the game is a metaphor for professional baseball. The boys chew gum, cheer, or even fight in their social imaginaries of professional players. Similarly, walking in the woods (the "temple of nature") to find mushrooms promotes environmental concern and reverence for nature. The tight, greasy, and loud backstage worlds of kitchens and the calm, clean, and bureaucratically ordered offices of meteorologists similarly channel the routines of participants. The arena provides a context by which some performances are encouraged and others rejected. Even when a group has no single space for gathering, such as folk art collectors or political activists, the group transforms ordinary spaces into personal venues. When such a group meets for an opening, auction, meeting, foray, or tournament, its members understand that their shared arena leads to common expectations.

The ability to provision space is essential for group life. Ongoing social worlds, even those of voluntary or leisure groups, depend on an authority structure—whether within the group or outside it—that provides resources to achieve group goals. Someone must select and maintain the place. Lacking such an authority structure, the continuation of community life is uncertain. At one point a local mushroom club almost foundered over heated debates about where their meetings were to be held. Did they wish to meet in a university space with microscopes for examining specimens, or would that make the club a scientific gathering? Did they want to pay to rent a central location or meet at a more distant locale for free? These choices proved controversial.

Groups use arenas to make local rules tacit; places are invitations to a particular definition of the situation. Through experience in similar domains, participants develop shared expectations of what behavior is permissible. Just as groups colonize settings, settings colonize groups. In discussing "third places," Ray Oldenburg (1989) argues that groups use an array of spaces, separate from home and work, to develop a community. Third places and third groups are inescapably linked.

*Relations*    A core challenge for scholar and novice alike is to read the interactional map and discern ties, both affective and material. The examination of social relations reveals the interpenetration of structure, culture, and interaction. If interaction is a performance, it is a performance that is shaped to satisfy an audience (Smith 2009). Performances not only are set in place but rely on a *social cartography*. As Goffman (1983, 4) notes in "The Interaction Order": "Each participant enters a social situation carrying an already established biography of prior dealings with the other participants."

A scene is constituted by social ties as well as by material conditions. These relations—the interpersonal context of action—channel emotional energy (Collins 2004). As Mustafa Emirbayer and Mimi Sheller (1999, 174) argue, this context of action "includes relatively long-lasting durable matrices of attachment and emotional solidarity, as well as negatively toned currents of hostility and aggression. The nodes in these processes-in-relations are not 'positions' . . . or 'symbols' . . . but rather whole persons, aspects of persons, fantasized substitutes for persons, or ideals." In other words, scenes are built on the relations within the group and depend on trust in known others. At National Weather Service offices, work practices depended on those on duty. The office could be raucous with joking about "mad scientist" experiments or quietly contemplative, the atmosphere punctuated only by meteorological mutterings. Examining similar groups within the same cultural field, whether Little League baseball teams, kitchen crews, or local meteorology offices, reveals that relations among participants shape group cultures. Although these relations result from the agency of one or several participants, they become linked to a group culture through the responses of others: no actor can construct group life without mutual concurrence. Some Little League baseball teams have recognized leaders who help adult coaches instill instrumental values by creating customs or rituals; other leaders serve as counter-institutional rebels, undercutting the authority of the coach by using nicknames or making sarcastic remarks; still other teams lack a consensual leader and struggle, because of uncertain status relations, with commitment. Restaurant kitchens, too, are shaped by whether the chef promotes emotional stability and interpersonal harmony among the crowded group of workers and whether workers, often through teasing or joking, accept these claims. Kitchens in which employees feel that they are treated with respect operate with more deference than those in which workers believe that a politics of preference is operating.

In addition to shaping action directly through the energy derived from affective ties, the recognition of relations also shapes identity (Snow and Anderson 1987), which in turn shapes action. Social identity theorists argue that the ability to relate to a local community produces identity continuity (Turner 1987). How one defines oneself derives from the groups to which one belongs, to which one gives emotional salience, and with which one identifies (Stryker and Burke 2000). As Luc Boltanski (1999, 8; emphasis in the original) notes in discussing the local constitution of compassion, "It is precisely this conjunction of the possibility of knowing and the possibility of acting that defines a *situation* characterized by the fact that it offers the possibility of being involved, of a *commitment*." These social relations commit individuals to engagement in local scenes, creating boundaries with other scenes and establishing passageways to them.

Voluntary organizations are salient in this regard. It is not sufficient that people choose activities that they enjoy—they should enjoy those who share their interests. Leisure groups benefit when they emphasize the pleasure that members can take in each other's company. As one political leader repeated, his goal was to make his party a "party." Group organizers rely on *rituals of pleasure* to create affiliation and then identity, cementing commitment (Roy 1959–1960). The linkage of satisfaction with affiliation is central to solving the free-rider problem (Olson 1965). Interpersonal affection can overcome the costs of participation. The sociology of pleasure, dependent on the desire to be with others, is integral to the recognition of how local structures are stabilized and how contentious rituals are avoided. Thus, in voluntary political engagement the reality that means often serve as ends motivates participation (Jeffrey Goldfarb, personal communication, 2009). Social relations provide the conditions for the diffusion of local culture. As Charles Camic (1995) notes with regard to the cultures of academic departments, collegial ties provide the basis from which individuals collaborate to produce products that then are shared with others, affecting a wider network.

*Shared History*    Every ongoing gathering develops an idioculture, a set of references that permits groups to identify themselves as meaningful microcommunities. Groups as focused domains establish collective memories that define the group to participants. As Harvey Molotch, William Freudenberg, and Krista Paulsen (2000) point out, communities have their futures set through a shared recognition of local character and tradition that shapes subsequent decisions, a "rolling inertia." Gerald Suttles (1984) similarly recognizes that local cultures—both collective representations and material artifacts—are not merely residual features of communities but are drawn upon to allow citizens to think and to feel how their community should be organized, recognized, and publicized. For Suttles, this localism shapes development decisions, land-use planning, and shared identities. The common past that a group has experienced and to which new members have been socialized is crucial as shared meaning constructs the boundaries of the group, separating insiders from outsiders, and it also defines how members imagine their linked future. Typically, as Goffman (1983, 4) argued, we can find a "standing behavior pattern" that serves as the basis of group order (see also Barker 1968).

Beyond their material structure, groups revel in shared experiences; with stories and anecdotes at the heart of group life, communities have the purpose, in Hayden White's terms, of translating "knowing into telling" (White 1987, cited in Ikegami 2000, 996). Discourse woven around stories provides a moral basis of community (White 1995, 1044; Perrin 2005; Polletta 2006). To establish collective selfhood, the group must incorporate the past into an insistent present, cementing the group's recall by reminding members that to know and to narrate is to belong. This is evident in joking cultures as humor underscores common references, bolstering the continuation of social interaction (Fine and DeSoucey 2005). Humorous performances yield more than momentary laughs: as links to group history, they provide a power lacking in evanescent merriment.

Group culture has what Goffman (1981, 46) spoke of as a *referential afterlife*. For a time cultural elements can be shared with the belief that others will comprehend what is meant. In this sense, each reference is set in time. Even if lacking formal rituals, group culture is grounded in history; a local sociology is inevitably historical. However, as Goffman noted, what is recalled is not eternal, and what is remembered at one moment can be forgotten later. Through the shifting of personnel (staff turnover in restaurant kitchens, boys outgrowing Little League baseball teams, high school clubs changing with rising student cohorts), the group culture shifts while remaining recognizable.

Group culture is also forward looking in that cultural tools are available for subsequent action. As culture becomes elaborated, the reach of the group as a meaning-maker is expanded. Group life is an ongoing project, not a momentary scene. Thus, the incorporation of identity becomes essential as groups socialize new members. By participating in chess clubs, novice members (although not necessarily novice players) learn expectations about the level of talk during matches or the proper responses to victory and defeat. Adolescents in fantasy-gaming groups learn which fantasies to keep private. Through these claims and their acceptance, participants define themselves as belonging to the group.

Idiocultures provide the basis for the stable expectations that are crucial to collective comfort. Since ambiguity has a social cost (Cohen, March, and Olsen 1972; Smelser 1998), groups create routine practices that maximize clarity; most groups prefer continued interaction over systemic ruptures. Members expect that themes of interaction tomorrow will be similar to themes of interaction today. In this they are usually correct. Tradition and ritual—on both the societal level and the local level—are important to social organization (Shils 1981), whether in the daily meetings of restaurant cooks, in gatherings on the mound in Little League baseball, or in the identification of mushrooms after a foray. Randall Collins (2004) properly emphasizes the iteration of interaction ritual chains; traditions build on each other. The more rituals in a group, the more new or elaborated rituals will follow; culture spawns culture. Idiosyncratic actions become practices when they are recognized as serving group needs (Fine 1979b; Sherif et al. 1987; Eliasoph and Lichterman 2003). Once neophytes can read this interactional grammar, they are treated as competent members, differentiated from those outside group boundaries.

Even the most minute social units, such as couples and families (Oring 1984; Kauffman 2009), develop local cultures that encourage the building of future practices on those previously established and buffer participants from external demands. These practices reify group history, setting the terms for propriety and creating structure from talk. The existence of lines of action does not deny the need for negotiations or the possibility of shocks to the system, but their solidity reveals the costs of rapid change, even while their ongoing iteration may produce incremental change.

A critic might point to the smallness and apparent idiosyncrasy of those cultural forms. In group life unforeseen events often spark common knowledge. These "triggering events" cannot be guessed, but neither are they random. Events that shape collective life are readily predictable after the fact (reading backward) but cannot be predicted before they occur (looking forward). However, once they are seen as relevant for group identity, actors scramble to shape their behavior, aligning ongoing action with group culture (Stokes and Hewitt 1976). Even if we cannot predict the moments of everyday life, such as jokes, insults, flubs, or queries, when they occur participants attempt to incorporate them into an orderly meaning system. They do not always succeed in this goal, and an overly restraining routine is not desired, but predictability is comforting. This commitment to stability (Goffman 1974)—the desire for a smooth flow of action—allows actors to feel confident in their tacit expectations, even as new interpretations are generated and change and conflict are incorporated into group life.

## The Local as Lens

*Seeing the World Through Action*    Borrowing Goffman's (1967, 149) famous phrase, sociology has the mandate to study "where the action is," connecting place, community, and interpretation. Sociologists study actors, not persons (Garfinkel 2006). *Performance* is a form of personal action, even if shaped by a web of collective understandings. In treating performance as action, we must recognize that performative logic (Alexander and Mast 2006, 1) depends on local, in situ actions.

The sociological examination of action is a long-standing theoretical stream with distinguished practitioners, a diverse lineage that includes Georg Simmel, George Homans, Herbert Blumer, Erving Goffman, Alfred

Schutz, Harold Garfinkel, and even Talcott Parsons after a fashion.[3] All have proceeded from the assumption that sociology has a mandate to study not only invisible structures but also the visible, the negotiated, and the local. We are a discipline of people and process as well as a discipline of populations and patterns: we examine social facts on the ground as well as social facts in the air.

Any approach that places action at the center of sociological analysis argues for the primacy of coordination over cognition and constraint. The stability of groups through continuity and change emerges from adjusting lines of action. These actions are not haphazard but are ritually replicated. Certain ones come to be treated as proper, and unless special circumstances apply, these expectations hold sway. The importance of action is that it is performed within focused gatherings with feedback loops that alter, challenge, and direct future action. Actions may be *free*, but they have *costs* that encourage or inhibit repetition.

A sociology of action does not erase obdurate reality, but neither does it eliminate options. At each inflection point, choices are required. Perhaps responses are shaped by structures, but they are never fully determined by them. Whether we call these options "tools," "mechanisms," or "decisions," group members choose, particularly if other groups with greater resource power or moral authority permit the choices. The study of play, games, and sport—voluntary systems that depend on decisions—is revealing. For a contest to be worth engaging in, choice and uncertainty are crucial. Ballplayers and chess players alike draw from a range of potential moves, and the move that is selected affects the situation to which competitors respond. If only a single option existed, behavior would lack the gamelike uncertainty that motivates involvement.

Action alternatives allow participants to create their worlds and to be created by them. In intense idiocultures that require temporal, material, or emotional investments, this recursive shaping means that the standards of the group channel participants, even as members determine those standards. Elaborated and ongoing cultures are often very stable and protected by strong boundaries that increase entry costs and the extent of surveillance (Carley 1991).

The availability of options does not mean that local scenes permit unconstrained action. Although a vast array of behavior may be physically possible, much is not morally permissible, especially given that small and intense groups have more complete surveillance than larger institutions and communities. The feedback loops remind participants that others may define their performance as outside moral boundaries and that sanctions may be provoked. In observing organizations that supported those who had been accused of child abuse, I was struck by the presence of social control: talk that seemed mundane but was potentially stigmatizing and threatening to the group's image was redirected. One could not joke in this arena about hitting one's child or spouse, common jocular tropes in popular discourse (viz *The Simpsons*). Even if everyone knew what was "really" meant, some narratives were precluded for fear of alternative interpretations.

Yet in tight-knit, secure scenes, participants are often given considerable leeway, revealing the sympathetic willingness of others to accept behaviors that might otherwise be outside group boundaries. Still, "idiosyncrasy credits" are not unlimited (Hollander 1958). Every "favor bank" places limits on withdrawals. Group members may encourage deviants to accept consensual traditions before coalescing to solidify the boundary of the group to exclude or sequester the problematic member (Goffman 1971). Voluntary organizations transform deviants into nonpersons; their presence is no longer acknowledged, and participation becomes more difficult.

In sum, groups are dynamic action systems. Their self-referential quality suggests that the group stabilizes itself by adjusting to the responses of members. This is consistent with the argument in pragmatic philosophy and Meadian symbolic interaction that meaning (patterns of action) results from the responses of actors (Mead 1934). Social life involves a process of call and response (Goffman 1981). The intersection of meanings, expressed through the negotiation of lines of action, constitutes a community. Individuals enter groups with diverse perspectives and only eventually understand the meanings that others hold. This is evident in the research of Muzafer Sherif (1935) on the establishment of group norms in reaction to the autokinetic effect. Sherif discovered that when viewing a point of light in a darkened room that lacks visual cues, individuals express widely divergent assessments of the distance that the light appears to move. However, over a set of trials most groups develop a firm consensus; conformity becomes thoughtless, and norms shape perception. The same is true of evaluations of action: in time, new members learn what those who have more seniority, experience, or authority consider proper. At first judgments are explicit and considered, but eventually group standards shape an actor's mental calculations so that they become tacit and intuitive.

When group members realize that they will continue to interact when they are committed to these ongoing relations, when they accept authority and consensual power relations, and when they identify with their colleagues, they show deference, even in the face of centripetal forces (Goffman 1967; Munroe 2007). At first, disagreements may be concealed, but as individuals publicly assert shared values, those values come to be held and not just claimed. As a result, participants treat the local scene as an outpost of, and model for, society. Of course, divisive forces can overwhelm this desire for harmony as groups split and dissipate or alter boundaries, but cohesion is expected. Should these divisions and barriers become too prominent, a belief may take hold that society as a whole is as contentious as the local scene.

## A Particular Sociology

In attempting a sociology of the local, I have built on James Joyce's challenge to see the general within the particular. A sociology that theorizes the conditions under which action is generated is a sociology that recognizes that meaning and society are achievements. These are not simply achievements of individuals who congregate and negotiate but achievements of those who build on the past, on established relations, and on ordered places: these are achievements of groups. The group constitutes an opportunity structure for the development of stability and change. In this way, such a project is to be differentiated from projects that focus on the immediacy of interpersonal behavior. Negotiation is important, but the power of shared pasts must not be downplayed. No study of action should ignore the local histories in which it unfolds.

Building on the claim that networks are linked groups, I challenge a traditional microsociological model by arguing that social scenes are not isolated. Participants engage in multiple scenes, simultaneously and sequentially, and in the process become aware of other scenes that serve as models or as points of differentiation. Building on power differentials both within and between groups, inequality is reproduced through these models of action (Schwalbe 2008).

Whether consciously recognized or tacit, the experience and recognition of groups enables a local culture to reverberate through time and space, extending beyond local interaction orders. When connected, these tiny publics form institutions, communities, and ultimately societies that, although grounded in ongoing interaction scenes, are larger, more established, and more stable.

To have predictable effects, order cannot be momentary and evanescent; an interaction order depends on interaction being durable and continuing. The local context of action invests a social world with longevity as it builds on collective interpretations, common references, and shared identity.

Participation in continuing scenes is not random. Just as groups produce outcomes (treatment effects), they also recruit selectively (selection effects). Through the choices of individuals to participate and through participants' encouragement of new members, groups establish or reproduce social divisions. We should not downplay the reality of intake boundaries as the basis of social differentiation and structural discrimi-nation. Local cultures are produced and extended through decisions about who is able to participate in action scenes. The local produces stratification as well as community (Schwalbe 2008). Hierarchy operates within groups and among them.

Meso-level analysis of how context operates is based on the group. Across time and through networks, ongoing groups build on each other and become linked in expansive social orders. Intersecting groups and the forces of control that hold groups together, including surveillance and resource power, are what we refer to as the "social structure"—a metaphor we take as real.

Actors do not merely congregate for a moment—they are more than tourists in an ephemeral micropublic to which they hold little allegiance as they respond impetuously to the press of personal interests and idio-syncratic motivations. This view misses the power of interactional domains. Social stability is a routine and thoughtless achievement because it is part of the commitment that participants make to the tiny publics to which they belong.

Sociologists should treasure the local. The danger is that such a charge tends to homogenize groups to make its point. Yet, groups are not interchangeable and are not equally accessible to all. Local scenes divide and separate, just as they provide for integration within and between groups. And once institutions and systems of power are built—even if directed by groups—the performance of these systems may be erased as the relations among groups are treated as a reality that stands above the level of action. Explaining how this happens and why it need not is our inheritance, in Goffman's (1983, 17) words, and what we can bequeath.

In a meso-level sociology, the local is both a stage and a lens. It is a stage in that as a place (physical, affiliative, and historical) it provides meanings that set the propriety of action. Action results from adjust-ments to events and performances as participants are committed to creating workable lines of action. Even in conflict, these lines are pres-ent, directing changes in prevailing practices or provoking a restruc-turing of community boundaries. But the local is not limited to the metaphor of the stage. The local also provides a lens through which actors typify and sustain groups, gatherings, or publics. However, it is also where we establish boundaries and divisions and where we resist or reproduce inequalities. Groups may build and fracture, both internally and within the wider social system. Watching groups, we may see society—perhaps a subsociety (tied to class, race, gender, age, or region) or a local scene. Still, always what we are watching is not generic but particular.

## A Local World

If you give a child a hammer, everything becomes a nail. This book reveals some of that enthusiasm. But in fact the world is filled with nails. In my sociological imagination, groups seem to be everywhere, doing everything. But such zeal has its limits. Groups are important and consequential for the organization of contemporary and traditional societies, but large organizations, mass gatherings, and individual action exist as well. And they matter greatly.

This volume proclaims that the group, the local context, and the interaction order belong to a crucial meso-level of analysis. Despite being marginalized, groups deserve more recognition. Cultural codes, boundaries, and the bonds that constitute group life are at the heart of any rigorous social science.

I have argued throughout this volume that context and performance are central to how we conceptualize social order. But in the pendulum swing of sociology over the past several decades, particularism has been less influential than generalism. To ignore the local is to make the serious mistake of ignoring what should be a central concern for sociology: how institutions and persons are linked in practice. Were I to be George Homans, I would issue a clarion call to bring the group back in.

This perspective is related to, but distinct from, the traditional approach to presentation of self. Erving Goffman and his fellow dramaturgical social psychologists find processes at work in the formal conditions of interaction. They recognize the centrality of impression management and frames of meaning but without recognizing the role of history and of community. (A partial exception is Goffman's magisterial *Asylums*, 1961a, in which a mental hospital becomes a local community.) These processes are often not tethered to ongoing relations. However, despite the appeal of situationalism, conditions are not random, incapable of being analyzed. The social response to situations is a form of performance, one shaped not just by a culture that is tied to a larger social system but by the expectations of a social group that holds its own interpretation of the norms, values, beliefs, and cultural forms of a broader social system.

The local provides a link between structure and interaction by means of the recognition of culture. Culture is at the heart of a meso-level analysis, that space between agentic action and the structural constraints of institution and organization. The local focuses on the ongoing, recognizable social group. However, even if we accept the reality of structural conditions and the immediate choices of interaction, we still must explain how agentic choices coexist with obdurate reality. The answer is that local cultures organize social action into systems of constraints and expectations. Culture incorporates order into social life by the recognition of shared pasts and prospective futures (Katovich and Couch 1992).

The examination of localism crystallizes a distinctly sociological micro-analysis. Local structures provide for identity continuity (Sani 2005). How one perceives oneself derives from those groups to which one belongs and to which one gives salience, a point made half a century ago by the researchers who developed the Twenty Statements Test (Kuhn and McPartland 1954). These linkages operate not only on the cognitive and emotional level but also as a form of behavior, cementing individuals to local scenes, while producing borders and bridges to other scenes.

## The Group and the World

Drawing on forty years of research and writing, I have sketched how a local sociology might proceed, suggesting concepts that permit insight into the place of group culture and how it shapes interaction. Place, relations, community, agency, and memory are all central in the creation of a vibrant local sociology and one that can help validate networks and institutions. Sociology hopes to explain the world, but sociology also needs to explain the *worlds within the world* and how those worlds within have tendrils that stretch beyond their boundaries.

My call is for sociologists not to study only the group but rather to recognize and highlight how groups build on each other and are linked in generating and responding to larger social structures through a shared history. Social structure constitutes a network of local worlds—of idiocultures. These intersecting groups and the forces that stabilize them—often other groups with surveillance and resource power—become the social structure. The social structure is not one big thing but many little things that together become a big thing. Groups determine the actions of institutions, and institutions shape group life. To picture how social structures form and survive without recognizing that they are interactional units, with a past and a future, that exist in space and operate through feedback loops that regulate and stabilize interaction is to miss the reality of social life. It is in the truth of localities of action that the work of establishing a social system gets done. As participants in an array of tiny publics, we are citizens of institutions, nations, and the world writ large.

James Joyce did not write about Dublin—he wrote about gatherings, relations, and corners in Dublin. With his miniaturist microscope, he created a world that we know we know because those scenes are ours as well.

# ═ Notes ═

## Chapter 1

1. The extent of virtual communication has expanded greatly since Bales's definition, leaving open whether "face-to-face" presence is a necessary feature of the definition or whether "virtual" communication suffices. Certainly cyber-communities have some features similar to those of interactional spaces (Boellstorff 2008), but in many of these communities there is a push to meet in a physical arena to bolster the reality of the community.

2. Although I use the term "association," I contrast this discussion of associations with how the concept of association is frequently used in discussions of democratic theory, social capital, and civil society, which typically ignore the size of the interest group and combine interacting groups with large organizations. Any perspective that combines the National Rifle Association with a bowling team ignores critical aspects of allegiance and shared identity.

## Chapter 2

1. Attention has been paid to the dynamics of culture within what used to be described as tribal societies, but typically these tribes are larger and more like quasi-states than face-to-face groups.

2. The cultural elements disseminated by mass media organizations (television, radio, newspapers) or in mass settings (rock concerts, rallies, sporting events) are apparent exceptions. However, even in these isolated or mass settings, audiences are composed not of discrete individuals but of a collection of small groups that structure the meaning of the event for participants. Printed matter is notable for the non-interactional acquisition of cultural knowledge, although even here the material is often the basis for discourse—as Jürgen Habermas (1991) points out for the creation of a public sphere in salon society or coffeehouses.

3. I coined the new term "idioculture" because the most local term, "group culture," had been used previously with several distinct meanings (Thelen 1954; Rossel 1976; McFeat 1974).

4. This observation was made during the 1970s; surely reactions would be stronger today.

## Chapter 3

1. Collins's (2004) most influential concept is that of "interaction ritual chains": the creation of social structure through the accretion of predictable behaviors. However, Collins assumes that the existence and motivating quality of microresources are presuppositions of a macrosociological perspective. He uses these resources (such as emotional resources and local cultures) to connect the individual to the production of shared social meanings. Collins's "linkage" perspective has not been fully accepted by either macro- or microsociologists: each discovers disreputable images of themselves. Microsociologists claim that Collins writes as a macrosociologist seeking to understand how social order transcends the individuals' actions that it builds upon (Denzin 1987) and that he ignores the negotiated and contingent character of meaning. His emphasis on ritual and collective action is taken as a structural bow in the direction of behavior, but one that ignores the negotiated and phenomenological character of that behavior. Others, noting his presentation of a strong individual actor, his belief in the efficacy of interaction ("ritual chains"), and his heavier emphasis on agency than structure, deem him a microsociologist (Ritzer 1985). Still, Collins makes microsociology primary and preliminary to the doing of macrosociology and lays down this challenge: "The dynamics as well as the inertia in any causal explanation of social structure must be microsituational; all macroconditions have their effects by impinging upon actors' situational motivations" (Collins 1981, 990).

2. Meso-theory has several potential points of reference. Some scholars use it to explore extended organizations, drawing a distinction between organizations and the society (or world-system). Drawing on the understandings of meso-level analysis in interaction, I focus on interaction realms.

3. To Collins's credit, his analysis extends beyond the commonplace conceit that the world is divided into micro and macro. His division of the person, the small group, the crowd/organization, the community, and the territorial society, based on population size and spatial territory, relaxes the macro/micro division. Levels smaller in population and size nest within larger ones. Within each increasingly macro level are numerous smaller ones. This distinction could be made finer still, as groups nest in groups (for example, the nuclear family in the extended family or the clique in the classroom) or communities in communities (neighborhoods in a town). Persons often participate in several small groups, just as the small group must have two or more persons. Levels of organization are always cross-cutting.

4. Durkheim in *The Rules of Sociological Method* (1964, 2–3) argued: "If I do not submit to the conventions of society, if in my dress I do not conform to the customs observed in my country and in my class, the ridicule I provoke, the social isolation in which I am kept, produce, although in an attenuated form, the same effects as a punishment in the strict sense of the word. The constraint is nonetheless efficacious for being indirect. . . . Even when I free

myself from these rules and violate them successfully, I am always compelled to struggle with them. When finally overcome, they make their constraining power sufficiently felt by the resistance they offer." This approach harmonizes with the approach that recognizes that people can behave as they wish, but they must live with sometimes painful consequences and struggle with those rules they do not accept.

5. I use the term "obdurate"—a concept frequently met in interactionist writing (see, for example, Blumer 1969)—to refer to unchanging, non-negotiable contingencies that actors must respond to or suffer consequences. Admittedly, the implications vary, depending, for instance, on the power of social sanctions or the extent of surveillance, but the concept implies something given, unproblematic, and temporally stable.

6. In some measure, tradition is the temporal dimension of culture (Molotch, Freudenburg, and Paulsen 2000). Some cultural elements are not traditional, although they too have external, normative effects on individuals.

7. We can specify two classes of expectations: those based on regularities of human behavior (microexpectations) and those based on organizations' and other collective actors' demands (macroexpectations). Both constitute social control over individual behavior, but the level of control differs, as does the source of power.

## Chapter 4

1. All quotes in this section are taken from my field notes for *Morel Tales* (Fine 1998).

## Chapter 5

1. Mushroomers have bitter debates over the question of regulating "commercial" enterprises, particularly firms that export mushrooms. In this case, the discussion about "overpicking" became tied to a discourse about ecological nationalism and unemployment rates in the logging industry (Fine 1997).

2. Gieryn (1983) proposed that scientists are similar to laypeople in this regard—they also are guided by dominant cultural images, metaphors, and folk ideas in doing their research and constructing or maintaining the boundaries of "science."

3. Gieryn (1983, 783) suggested that ideologies may have stylistic variations (the use of hyperbole, irony, sarcasm, etc.) and argued that analysts need to "specify the social conditions in which ideologies might be expected to take one or another stylistic form."

4. Garrett Hardin (1974, x) suggests that the existence of a label may also provoke a counter-movement, which then perceives that it has something to defend.

5. Ideologies also can evoke emotions and, at the extreme, lead to "ideological passion." Such passion is particularly likely when the public is mobilized

and demonstrating a high degree of activism. Under these conditions, the public can be aroused to emotion through rhetoric that activates their ideological beliefs—a process of "ideological heating" (Sartori 1969, 403). Playing on the core of ideological beliefs can lead to intense emotional reactions and, in extreme cases, to war and violence (Blain 1988).

6. Arlie Hochschild (1979) provides an explicit, albeit brief, discussion of the relationship between emotion and ideology. However, her analysis examines the effects of ideology on the social construction of emotion and particularly on feeling rules (without specifying how particular ideologies do this). Her causal model leads from ideology to emotional display. In contrast, I focus on how emotion constrains and channels the development of ideology; I consider emotion not as an outcome of ideology but as a contributing feature.

7. This feeling is not localized to a single cultural system, a view supported by a wide array of cross-cultural evidence (Nash 1989). A powerful bond exists between people and their world, a bond that transcends cultural systems. As human society depends for its survival and satisfaction on the natural environment, an attempt to connect oneself to this reality is faced by all (or most) human systems. "Nature" is a party to the division of labor, and so its inclusion within the idea of community is to be expected.

## Chapter 6

1. I refer to unpublished research by Ann Jamison on the Lebowski Fest, a pure example of a wispy community. A convocation of fans (self-labeled "achievers") of the cult film *The Big Lebowski,* the Lebowski Fest is a tradition that began in 2002 in Louisville, Kentucky, as an annual gathering. By 2009, Lebowski Fests were being held in fourteen cities.

2. Many leisure communities have a shared literature, such as the fanzines found in science fiction worlds (Bacon-Smith 2000; Jenkins 1992). Jargon, while certainly not as extensive as language, allows participants to communicate separate from outsiders.

3. Within communities, some individuals may press others hard for commitment that goes beyond the occasion, especially in scenes that require an infrastructure for the continuation of the activity. Yet, these active engagers are typically under little pressure themselves to enforce their own commitments on their fellows.

4. Although I do not focus on virtual communities in this volume, such communities can be seen as wispy. They do not require long-term, continually face-to-face interaction, and in most such domains individuals can enter and leave at any time. These communities often have moments of intense activity that fades rapidly when interest wanes, but the community remains available for renewed activation. Further research is warranted on the intersection of Internet exchange and a groups model of social life.

## Chapter 7

1. I do not differentiate these closely related but separate concepts (Calhoun 2001a, 2001b). When I speak of a civil society, I assume a social system with a vigorous public sphere.

2. Reinhart Koselleck (1988, 66, 85) claimed that even seemingly apolitical groups are in fact political, a claim that Habermas doubts (Cohen and Arato 1992, 212).

3. The influence of small groups is not limited to the creation of Western civic society. Nehemia Levtzion (2002, 110–16) points to Sufi brotherhood lodges as helping to create a Muslim public sphere.

4. In his early work, Habermas emphasized the importance of groups, but much of his later theory focused on the role of communicative technology. For Habermas, group interaction is not an end in itself but a means by which a critical audience develops for literary work (Cohen and Arato 1992, 215). The group is an incubator of audiences, not a social-psychological microcommunity.

5. In contrast to this approach, these theorists have a specialized conception of the type of small groups that contribute to the public sphere. Habermas (1991, 163) argues that the presence of political and literary debate characterizes sociable groups and creates a "public." I have a more expansive view of the role of group culture in civil society.

6. In examining the relationship of small groups to civil society, I do not assume that groups hold any particular position with regard to politics or civic investment. Members of a small group can share any stance, or as is often the case they may have no explicit or elaborated social or political position (Eliasoph 1998). Indeed, they may disagree within the group, preventing a shared front. However, this diversity or even attitudinal apathy does not prevent the group from influencing civil society.

7. It is true, as Eliasoph (1998) notes, that groups may also pull individuals into civic nonparticipation or collective apathy, creating a culture in which involvement is seen as undesirable.

8. Putnam (1995) acknowledges this development and considers how it may distort his findings, based on data from established organizations such as the Elks Club.

## Chapter 8

1. As Small (2009, 172) properly notes for day care centers—and as is true more generally—groups differ in their connectedness with other groups and thus in their ability to provide participants with social capital.

2.  "Small world experiments" (Travers and Milgram 1969; Korte and Milgram 1970) reveal that some network strands are shorter than others: not all ties have six degrees of separation, since groups (and individuals) can be more or less integrated.

## Chapter 9

1.  One can see this strain in Goffman's (1983) consummatory "The Interaction Order," an undelivered oration that warns against "rampant situational-ism" while recognizing the shared basis of an understanding of that inter-action order. A similar tension exists within ethnomethodology between approaches that see interpretations as freshly constructed in situ as local projects (for example, Garfinkel 1967, ch. 3) and those that depend on the existence of ongoing local cultures (for example, Garfinkel 1967, ch. 2). Essentially, Harold Garfinkel's argument is that local cultures constitute the default condition of interpretations and that responses to disruption consti-tute a measure of just how preferential those cultures are. Although lacking space here to treat fully the ethnomethodological attention to local context, I recognize that tradition's emphasis on particularity (see, for example, Heritage 1984; Schegloff 1986; Maynard 2003). Yet, much of the focus in con-versation analysis has been precisely on how interactional strangers strug-gle to create meaning in the absence of local traditions.

2.  The meso-level of analysis, while separate from microanalysis and macro-analysis, has several different meanings and references, including the exam-ination of organizations and communities and, as used here, a focus on groups and ongoing interaction systems. For a discussion of the range of meso-theory, see Turner (2005).

3.  The Parsonian project (Parsons and Shils 1954) to create a "General Theory of Action" is engaged in colonizing action in order to make a structural sociology complete.

# References

Adler, Patricia, and Peter Adler. 1998. *Peer Power: Preadolescent Culture and Identity.* New Brunswick, N.J.: Rutgers University Press.

Agulhon, Maurice. 1982. *The Republic in the Village: The People of the Var from the French Revolution to the Second Republic.* Cambridge: Cambridge University Press.

Aldrich, Howard. 1971. "The Sociable Organization: A Case Study of Mensa and Some Propositions." *Sociology and Social Research* 55: 429–44.

Alexander, Jeffrey C. 1982. *Positivism, Presuppositions, and Current Controversies.* Berkeley: University of California Press.

———. 2003. *The Meanings of Social Life: A Cultural Sociology.* New York: Oxford University Press.

———. 2004. "From the Depths of Despair: Performance and Counter-Performance on September 11." *Sociological Theory* 21: 88–105.

———. 2006. *The Civil Sphere.* New York: Oxford University Press.

Alexander, Jeffrey C., and Bernhard Giesen. 1987. "From Reduction to Linkage: The Long View of the Micro-Macro Link." In *The Micro-Macro Link,* edited by Jeffrey C. Alexander, Bernhard Giesen, Richard Munch, and Neil J. Smelser. Berkeley: University of California Press.

Alexander, Jeffrey C., and Jason Mast. 2006. "Introduction: Symbolic Action in Theory and Practice: The Cultural Pragmatics of Symbolic Action." In *Social Performance: Symbolic Action, Cultural Pragmatics, and Ritual,* edited by Jeffrey C. Alexander, Bernhard Giesen, and Jason Mast. New York: Cambridge University Press.

Althusser, Louis. 1971. *Lenin and Philosophy and Other Essays.* New York: Monthly Review Press.

Amann, Peter. 1975. *Revolution and Mass Democracy: The Paris Club Movement in 1948.* Princeton, N.J.: Princeton University Press.

Anderson, Benedict O. 1991. *Imagined Communities: Reflections on the Origin and Spread of Nationalism,* rev. ed. London: Verso.

Anderson, Elijah. 1979. *A Place on the Corner.* Chicago: University of Chicago Press.

Arendt, Hannah. 1972. *Crises of the Republic.* New York: Harcourt Brace Jovanovich.

Argami, Marc, and Lisa van den Scott. 2010. "Framing the Early Framers: The Contributions Towards the Concept of *Frame* in the Research of the 1930s and 1940s." Unpublished paper, Universitat Autonoma de Barcelona, Spain.

Arieli, Yehoshua. 1964. *Individualism and Nationalism in American Ideology.* Cambridge, Mass.: Harvard University Press.

Aries, Elizabeth J. 1976. "Interaction Patterns and Themes of Male, Female, and Mixed Groups." *Small Group Research* 7: 7–18.

Armstrong, Gail, and Mary Wilson. 1973. "City Politics and Deviancy Amplification." In *Politics and Deviance,* edited by Ian Taylor and Laurie Taylor. Harmondsworth, U.K.: Penguin.

Arnold, David O. 1970. "A Process Model of Subcultures." In *Subcultures,* edited by David O. Arnold. Berkeley, Calif.: Glendessary.

Ashley, David. 1984. "Historical Materialism and Ideological Practice: How Do Ideologies Dominate People?" *Current Perspectives in Social Theory* 5: 1–20.

Athens, Lonnie. 1980. *Violent Criminal Acts and Actors.* London: Routledge & Kegan Paul.

———. 2005. "The Self as a Soliloquy." *Sociological Quarterly* 35: 521–32.

Austin, J. L. 1975. *How to Do Things with Words.* Cambridge, Mass.: Harvard University Press.

Aveni, Adrian. 1977. "The Not-So-Lonely Crowd: Friendship Groups in Collective Behavior." *Sociometry* 40: 96–99.

Back, Kurt, and Donna Polisar. 1983. "Salons und Kaffeehauser." *Kolner Zeitschrift fur Soziologie und Sozialpsychologie* 25: 276–28.

Bacon-Smith, Camille. 1992. *Enterprising Women: Television Fandom and the Creation of Popular Myth.* Philadelphia: University of Pennsylvania Press.

———. 2000. *Science Fiction Culture.* Philadelphia: University of Pennsylvania Press.

Baiocchi, Gianpaolo. 2003. "Emergent Public Spheres: Talking Politics in Participatory Governance." *American Sociological Review* 68: 52–74.

Bales, Robert Freed. 1950. *Interaction Process Analysis: A Method for the Study of Small Groups.* Cambridge: Addison-Wesley.

———. 1970. *Personality and Interpersonal Behavior.* New York: Holt, Rinehart and Winston.

Bales, Robert Freed, and Stephen P. Cohen. 1979. *SYMLOG: A System for the Multiple Level Observation of Groups.* New York: Free Press.

Banfield, Edward. 1958. *The Moral Basis of a Backward Society.* Glencoe, Ill.: Free Press.

Barker, Roger G. 1968. *Ecological Psychology.* Stanford, Calif.: Stanford University Press.

Barley, Steven. 1988. "The Social Construction of a Machine: Ritual, Superstition, Magical Thinking, and Other Pragmatic Responses to Running a CT Scanner." In *Bio-medicine Examined,* edited by Margaret Lock and Deborah Gordon. Dordrecht, Netherlands: Kluwer Academic Publishers.

Barnes, J. A. 1969. "Networks and Political Process." In *Social Networks in Urban Situations,* edited by J. Clyde Mitchell. Manchester, U.K.: Manchester University Press.

Bateson, Gregory. 1972. "A Theory of Play and Phantasy." In *Steps to an Ecology of Mind,* edited by Gregory Bateson. New York: Ballantine Books.

Baumeister, Roy F. 1991. *Escaping the Self: Alcoholism, Spirituality, Masochism, and Other Flights from the Burden of Selfhood.* New York: Basic Books.

Bearman, Peter S. 1991. "Desertion as Localism: Army Unit Solidarity and Group Norms in the U.S. Civil War." *Social Forces* 70: 321–42.

Becker, Howard S. 1974. "Art as Collective Action." *American Sociological Review* 39: 767–76.

———. 1982. *Art Worlds.* Berkeley: University of California Press.

Becker, Howard S., and Blanche Geer. 1960. "Latent Culture: A Note on the Theory of Latent Social Roles." *Administration Science Quarterly* 5: 304–13.

Becker, Howard S., Blanche Geer, Everett C. Hughes, and Anselm Strauss. 1961. *Boys in White.* Chicago: University of Chicago Press.

Bellah, Robert, Richard Madsen, William M. Sullivan, Ann Swidler, and Steven M. Tipton. 1985. *Habits of the Heart: Individualism and Commitment in American Society.* Berkeley: University of California Press.

———. 1991. *The Good Society.* New York: Knopf.

Benford, Robert D., and Scott A. Hunt. 1992. "Dramaturgy and Social Movements: The Social Construction and Communication of Power." *Sociological Inquiry* 62: 36–55.

Bennett, Andy, and Keith Kahn-Harris. 2004. "Introduction." In *After Subculture: Critical Studies in Contemporary Youth Culture,* edited by Andy Bennett and Keith Kahn-Harris. New York: Palgrave-Macmillan.

Bentham, Jeremy. 1996. *Introduction to Principles of Morals and Legislation.* New York: Oxford University Press. (Originally published in 1789.)

Ben-Yehuda, Nachman. 1985. *Deviance and Moral Boundaries.* Chicago: University of Chicago Press.

Berger, Joseph, Susan J. Rosenholtz, and Morris Zelditch. 1980. "Status Organizing Processes." *Annual Review of Sociology* 6: 479–508.

Berger, Peter, and Thomas Luckmann. 1967. *The Social Construction of Reality.* New York: Anchor.

Bergmann, Jorg. 1993. *Discrete Indiscretions: The Social Organization of Gossip.* Hawthorne, N.Y.: Aldine.

Best, Joel. 1999. *Random Violence: How We Talk About New Crimes and New Victims.* Berkeley: University of California Press.

Bey, Hakim. 2008. *The Temporary Autonomous Zone, Ontological Anarchy, Poetic Terrorism.* Brooklyn, N.Y.: Autonomedia.

Billig, Michael. 1987. *Arguing and Thinking.* Cambridge: Cambridge University Press.

———. 1995. *Banal Nationalism.* London: Sage Publications.

Blain, Michael. 1988. "Fighting Words: What We Can Learn from Hitler's Hyperbole." *Symbolic Interaction* 11: 257–76.

Blau, Judith. 1984. *Architects and Firms.* Cambridge, Mass.: MIT Press.

Bloustien, Gerry. 2004. "Buffy Night at the Seven Stars: A 'Subcultural' Happening at the 'Glocal' Level." In *After Subculture: Critical Studies in Contemporary Youth Culture,* edited by Andy Bennett and Keith Kahn-Harris. New York: Palgrave-Macmillan.

Blumer, Herbert. 1969. *Symbolic Interactionism.* Englewood Cliffs, N.J.: Prentice-Hall.

Boellstorff, Thomas. 2008. *Coming of Age in Second Life: An Anthropologist Explores the Virtually Human.* Princeton, N.J.: Princeton University Press.

Boltanski, Luc. 1999. *Distant Suffering: Morality, Media, and Politics.* Cambridge: Cambridge University Press.

Boorstin, Daniel. 1961. *The Image: A Guide to Pseudo-Events in America.* New York: Atheneum.

Borgatta, Edgar G., and Robert Freed Bales. 1953. "Task and Accumulation of Experience as Factors in the Interaction of Small Groups." *Sociometry* 16: 239–52.

Borneman, John, and Stefan Senders. 2000. "Politics Without a Head: Is the 'Love Parade' a New Form of Political Identification?" *Cultural Anthropology* 15: 294–317.

Bourdieu, Pierre. 1977. *Outline of a Theory of Practice.* New York: Cambridge University Press.

———. 1984. *Distinction: A Social Critique of the Judgment of Taste.* Cambridge, Mass.: Harvard University Press.

Bourdieu, Pierre, and Loïc Wacquant. 1992. *An Invitation to Reflexive Sociology.* Chicago: University of Chicago Press.

Brake, Michael. 1985. *Comparative Youth Culture.* New York: Routledge & Kegan Paul.

Brissett, Dennis, and Charles Edgley, eds. 2005. *Life as Theater: A Dramaturgical Sourcebook,* 2nd ed. New Brunswick, N.J.: Transaction.

Brown, Laurence. 1973. *Ideology.* Harmondsworth, U.K.: Penguin.

Brown, Phil. 1997. "Popular Epidemiology Revisited." *Current Sociology* 45: 137–56.

Brown, Richard. 1977. *A Poetic for Sociology.* Chicago: University of Chicago Press.

Brown-Saracino, Japonica. 2009. *A Neighborhood That Never Changes: Gentrification, Social Preservation, and the Search for Authenticity.* Chicago: University of Chicago Press.

Brubaker, Rogers, and Frederick Cooper. 2000. "Beyond 'Identity.' " *Theory and Society* 29: 1–47.

Bryan, Frank M. 2004. *Real Democracy: The New England Town Meeting and How It Works.* Chicago: University of Chicago Press.

Burawoy, Michael 1979. *Manufacturing Consent: Changes in the Labor Process Under Monopoly Capitalism.* Chicago: University of Chicago Press.

———. 1991. *Ethnography Unbound: Power and Resistance in the Urban Metropolis.* Berkeley: University of California Press.

———. 2009. *The Extended Case Method: Four Countries, Four Decades, Four Great Transformations, and One Theoretical Tradition.* Berkeley: University of California Press.

Burgess, Jean, and Joshua Green. 2009. *YouTube: Online Video and Participatory Culture.* Cambridge: Polity Press.

Burke, Kenneth. 1984. *Permanence and Change: An Anatomy of Purpose,* 3rd ed. Berkeley: University of California Press.

Burke, Peter, and Jan Stets. 2009. *Identity Theory.* New York: Oxford University Press.

Burt, Ronald S. 1992. *Structural Holes: The Social Structure of Competition.* Cambridge, Mass.: Harvard University Press.

———. 2005. *Brokerage and Closure.* Oxford: Oxford University Press.

———. 2010. *Neighbor Networks: Competitive Advantage Local and Personal.* Oxford: Oxford University Press.

Busch, Lawrence. 1980. "Structure and Negotiation in the Agricultural Sciences." *Rural Sociology* 45: 26–48.

Cahill, Spencer. 1989. "Fashioning Males and Females: Appearance Management and the Social Reproduction of Gender." *Symbolic Interaction* 12: 281–98.

———. 1998. "Towards a Sociology of the Person." *Sociological Theory* 16: 131–48.

Calhoun, Craig. 1982. *The Question of Class Struggle: Social Foundations of Popular Radicalism During the Industrial Revolution.* Chicago: University of Chicago Press.

———. 1993. "Introduction: Habermas and the Public Sphere." In *Habermas and the Public Sphere,* edited by Craig Calhoun. Cambridge, Mass.: MIT Press.

———. 2001a. "Civil Society/Public Sphere: History of the Concepts." In *International Encyclopedia of the Social and Behavioral Sciences.* Amsterdam: Elsevier.

———. 2001b. "Public Sphere: Nineteenth and Twentieth Century History." In *International Encyclopedia of the Social and Behavioral Sciences.* Amsterdam: Elsevier.

Camic, Charles. 1995. "Three Departments in Search of a Discipline: Localism and Interdisciplinary Interaction in American Sociology, 1890–1940." *Social Research* 62: 1003–33.

Cardozo-Freeman, Inez. 1984. *The Joint: Language and Culture in a Maximum-Security Prison.* Springfield, Ill.: Charles C Thomas.

Carley, Kathleen. 1991. "A Theory of Group Stability." *American Sociological Review* 56: 331–54.

Cartwright, Dorwin, and Alvin Zander, eds. 1953. *Group Dynamics.* Evanston, Ill.: Row, Peterson.

Caughey, John. 1984. *Imaginary Social Worlds: A Cultural Approach.* Lincoln: University of Nebraska Press.

Chaney, David. 2004. "Fragmented Culture and Subcultures." In *After Subculture: Critical Studies in Contemporary Youth Culture,* edited by Andy Bennett and Keith Kahn-Harris. New York: Palgrave-Macmillan.

Chen, Katherine. 2009. *Enabling Creative Chaos: The Organization Behind the Burning Man Event.* Chicago: University of Chicago Press.

Chong, Dennis. 1990. *Collective Action and the Civil Rights Movement.* Chicago: University of Chicago Press.

Christakis, Nicholas A., and James H. Fowler. 2009. *Connected: How Your Friends' Friends' Friends Affect Everything You Feel, Think, and Do.* Boston: Little, Brown.

Clarke, Lee. 2005. *Worst Cases: Terror and Catastrophe in the Popular Imagination.* Chicago: University of Chicago Press.

Cohen, Albert K. 1955. *Delinquent Boys.* Glencoe, Ill.: Free Press.

Cohen, Ira. 1987. "Structuration Theory and Social Praxis." In *Social Theory Today,* edited by Anthony Giddens and Jonathan Rimer. Cambridge: Polity Press.

Cohen, Jean L., and Andrew Arato. 1992. *Civil Society and Political Theory.* Cambridge, Mass.: MIT Press.

Cohen, Jere. 1978. "Conformity and Norm Formation in Small Groups." *Pacific Sociological Review* 21: 441–66.

Cohen, Joseph. 1989. "About Steaks Liking to Be Eaten: The Conflicting Views of Symbolic Interactionists and Talcott Parsons Concerning the Nature of Relations Between Persons and Nonhuman Objects." *Symbolic Interaction* 12: 191–213.

Cohen, Michael D., James G. March, and Johan P. Olsen. 1972. "A Garbage Can Model of Organizational Choice." *Administrative Science Quarterly* 17: 1–25.

Cohen, Stanley. 1964. *Folk Devils and Moral Panics*. London: MacGibbon & Kee.

Coleman, James, Elihu Katz, and Herbert Menzel. 1966. *Medical Innovation: A Diffusion Study*. New York: Bobbs-Merrill.

Collins, Harry. 1992. *Replication and Induction in Scientific Practice*, 2nd ed. Chicago: University of Chicago Press.

Collins, Randall. 1981. "On the Microfoundations of Macrosociology." *American Journal of Sociology* 86: 984–1014.

———. 1998. *The Sociology of Philosophies*. Cambridge, Mass.: Harvard University Press.

———. 1999. "Socially Unrecognized Cumulation." *American Sociologist* 30: 41–61.

———. 2004. *Interaction Ritual Chains*. Princeton, N.J.: Princeton University Press.

Cook, Karen S., and Richard M. Emerson. 1978. "Power, Equity, and Commitment in Exchange Networks." *American Sociological Review* 43: 721–39.

Cooley, Charles Horton. 1964. *Human Nature and the Social Order*. New York: Schocken. (Originally published in 1902.)

Corsaro, William. 2003. *We're Friends Right? Inside Kids' Culture*. Washington, D.C.: Joseph Henry Press.

Corsaro, William, and Thomas Rizzo. 1988. "Discussione and Friendship: Socialization Processes in the Peer Culture of Italian Nursery School Children." *American Sociological Review* 55: 879–94.

Coser, Lewis. 1974. *Greedy Institutions: Patterns of Undivided Commitment*. New York: Free Press.

Costello, Donald P. 1972. "From Counterculture to Anticulture." *Journal of Politics* 34: 187–93.

Couch, Carl. 1984. "Symbolic Interaction and Generic Sociological Principles." *Symbolic Interaction* 7: 1–13.

———. 1989. *Social Processes and Relationships*. Dix Hills, N.Y.: General Hall.

Couch, Carl, and Marion W. Weiland. 1986. "A Study of the Representative-Constituent Relationship." In *Studies in Symbolic Interaction*, supp. 2, edited by Carl J. Couch, Stanley L. Saxton, and Michael A. Katovich. Greenwich, Conn.: JAI Press.

Cravalho, Mark Andrew. 1996. "Toast on Ice: The Ethnopsychology of the Winter-over Experience in Antarctica." *Ethos* 24: 628–56.

Csikszentmihalyi, Mihalyi. 1975. *Beyond Boredom and Anxiety*. San Francisco: Jossey-Bass.

Curtis, James, Douglas Baer, and Edward Grabb. 2001. "Nations of Joiners: Explaining Voluntary Association Membership in Democratic Societies." *American Sociological Review* 66: 783–805.

Curtis, James, Edward Grabb, and Douglas Baer. 1992. "Voluntary Association Membership in Fifteen Countries: A Comparative Analysis." *American Sociological Review* 57: 139–52.

Davis, Joseph E. 2002. *Stories of Change: Narrative and Social Movements.* Albany: State University of New York Press.

Davis, Murray. 1973. *Intimate Relations.* New York: Free Press.

———. 1993. *What's So Funny? The Comic Conception of Culture and Society.* Chicago: University of Chicago Press.

Dawkins, Richard. 1976. *The Selfish Gene.* New York: Oxford University Press.

Dayan, Daniel. 1986. "Review Essay: Copyrighted Subcultures." *American Journal of Sociology* 91: 1219–28.

de Tocqueville, Alexis. 1966. *Democracy in America.* New York: Harper & Row. (Originally published in 1835.)

Deaux, Kay. 1984. "From Individual Differences to Social Categories: Analysis of a Decade's Research on Gender." *American Psychologist* 39: 105–16.

Dégh, Linda, and Andrew Vazsonyi. 1975. "The Hypothesis of Multi-Conduit Transmission in Folklore." In *Folklore: Performance and Communication,* edited by Dan Ben-Amos and Kenneth Goldstein. The Hague: Mouton.

Dentler, R. A., and Kai Erikson. 1959. "The Functions of Deviance in Groups." *Social Problems* 7: 98–107.

Denzin, Norman K. 1977a. *Childhood Socialization.* San Francisco: Jossey-Bass.

———. 1977b. "Notes on the Criminogenic Hypothesis: A Case Study of the American Liquor Industry." *American Sociological Review* 42: 905–20.

———. 1985. "Emotion as Lived Experience." *Symbolic Interaction* 8: 223–40.

———. 1987. "The Death of Sociology in the 1980s: Comment on Collins." *American Journal of Sociology* 93: 180–84.

Denzin, Norman K., and Charles M. Keller. 1981. "Frame Analysis Reconsidered." *Contemporary Sociology* 10: 52–60.

DeSoucey, Michaela. 2010. "Gastronationalism: Food Traditions and Authenticity Politics in the European Union." *American Sociological Review* 75: 432–55.

Dewey, John. 1927. *The Public and Its Problems.* Denver: Alan Swallow.

DiFonzo, Nicholas. 2008. *The Watercooler Effect: A Psychologist Explores the Extraordinary Power of Rumors.* New York: Avery.

DiMaggio, Paul. 1997. "Culture and Cognition." *Annual Review of Sociology* 23: 263–87.

DiMaggio, Paul, and Hugh Louch. 1998. "Socially Embedded Consumer Transactions: For What Kinds of Purchases Do People Most Often Use Networks?" *American Sociological Review* 63: 619–37.

Douglas, Mary. 1967. *Purity and Dirt.* London: Penguin.

———. 1985. *How Institutions Think.* Syracuse, N.Y.: Syracuse University Press.

Douglas, Mary, and Aaron Wildavsky. 1982. *Risk and Culture.* Berkeley: University of California Press.

Dowd, Timothy J., Kathleen Liddle, and Jenna Nelson. 2004. "Music Festivals as Scenes: Examples from Serious Music, Womyn's Music, and SkatePunk." In *Music Scenes: Local, Translocal, and Virtual,* edited by Andy Bennett and Richard A. Peterson. Nashville: Vanderbilt University Press.

Duncan, Hugh D. 1968. *Symbols in Society.* New York: Oxford University Press.

Dundes, Alan. 1972. "Folk Ideas as Units of World View." *Journal of American Folklore* 84: 93–103.

Duneier, Mitchell. 1999. *Sidewalk.* New York: Farrar, Straus, Giroux.

Durkheim, Émile. 1964. *The Rules of Sociological Method.* New York: Free Press.

———. 1965. *The Elementary Forms of the Religious Life,* translated by Joseph Ward Swain. New York: Free Press. (English translation originally published in 1915.)

DuWors, Richard E. 1952. "Persistence and Change in Local Values of Two New England Communities." *Rural Sociology* 17: 207–17.

Eder, Donna. 1985. "The Cycle of Popularity: Interpersonal Relations Among Female Adolescents." *Sociology of Education* 58: 154–65.

Edgerton, Robert. 1979. *Alone Together: Social Order on an Urban Beach.* Berkeley: University of California Press.

Eliasoph, Nina. 1998. *Avoiding Politics: How Americans Produce Apathy in Everyday Life.* New York: Cambridge University Press.

Eliasoph, Nina, and Paul Lichterman. 2003. "Culture in Interaction." *American Journal of Sociology* 108: 735–94.

Ellickson, Robert C. 1991. *Order Without Law: How Neighbors Settle Disputes.* Cambridge, Mass.: Harvard University Press.

Emerson, Richard M. 1962. "Power-Dependence Relations." *American Sociological Review* 27: 31–41.

Emerson, Robert M., and Sheldon L. Messinger. 1977. "The Micro-Politics of Trouble." *Social Problems* 25: 121–34.

Emirbayer, Mustafa. 1997. "Manifesto for a Relational Sociology." *American Journal of Sociology* 103: 281–317.

Emirbayer, Mustafa, and Mimi Sheller. 1999. "Publics in History." *Theory and Society* 28: 145–97.

Erickson, Karla. 2009. *The Hungry Cowboy: Service and Community in a Neighborhood Restaurant.* Jackson: University of Mississippi Press.

Etzioni, Amitai. 1993. *The Spirit of Community.* New York: Crown.

Evans, Sara, and Harry Boyte. 1986. *Free Spaces: The Sources of Democratic Change in America.* New York: Harper & Row.

Evreinoff, Nicolas. 1927. *The Theatre in Life,* translated by Alexander Nazaroff. New York: Brentano's.

Fantasia, Rick. 1988. *Cultures of Solidarity.* Berkeley: University of California Press.

Farberman, Harvey. 1975. "A Criminogenic Market Structure: The Automobile Industry." *Sociological Quarterly* 16: 438–57.

Farrell, Michael. 2001. *Collaborative Circles: Friendship Dynamics and Creative Work.* Chicago: University of Chicago Press.

Fenstermaker, Sarah, and Candace West. 2002. *Doing Gender, Doing Change: Inequality, Power, and Institutional Change.* New York: Routledge.

Festinger, Leon, Henry Riecken, and Stanley Schachter. 1956. *When Prophecy Fails.* New York: Harper & Row.

Feuer, Lewis. 1975. *Ideology and the Ideologists.* New York: Harper & Row.

Fine, Gary Alan. 1977. "Popular Culture and Social Interaction." *Journal of Popular Culture* 11: 453–66.

———. 1979a. "Folklore Diffusion Through Interactive Social Networks." *New York Folklore* 5: 99–125.

———. 1979b. "Small Groups and Cultural Creation: The Idioculture of Little League Baseball Teams." *American Sociological Review* 44: 733–45.

———. 1983. *Shared Fantasy: Role-Playing Games as Social Worlds*. Chicago: University of Chicago Press.

———. 1985. "Occupational Aesthetics: How Trade School Students Learn to Cook." *Urban Life* 14: 3–32.

———. 1987a. "Community and Boundary: Personal Experience Stories of Mushroom Collectors." *Journal of Folklore Research* 24: 223–40.

———. 1987b. *With the Boys: Little League Baseball and Preadolescent Culture*. Chicago: University of Chicago Press.

———. 1989. "Mobilizing Fun: Provisioning Resources in Leisure Worlds." *Sport Sociology Journal* 6: 319–34.

———. 1992. "Agency, Structure, and Comparative Contexts: Toward a Synthetic Interactionism." *Symbolic Interaction* 15: 87–107.

———. 1995. "Public Narration and Group Culture: Discerning Discourse in Social Movements." In *Social Movements and Culture*, edited by Hank Johnston and Bert Klandermans. Minneapolis: University of Minnesota Press.

———. 1996. *Kitchens: The Culture of Restaurant Work*. Berkeley: University of California Press.

———. 1997. "Naturework and the Taming of the Wild: The Problem of 'Overpick' in the Culture of Mushroomers." *Social Problems* 44(1): 68–88.

———. 1998. *Morel Tales: The Culture of Mushrooming*. Cambridge, Mass.: Harvard University Press.

———. 2001. *Gifted Tongues: High School Debate and Adolescent Culture*. Princeton, N.J.: Princeton University Press.

———. 2003a. "On the Trail of Tribal Sociology." *Sociological Forum* 18: 653–65.

———. 2003b. "Toward a Peopled Ethnography: Developing Theory from Group Life." *Ethnography* 4: 41–60.

———. 2004. *Everyday Genius: Self-Taught Art and the Culture of Authenticity*. Chicago: University of Chicago Press.

———. 2007. *Authors of the Storm: Meteorology and the Culture of Prediction*. Chicago: University of Chicago Press.

Fine, Gary Alan, and Michaela DeSoucey. 2005. "Joking Cultures: Humor Themes as Social Regulation in Group Life." *Humor* 18: 1–22.

Fine, Gary Alan, and Tim Hallett. 2003. "Dust: A Study in Sociological Miniaturism." *Sociological Quarterly* 25: 121–34.

Fine, Gary Alan, Tim Hallett, and Michael Sauder. 2004. "The Myth and Meaning of Bowling Alone." *Society* (July–August): 47–49.

Fine, Gary Alan, Brooke Harrington, and Sandro Segre. 2008. "Politics in the Public Sphere: The Power of Tiny Publics in Classical Sociology." *Sociologica* 1 (online). Available at: http://www.sociologica.mulino.it/journal/article/index/Article/Journal:ARTICLE:156/Item/Journal:ARTICLE:156 (accessed January 22, 2012).

Fine, Gary Alan, and Lori Holyfield. 1996. "Secrecy, Trust, and Dangerous Leisure: Generating Group Cohesion in Voluntary Organizations." *Social Psychology Quarterly* 59: 22–38.

Fine, Gary Alan, and Sherryl Kleinman. 1979. "Rethinking Subculture: An Interactionist Analysis." *American Journal of Sociology* 85: 1–20.

———. 1983. "Network and Meaning: An Interactionist Approach to Structure." *Symbolic Interaction* 6: 97–110.

Fine, Gary Alan, and Laura Leighton. 1993. "Nocturnal Omissions: Steps Toward a Sociology of Dreams." *Symbolic Interaction* 16: 95–104.

Fine, Gary Alan, and Jay Mechling. 1991. "Minor Difficulties: Changing Children in the Late Twentieth Century." In *America at Century's End*, edited by Alan Wolfe. Berkeley: University of California Press.

Fine, Gary Alan, and Randy Stoecker. 1985. "Can the Circle Be Unbroken: Small Groups and Social Movements." *Advances in Group Process* 2: 1–28.

Fine, Gary Alan, and Patricia Turner. 2001. *Whispers on the Color Line: Rumor and Race in America.* Berkeley: University of California Press.

Fischer, Claude. 1982. *To Dwell Among Friends: Personal Networks in Town and City.* Chicago: University of Chicago Press.

Fischer, J. L. 1968. "Microethnology: Small-Scale Comparative Studies." In *Introduction to Cultural Anthropology*, edited by J. A. Clifton. Boston: Houghton Mifflin.

Flaherty, Michael. 2000. *A Watched Pot: How We Experience Time.* New York: New York University Press.

Flaherty, Michael, and Gary Alan Fine. 2001. "Present, Past and Future: Conjugating Mead's Perspective of Time." *Time and Society* 10: 147–61.

Foucault, Michel. 1977. *Discipline and Punish: The Birth of the Prison.* New York: Pantheon.

Fraser, Nancy. 1992. "Rethinking the Public Sphere: A Contribution to the Critique of Actually Existing Democracy." In *Habermas and the Public Sphere*, edited by Craig Calhoun. Cambridge, Mass.: MIT Press.

Freud, Sigmund. 1922. *Group Psychology and the Analysis of the Ego.* New York: Boni and Liveright.

Friedson, Eliot. 1953. "Communications Research and the Concept of the Mass." *American Sociological Review* 18: 313–17.

Fry, William F., Jr. 1963. *Sweet Madness: A Study of Humor.* Palo Alto, Calif.: Pacific Books.

Furman, Frida Kerner. 1997. *Facing the Mirror: Older Women and Beauty Shop Culture.* New York: Routledge.

Gamson, William, Bruce Fireman, and Steven Rytina. 1982. *Encounters with Unjust Authority.* Homewood, Ill.: Dorsey Press.

Garfinkel, Harold. 1967. *Studies in Ethnomethodology.* Englewood Cliffs, N.J.: Prentice-Hall.

———. 2006. *Seeing Sociologically: The Routine Grounds of Social Action.* Boulder, Colo.: Paradigm.

Geary, Ida. 1982. "Hunting the Wild Morels." *California* (May): 72.

Gecas, Viktor. 1994. "Self and Identity." In *Sociological Perspectives on Social Psychology*, edited by Karen S. Cook, Gary Alan Fine, and James House. Boston: Allyn and Bacon.

Gecas, Viktor, and Michael Schwalbe. 1983. "Beyond the Looking Glass Self: Social Structure and Efficiency-Based Self-Esteem." *Social Psychology Quarterly* 46: 77–88.

Geertz, Clifford. 1973. *The Interpretation of Cultures*. New York: Basic Books.
———. 1978. "The Bazaar Economy: Information and Search in Peasant Marketing." *American Economic Review* 62: 28–32.
———. 1983. *Local Knowledge: Further Essays in Interpretive Anthropology*. New York: Basic Books.
Gergen, Kenneth. 1991. *The Saturated Self: Dilemmas of Identity in Everyday Life*. New York: Basic Books.
Gerlach, Luther, and Virginia Hine. 1970. *People, Power, Change: Movements of Social Transformation*. Indianapolis: Bobbs-Merrill.
Ghaziani, Amin. 2009. "An Amorphous Mist? The Problem of Measurement in the Study of Culture." *Theory and Society* 38: 581–612.
Giallombardo, Rose. 1974. *The Social World of Imprisoned Girls*. New York: Wiley.
Gibson, David. 2000. "Seizing the Moment: The Problem of Conversational Agency." *Sociological Theory* 18: 369–82.
———. 2005. "Taking Turns and Talking Ties: Network Structure and Conversational Sequences." *American Journal of Sociology* 110: 1561–97.
Giddens, Anthony. 1978. *Durkheim*. Glasgow: Fontana.
———. 1984. *The Constitution of Society: Outline of the Theory of Structuration*. Berkeley: University of California Press.
Gieryn, Thomas F. 1983. "Boundary-Work and the Demarcation of Science from Non-Science: Strains and Interests in Professional Ideologies of Scientists." *American Sociological Review* 48: 781–95.
———. 2000. "A Space for Place in Sociology." *Annual Review of Sociology* 26: 463–96.
Giesen, Bernhard. 2001. "Cosmopolitans, Patriots, Jacobins, and Romantics." In *Public Spheres and Collective Identities*, edited by Shmuel N. Eisenstadt, Wolfgang Schlucter, and Bjorn Wittrock. New Brunswick, N.J.: Transaction.
Gladwell, Malcolm. 2000. *The Tipping Point: How Little Things Can Make a Big Difference*. Boston: Little, Brown.
Glaeser, Andreas. 2003. "Power/Knowledge Failure: Epistemic Practices and Ideologies in the Secret Police of Former East Germany." *Social Analysis* 47: 10–26.
Glaser, Barney, and Anselm Strauss. 1967. *The Discovery of Grounded Theory: Strategies for Qualitative Research*. New York: Aldine.
Gmelch, George J. 1971. "Baseball Magic." *Transaction* 8(8): 39–41, 54.
Goffman, Erving. 1959. *Presentation of Self in Everyday Life*. New York: Anchor.
———. 1961a. *Asylums: Essays on the Social Situation of Mental Patients and Other Inmates*. New York: Anchor.
———. 1961b. *Encounters: Two Studies in the Sociology of Interaction*. Indianapolis: Bobbs-Merrill.
———. 1963. *Behavior in Public Places: Notes on the Social Organization of Gatherings*. New York: Free Press.
———. 1967. *Interaction Ritual: Essays on Face-to-Face Behavior*. New York: Anchor.
———. 1971. *Relations in Public*. New York: Basic Books.
———. 1974. *Frame Analysis: An Essay in the Organization of Experience*. Cambridge, Mass.: Harvard University Press.
———. 1981. *Forms of Talk*. Philadelphia: University of Pennsylvania Press.
———. 1983. "The Interaction Order." *American Sociological Review* 48: 1–17.

Goldfarb, Jeffrey. 2006. *The Politics of Small Things: The Power of the Powerless in Dark Times.* Chicago: University of Chicago Press.

Gonos, George. 1977. " 'Situation' Versus 'Frame': The 'Interactionist' and the 'Structuralist' Analysis of Everyday Life." *American Sociological Review* 42: 854–67.

Gordon, H. S. 1954. "The Economic Theory of a Common-Property Resource: A Fishery." *Journal of Political Economy* 62: 124–42.

Gordon, Milton M. 1947. "The Concept of the Sub-Culture and Its Application." *Social Forces* 26: 40–42.

———. 1964. *Assimilation in American Life.* New York: Oxford University Press.

Gould, Roger. 1993. "Trade Cohesion, Class Unity, and Urban Insurrection: Artisanal Activism in the Paris Commune." *American Journal of Sociology* 98: 721–54.

Gouldner, Alvin. 1970. *The Coming Crisis of Western Sociology.* New York: Basic Books.

———. 1976. *The Dialectic of Ideology and Technology.* New York: Seabury.

Gramsci, Antonio. 1992. *Prison Notebooks,* vol. 1, edited and translated by Joseph Buttigieg. New York: Columbia University Press.

Grannis, Rick. 2009. *From the Ground Up: Translating Geography into Community Through Neighbor Networks.* Princeton, N.J.: Princeton University Press.

Granovetter, Mark. 1973. "The Strength of Weak Ties." *American Journal of Sociology* 78: 1360–80.

———. 1977. "Threshold Models of Collective Behavior." *American Journal of Sociology* 82: 1420–42.

Gray, Jonathan, Cornel Sandvoss, and C. Lee Harrington. 2007. "Why Study Fans?" In *Fandom: Identities and Communities in a Mediated World,* edited by Jonathan Gray, Cornel Sandvoss, and C. Lee Harrington. New York: New York University Press.

Green, Arnold W. 1946. "Sociological Analysis of Horney and Fromm." *American Journal of Sociology* 51: 533–40.

Greenfeld, Liah. 1992. *Nationalism: Five Roads to Modernity.* Cambridge, Mass.: Harvard University Press.

Griswold, Wendy. 1994. *Cultures and Societies in a Changing World.* Thousand Oaks, Calif.: Pine Forge.

Gross, Edward. 1986. "The Social Construction of Historical Events Through Public Drama." *Symbolic Interaction* 9: 179–200.

Gross, Neil. 2009. "A Pragmatist Theory of Social Mechanisms." *American Sociological Review* 74: 358–79.

Gurr, Ted. 1970. *Why Men Rebel.* Princeton, N.J.: Princeton University Press.

Gusfield, Joseph. 1976. "The Literary Rhetoric of Science: Comedy and Pathos in Drinking Driving Research." *American Sociological Review* 41: 16–33.

Haas, Peter M. 1992. "Epistemic Communities and International Policy Coordination." *International Organization* 46: 1–35.

Habermas, Jürgen. 1970. *Toward a Rational Society.* Boston: Beacon Press.

———. 1991. *The Structural Transformation of the Public Sphere: An Inquiry into a Category of Bourgeois Society,* translated by Thomas Burger. Cambridge, Mass.: MIT Press.

Hall, Peter, and Dee Spencer-Hall. 1982. "The Social Conditions of the Negotiated Order." *Urban Life* 11: 328–49.

Hall, Stuart. 1986. "The Problem of Ideology: Marxism Without Guarantees." *Journal of Communication* 10: 28–44.

Hall, Stuart, and Tony Jefferson, eds. 1976. *Resistance Through Rituals: Youth Subcultures in Post-War Britain.* London: Hutchinson.

Hallett, Tim. 2003. "Symbolic Power and Organizational Culture." *Sociological Theory* 21: 128–49.

Hallett, Tim, and Marc Ventresca. 2006. "Inhabited Institutions: Social Interaction and Organizational Forms in Gouldner's *Patterns of Industrial Bureaucracy.*" *Theory and Society* 35: 213–36.

Hardin, Garrett. 1974. "Foreword." In *Should Trees Have Standing?* by Christopher D. Stone. Los Altos, Calif.: William Kaufmann.

Hare, A. Paul. 1976. *Handbook of Small Group Research,* 2nd ed. New York: Free Press.

———. 1982. *Creativity in Small Groups.* Beverly Hills, Calif.: Sage Publications.

Harrington, Brooke. 2001. "Organizational Performance and Social Capital: A Contingency Model." *Research in the Sociology of Organizations* 18: 83–106.

Harrington, Brooke, and Gary Alan Fine. 2000. "Opening the Black Box: Small Groups and Twenty-First-Century Sociology." *Social Psychology Quarterly* 63: 312–23.

Hart, Paul 't. 1994. *Groupthink in Government: A Study of Small Groups and Policy Failure.* Baltimore: Johns Hopkins University Press.

Hartz, Louis. 1955. *The Liberal Tradition: An Interpretation of American Political Thought Since the Revolution.* New York: Harcourt, Brace.

Heath, Chip, Chris Bell, and Emily Sternberg. 2001. "Emotional Selection in Memes: The Case of Urban Legends." *Journal of Personality and Social Psychology* 81: 1028–41.

Heath, Chip, and Dan Heath. 2007. *Made to Stick: Why Some Ideas Survive and Others Die.* New York: Random House.

Hebb, Donald O. 1974. "What Psychology Is About." *American Psychologist* 29: 71–87.

Hebdige, Dick. 1981. *Subculture: The Meaning of Style.* London: Routledge.

Hechter, Michael. 1987. *Principles of Group Solidarity.* Berkeley: University of California Press.

Hedström, Peter, and Richard Swedberg, eds. 1998. *Social Mechanisms: An Analytical Approach to Social Theory.* Cambridge: Cambridge University Press.

Heimer, Carol, and Arthur Stinchcombe. 1980. "Love and Irrationality: It's Got to Be Rational to Love You Because It Makes Me So Happy." *Social Science Information* 19: 697–754.

Heise, David R. 1979. *Understanding Events: Affect and the Construction of Social Action.* New York: Cambridge University Press.

Hellekson, Karen. 2006. *Fan Fiction and Fan Communities in the Age of the Internet.* Jefferson, N.C.: McFarland.

Henke, Christopher, and Thomas Gieryn. 2008. "Sites of Scientific Practice: The Enduring Importance of Place." In *The Handbook of Science and Technology Studies,* edited by Edward J. Hackett. Cambridge, Mass.: MIT Press.

Heritage, John. 1984. *Garfinkel and Ethnomethodology.* Cambridge: Polity Press.

Hewitt, John. 1984. "Stalking the Wild Identity." Unpublished paper.

———. 1989. *Dilemmas of the American Self.* Philadelphia: Temple University Press.

Hillery, George. 1955. "Definitions of Community: Areas of Agreement." *Rural Sociology* 20: 111–23.

Hillmann, Henning. 2008. "Localism and the Limits of Political Brokerage: Evidence from Revolutionary Vermont." *American Journal of Sociology* 114: 287–331.

Hills, Matthew. 2002. *Fan Cultures.* New York: Routledge.

Hirsch, Paul. 1986. "The Creation of Political Solidarity in Social Movement Organizations." *Sociological Quarterly* 27: 378–87.

Hitlin, Steven. 2008. *Moral Selves, Evil Selves: The Social Psychology of Conscience.* New York: Palgrave-Macmillan.

Hobbes, Thomas. 1886. *Leviathan, Or the Matter, Form, and Power of a Commonwealth.* London: Routledge.

Hobsbawm, Eric, and Terrence Ranger, eds. 1983. *The Invention of Tradition.* Cambridge: Cambridge University Press.

Hochschild, Arlie. 1979. "Emotion Work, Feeling Rules, and Social Structure." *American Journal of Sociology* 85: 551–75.

———. 1983. *The Managed Heart: Commercialization of Human Feeling.* Berkeley: University of California Press.

Hoffman, Steve. 2006. "How to Punch Someone and Stay Friends: An Inductive Theory of Simulation." *Sociological Theory* 24(2): 170–93.

Hoggett, Paul, and Jeff Bishop. 1986. *Organizing Around Enthusiasms: Patterns of Mutual Aid and Leisure.* London: Comedia Publishing Group.

Hollander, Edwin. 1958. "Conformity, Status, and Idiosyncrasy Credit." *Psychological Review* 65: 117–27.

Hollingshead, August B. 1939. "Behavior Systems as a Field for Research." *American Sociological Review* 4: 816–22.

Holstein, James A., and Jaber F. Gubrium. 2000. *The Self We Live By: Narrative Identity in a Postmodern World.* New York: Oxford University Press.

Homans, George C. 1964. "Bringing Men Back In." *American Sociological Review* 29: 809–18.

Horne, Christine. 2001. "The Enforcement of Norms: Group Cohesion and Metanorms." *Social Psychology Quarterly* 64: 253–66.

Horowitz, Ruth. 1983. *Honor and the American Dream: Culture and Identity in a Chicano Community.* New Brunswick, N.J.: Rutgers University Press.

Horton, Donald, and R. Richard Wohl. 1956. "Mass Communication and Para-social Interaction: Observations on Intimacy at a Distance." *Psychiatry* 19: 215–29.

Hughes, Linda. 1983. "Beyond the *Rules* of the Game: Why Are *Rooie Rules* Nice?" In *The World of Play,* edited by Frank E. Manning. West Point, N.Y.: Leisure Press.

Hunt, Pamela. 2008. "From Festies to Tourrats: Examining the Relationship Between Jamband Subculture Involvement and Role Meanings." *Social Psychology Quarterly* 71: 356–78.

Hunter, Albert, and Gerald Suttles. 1972. "The Expanding Community of Limited Liability." In *The Social Construction of Communities,* edited by Gerald Suttles. Chicago: University of Chicago Press.

Ikegami, Eiko. 2000. "A Sociological Theory of Publics: Identity and Culture as Emergent Properties in Networks." *Social Research* 67: 989–1029.

Jackall, Robert. 1988. *Moral Mazes: The World of Corporate Managers*. New York: Oxford University Press.

Jacobs, R. C., and Donald T. Campbell. 1961. "The Perpetuation of an Arbitrary Tradition Through Several Generations of a Laboratory Microculture." *Journal of Abnormal and Social Psychology* 62: 649–58.

James, Alison, Chris Jenks, and Alan Prout. 1998. *Theorizing Childhood*. Oxford: Blackwell.

Janowitz, Morris. 1952. *The Community Press in an Urban Setting*. Glencoe, Ill.: Free Press.

Jenkins, Henry. 1992. *Textual Poachers: Television Fans and Participatory Culture*. New York: Routledge.

Jenks, Chris. 2004. *Subculture: The Fragmentation of the Social*. London: Sage Publications.

Jindra, Michael. 1994. "Star Trek Fandom as a Religious Phenomenon." *Sociology of Religion* 55: 27–51.

Johnson, Harry M. 1968. "Ideology and the Social System." *International Encyclopedia of the Social Sciences* 7: 76–85.

Johnston, Hank. 1991. *Tales of Nationalism: Catalonia, 1939–1979*. New Brunswick, N.J.: Rutgers University Press.

Katovich, Michael. 1987. "Identity, Time, and Situated Activity: An Interactionist Analysis of Dyadic Transactions." *Symbolic Interaction* 10: 187–208.

Katovich, Michael A., and Carl J. Couch. 1992. "The Nature of Social Pasts and Their Uses as Foundations for Situated Action." *Symbolic Interaction* 15: 25–48.

Katz, Elihu, and Paul F. Lazarsfeld. 1955. *Personal Influence*. New York: Free Press.

Katz, Jack. 1989. *Seductions of Crime*. New York: Basic Books.

Kauffman, Jean-Claude. 2009. *Gripes: The Little Quarrels of Couples*. Cambridge: Polity.

Kaufman, Jason A. 1999. "Three Views of Associationalism in Nineteenth-Century America: An Empirical Examination." *American Journal of Sociology* 104: 1296–1345.

———. 2003. *For the Common Good? American Civic Life and the Golden Age of Fraternity*. New York: Oxford University Press.

Kaufman, Wallace. 1983. "Tree Oysters." *Coltsfoot* 4(November-December): 7–9.

Kelly, Harold. 1967. "Attribution Theory in Social Psychology." In *Nebraska Symposium on Motivation*, edited by David Levine. Lincoln: University of Nebraska Press.

Kelman, Herbert C. 1973. "Violence Without Moral Restraints: Reflections on the Dehumanization of Victims and Victimizers." *Journal of Social Issues* 29: 25–61.

Kinloch, Graham C. 1981. *Ideology and Contemporary Sociological Theory*. Englewood Cliffs, N.J.: Prentice-Hall.

Kleinman, Sherryl. 1984. *Equals Before God*. Chicago: University of Chicago Press.

Kling, Rob, and Elihu Gerson. 1977. "The Social Dynamics of Technical Innovation in the Computing World." *Symbolic Interaction* 1: 132–46.

Knorr-Cetina, Karin. 1999. *Epistemic Cultures: How the Sciences Make Knowledge*. Cambridge, Mass.: Harvard University Press.

Korte, Charles, and Stanley Milgram. 1970. "Acquaintance Networks Between Racial Groups." *Journal of Personality and Social Psychology* 15: 101–8.

Koselleck, Reinhart. 1988. *Critique and Crisis: Enlightenment and the Pathogenesis of Modern Society.* Cambridge, Mass.: MIT Press.

Kozinets, Robert. 2002. "Can Consumers Escape the Market? Emancipatory Illuminations from Burning Man." *Journal of Consumer Research* 29: 20–38.

Kroeber, A. L. 1917. "The Superorganic." *American Anthropologist* 19: 263–73.

Kuhn, Manford H., and Thomas S. McPartland. 1954. "An Empirical Investigation of Self-Attitudes." *American Sociological Review* 19: 68–76.

Lachmann, Richard. 1988. "Graffiti as Career and Ideology." *American Journal of Sociology* 94: 229–50.

Lakoff, George. 2006. *Moral Politics: How Liberals and Conservatives Think.* Chicago: University of Chicago Press.

Lakoff, George, and Mark Johnson. 1980. *Metaphors We Live By.* Chicago: University of Chicago Press.

Lamont, Michele. 1992. *Money, Morals, and Manners: The Culture of the French and the American Upper-Middle Class.* Chicago: University of Chicago Press.

Lamont, Michele, and Marcel Fournier. 1993. *Cultivating Differences: Symbolic Boundaries and the Making of Inequality.* Chicago: University of Chicago Press.

Lasch, Christopher. 1978. *The Culture of Narcissism: American Life in an Age of Diminishing Expectations.* New York: W. W. Norton.

Latour, Bruno. 1988. *Science in Action.* Cambridge, Mass.: Harvard University Press.

Latour, Bruno, and Steven Woolgar. 1979. *Laboratory Life.* Beverly Hills, Calif.: Sage Publications.

Lawler, Edward. 1992. "Affective Attachments to Nested Groups: A Choice-Process Theory." *American Sociological Review* 57: 327–39.

Lawler, Edward, Shane R. Thye, and Jeongkoo Yoon. 2009. *Social Commitments in a Depersonalized World.* New York: Russell Sage Foundation.

Lears, T. J. Jackson. 1981. *No Place of Grace: Antimodernism and the Transformation of American Culture.* New York: Pantheon.

Lee, Alfred McClung. 1954. "Attitudinal Multivalence in Relation to Culture and Personality." *American Journal of Sociology* 60: 294–99.

Lemann, Nicolas. 1996. "Kicking in Groups." *Atlantic Monthly* (April): 22–26.

Levtzion, Nehemia. 2002. "The Dynamics of Sufi Brotherhoods." In *The Public Sphere in Muslim Societies,* edited by Miriam Hoexter, Shmuel N. Eisenstadt, and Nehemia Levtzion. Albany: State University of New York Press.

Lewin, Kurt. 1936. *Principles of Topological Psychology.* New York: McGraw-Hill.

Lichterman, Paul. 1996. *The Search for Political Community.* New York: Cambridge University Press.

———. 2005. *Elusive Togetherness: Church Groups Trying to Bridge America's Divisions.* Princeton, N.J.: Princeton University Press.

Liebow, Elliott. 1967. *Tally's Corner: A Study of Negro Streetcorner Men.* Boston: Little, Brown.

Lifton, Robert Jay. 1987. *The Future of Immortality.* New York: Basic Books.

Lincoln, Sian. 2004. "Teenage Girls' 'Bedroom Culture': Codes versus Zones." In *After Subculture: Critical Studies in Contemporary Youth Culture,* edited by Andy Bennett and Keith Kahn-Harris. New York: Palgrave-Macmillan.

Lipset, Seymour Martin. 1985. "Canada and the United States: The Cultural Dimension." In *Canada and the United States,* edited by C. E. Doran and J. H. Sigler. Englewood Cliffs, N.J.: Prentice-Hall.

———. 1996. *American Exceptionalism: A Double-Edged Sword.* New York: Norton.

Lizardo, Omar. 2006. "Cultural Tastes and Personal Networks." *American Sociological Review* 71: 778–807.

———. 2008. "Defining and Theorizing Terrorism: A Global Actor-Centered Approach." *Journal of World Systems Research* 14: 91–118.

Lofland, Lyn. 1973. *A World of Strangers: Order and Action in Urban Public Space.* New York: Basic Books.

Lois, Jennifer. 1999. "Socialization to Heroism: Individualism and Collectivism in a Voluntary Search and Rescue Group." *Social Psychology Quarterly* 62: 117–35.

Long, Elizabeth. 2003. *Book Clubs: Women and the Uses of Reading in Everyday Life.* Chicago: University of Chicago Press.

Loseke, Donileen. 2003. *Thinking About Social Problems: An Introduction to Constructionist Perspectives.* Chicago: Aldine.

Lovaglia, Michael J., and Jeffrey A. Houser. 1996. "Emotional Reactions and Status in Groups." *American Sociological Review* 61: 864–80.

Lyng, Stephen, ed. 2004. *Edgework: The Sociology of Risk-Taking.* New York: Routledge.

Lyons, Elizabeth. 1983. "Demographic Correlates of Landscape Preference." *Environment and Behavior* 15: 487–511.

MacNeil, Mark K., and Muzafer Sherif. 1976. "Norm Change over Subject Generations as a Function of Arbitrariness of Prescribed Norms." *Journal of Personality and Social Psychology* 34: 762–73.

Maffesoli, Michel. 1996. *The Time of the Tribes: The Decline of Individualism in Mass Society.* Thousand Oaks, Calif.: Sage Publications.

Maines, David. 1977. "Social Organization and Social Structure in Symbolic Interactionist Thought." *Annual Review of Sociology* 3: 235–59.

———. 1982. "In Search of Mesostructure: Studies in the Negotiated Order." *Urban Life* 11: 267–79.

———. 1988. "Myth, Text, and Interactionist Complicity in the Neglect of Blumer's Macrosociology." *Symbolic Interaction* 11: 43–57.

———. 1999. "Information Pools and Racialized Narrative Structures." *Sociological Quarterly* 40: 316–26.

Maines, David, and Thomas Morrione. 1990. "On the Breadth and Relevance of Blumer's Perspective: Introduction to His Analysis of Industrialization." In *Industrialization as an Agent of Social Change,* by Herbert Blumer. New York: Aldine.

Maines, David, Noreen Sugrue, and Michael Katovich. 1983. "G. H. Mead's Theory of the Past." *American Sociological Review* 48: 161–73.

Mannheim, Karl. 1936. *Ideology and Utopia.* New York: Harcourt.

———. 1952. "The Problem of Generations." In *Essays in the Sociology of Knowledge.* London: Routledge & Kegan Paul.

Manning, David J. 1976. *Liberalism.* New York: St. Martin's Press.

———. 1980. "The Place of Ideology in Political Life." In *The Form of Ideology,* edited by David J. Manning. London: Allen and Unwin.

Martin, Daniel, and Gary Alan Fine. 1991. "Satanic Cults, Satanic Play: Is Dungeons and Dragons a Breeding Ground for the Devil?" In *The Satanism Scare,* edited by James Richardson, David Bromley, and Joel Best. New York: Aldine de Gruyter.

Martin, Joanne, and Melanie Powers. 1983. "Organizational Stories: More Vivid and Persuasive Than Quantitative Data." In *Psychological Foundations of Organizational Behavior,* edited by Barry Staw. Glenview, Ill.: Scott, Foresman.

Martin, Karin A. 1998. "Becoming a Gendered Body: Practices of Preschools." *American Sociological Review* 63: 494–511.

Marx, Karl, and Friedrich Engels. 1976. "The German Ideology." In *Karl Marx-Friedrich Engels Collected Works,* vol. 5. New York: International Publishers. (Originally published in 1846.)

Matza, David. 1964. *Delinquency and Drift.* New York: Wiley.

Mayer, Adrian C. 1966. "The Significance of Quasi-Groups in the Study of Complex Societies." In *The Social Anthropology of Complex Societies,* edited by Michael Banton. London: Tavistock.

Maynard, Douglas W. 2003. *Bad News, Good News: Conversational Order in Everyday Talk and Clinical Settings.* Chicago: University of Chicago Press.

McAdam, Douglas. 1986. "Recruitment to High-Risk Activism: The Case of Freedom Summer." *American Journal of Sociology* 82: 64–90.

McBride, Glen. 1975. "Interactions and the Control of Behavior." In *Organization of Behavior in Face-to-Face Interaction,* edited by Adam Kendon, Richard M. Harris, and Mary Ritchie Kay. The Hague: Mouton.

McCarthy, John, and Mayer Zald. 1977. "Resource Mobilization and Social Movements: A Partial Theory." *American Journal of Sociology* 82: 1212–41.

McCloskey, Donald. 1990. *If You're So Smart: The Narrative of Economic Expertise.* Chicago: University of Chicago Press.

McFeat, Tom. 1974. *Small-Group Cultures.* New York: Pergamon.

McLean, Scott L., David A. Schultz, and Manfred Steger, eds. 2002. *Social Capital: Critical Perspectives on Community and "Bowling Along."* New York: NYU Press.

McLellan, David. 1986. *Ideology.* Minneapolis: University of Minnesota Press.

McPhail, Clark. 1991. *The Myth of the Madding Crowd.* New York: Aldine.

———. 2008. "Gatherings as Patchworks." *Social Psychology Quarterly* 71: 1–5.

McPherson, Miller, Lynn Smith-Lovin, and Matthew Brashears. 2006. "Social Isolation in America: Changes in Core Discussion Networks over Two Decades." *American Sociological Review* 71: 353–75.

McRobbie, Angela, and Jenny Garber. 1976. "Girls and Subcultures: An Exploration." In *Resistance Through Rituals: Youth Subcultures in Post-War Britain,* edited by Stuart Hall and Tony Jefferson. London: Hutchinson.

Mead, George Herbert. 1934. *Mind, Self, and Society.* Chicago: University of Chicago Press.

———. 1936. *Movements of Thought in the Nineteenth Century.* Chicago: University of Chicago Press.

Mechling, Jay. 2001. *On My Honor: Boy Scouts and the Making of American Youth.* Chicago: University of Chicago Press.

Messick, David, and Charles G. McClintock. 1968. "Motivational Bases of Choice in Experimental Games." *Journal of Experimental Social Psychology* 4: 1–25.

Messinger, Sheldon, Harold Sampson, and Robert Towne. 1962. "Life as Theater: Some Notes on the Dramaturgical Approach to Social Reality." *Sociometry* 25: 98–110.

Milgram, Stanley. 1967. "The Small-World Problem." *Psychology Today* 1(May): 62–67.

———. 1974. *Obedience to Authority: An Experimental View.* New York: HarperCollins.

Miller, Henry. 1936. *Black Spring.* Paris: Obelisk.

Miller, Walter B. 1958. "Lower Class Culture as a Generating Milieu of Gang Delinquency." *Journal of Social Issues* 14: 5–19.

Mills, C. Wright. 1959. *The Sociological Imagination.* New York: Oxford University Press.

Mische, Ann. 2007. *Partisan Publics: Communication and Contention Across Brazilian Youth Activist Networks.* Princeton, N.J.: Princeton University Press.

Mische, Ann, and Harrison White. 1998. "Between Conversation and Situation: Public Switching Dynamics Across Network-Domains." *Social Research* 65: 694–724.

Mitchell, Richard. 1983. *Mountain Experience.* Chicago: University of Chicago Press.

Molotch, Harvey, William Freudenburg, and Krista E. Paulsen. 2000. "History Repeats Itself, but How? City Character, Urban Tradition, and the Accomplishment of Place." *American Sociological Review* 65: 791–823.

Morgan, Jane, Rom Harré, and Christopher O'Neill. 1979. *Nicknames: Their Origins and Social Consequences.* London: Routledge & Kegan Paul.

Morris, Aldon. 1981. "Black Southern Sit-in Movement: An Analysis of Internal Organization." *American Sociological Review* 46: 744–67.

Mouffe, Chantal. 2005. *On the Political.* New York: Routledge.

Ms. Mushroom. 1984. "Etiquette." *Mushroom* 3(Summer): 28–29.

Muggleton, David. 2000. *Inside Subculture: The Postmodern Meaning of Style.* Oxford: Berg.

Mullins, Nicholas C. 1973. *Theories and Theory Groups in Contemporary American Sociology.* New York: Harper & Row.

Mullins, Willard A. 1972. "On the Concept of Ideology in Political Science." *American Political Science Review* 66: 498–510.

Muniz, Albert, Jr., and Thomas C. O'Guinn. 2001. "Brand Community." *Journal of Consumer Research* 27: 412–32.

Munroe, Paul T. 2007. "Deference." In *Blackwell Encyclopedia of Sociology,* edited by George Ritzer. Blackwell Reference Online, available to subscribers at: http://www.sociologyencyclopedia.com/subscriber/tocnode?id=g97814051 24331_chunk_g978140512433110_ss1-11 (accessed February 25, 2010).

Munroe, Robert L., and William L. Faust. 1976. "Psychological Determinants of Institutions in a Laboratory Microculture." *Ethos* 4: 449–62.

Nash, Roderick. 1989. *The Rights of Nature: A History of Environmental Ethics.* Madison: University of Wisconsin Press.

Nee, Victor, and Brett de Bary Nee. 1973. *Long Time Californ': Documentary Study of an American Chinatown.* New York: Pantheon.

Nisbet, Robert. 1966. *The Sociological Tradition.* New York: Basic Books.

———. 1976. *Sociology as an Art Form.* New York: Oxford University Press.

Oldenburg, Ray. 1989. *The Great Good Place.* St. Paul, Minn.: Paragon House.

Olick, Jeffrey K., and Joyce Robbins. 1998. "Social Memory Studies: From 'Collective Memory' to the Historical Sociology of Mnemonic Practices." *Annual Review of Sociology* 24: 105–40.

Olson, Mancur. 1965. *The Logic of Collective Action: Public Goods and the Theory of Groups.* Cambridge: Harvard University Press.

Opie, Iona, and Peter Opie. 1959. *The Lore and Language of School-Children.* Oxford: Clarendon.

Opp, Karl-Dieter, and Christiane Gern. 1993. "Dissident Groups, Personal Networks, and Spontaneous Cooperation: The East German Revolution of 1989." *American Sociological Review* 58: 659–80.

Oring, Elliott. 1984. "Dyadic Traditions." *Journal of Folklore Research* 21: 19–28.

Orzechowicz, David. 2008. "Privileged Emotional Managers: The Case of Actors." *Social Psychology Quarterly* 71: 143–56.

Osgood, Charles, George Suci, and Percy Tannenbaum. 1957. *The Measurement of Meaning.* Urbana: University of Illinois Press.

Ostrom, Elinor. 1990. *Governing the Commons: The Evolution of Institutions for Collective Action.* Cambridge: Cambridge University Press.

Parsons, Talcott. 1937. *The Structure of Social Action.* New York: McGraw-Hill.

———. 1951. *The Social System.* New York: Free Press.

———. 1967. *Sociological Theory and Modern Societies.* New York: Free Press.

Parsons, Talcott, and Edward Shils. 1954. *Toward a General Theory of Action.* Cambridge, Mass.: Harvard University Press.

Partridge, William L. 1973. *The Hippie Ghetto: The Natural History of a Subculture.* New York: Holt, Rinehart & Winston.

Patrick, James. 1973. *A Glasgow Gang Observed.* London: Eyre Methuen.

Paxton, Pamela. 1999. "Is Social Capital Declining? A Multiple Indicator Assessment." *American Journal of Sociology* 105: 88–127.

Pearson, Roberta. 2007. "Bachies, Bardies, Trekkies, and Sherlockians." In *Fandom: Identities and Communities in a Mediated World,* edited by Jonathan Gray, Cornel Sandvoss, and C. Lee Harrington. New York: New York University Press.

Pellegrin, Roland J. 1953. "The Achievement of High Statuses and Leadership in the Small Group." *Social Forces* 32: 10–16.

Perinbanayagam, Robert. 1986. "The Meaning of Uncertainty and the Uncertainty of Meaning." *Symbolic Interaction* 9: 105–26.

Perrin, Andrew J. 2005. "Political Microcultures: Linking Civic Life and Democratic Discourse." *Social Forces* 84: 1049–82.

Peterson, Richard, and Roger Kern. 1996. "Changing Highbrow Taste: From Snob to Omnivore." *American Sociological Review* 61: 900–907.

Pfaff, Steven. 1996. "Collective Identity and Informal Groups in Revolutionary Mobilization: East Germany in 1989." *Social Forces* 75: 91–118.

Piaget, Jean. 1969. *The Moral Judgment of the Child.* New York: Collier. (Originally published in 1932.)

Polanyi, Michael. 1964. *Personal Knowledge: Towards a Post-Critical Philosophy.* Chicago: University of Chicago Press.

Polletta, Francesca. 2002. *Freedom Is an Endless Meeting: Democracy in American Social Movements.* Chicago: University of Chicago Press.

———. 2006. *It Was Like a Fever: Storytelling in Protest and Politics.* Chicago: University of Chicago Press.

Pollner, Mel. 1987. *Mundane Reason.* Cambridge: Cambridge University Press.

Portes, Alejandro, and Julia Sensenbrenner. 1993. "Embeddedness and Immigration: Notes on the Social Determinants of Economic Action." *American Journal of Sociology* 98: 1320–50.

Posen, I. Sheldon. 1974. "Pranks and Practical Jokes and Children's Summer Camps." *Southern Folklore Quarterly* 38: 299–309.

Powell, Walter. 1987. "How the Past Informs the Present: The Uses and Liabilities of Organizational Memory." Unpublished paper, Stanford University.

Prus, Robert. 1987. "Generic Social Processes: Maximizing Conceptual Development in Ethnographic Research." *Journal of Contemporary Ethnography* 16: 250–93.

Puddephat, Antony. 2005. "Advancing in the Amateur Chess World." In *Doing Ethnography: Studying Everyday Life,* edited by Dorothy Pawluch, William Shaffir, and Charlene Miall. Toronto: Canadian Scholars' Press.

———. 2008. "Incorporating Ritual into Greedy Institution Theory: The Case of Devotion in Organized Chess." *Sociological Quarterly* 49: 155–80.

Purcell, Allen T. 1986. "Environmental Perception and Affect: A Schema Discrepancy Model." *Environment and Behavior* 18: 3–30.

Purvis, Trevor, and Alan Hunt. 1993. "Discourse, Ideology, Discourse, Ideology, Discourse, Ideology . . ." *British Journal of Sociology* 44: 473–99.

Putnam, Robert. 1995. "Bowling Alone: America's Declining Social Capital." *Journal of Democracy* 6(1): 65–78.

———. 2000. *Bowling Alone: The Collapse and Revival of American Community.* New York: Simon & Schuster.

Quillian, Lincoln, and Devah Pager. 2001. "Black Neighbors, Higher Crime? The Role of Racial Stereotypes in Evaluations of Neighborhood Crime." *American Journal of Sociology* 107: 717–67.

Rawls, Anne. 1987. "Interaction Sui Generis." *Sociological Theory* 5: 136–49.

Raynor, J. D. 1980. "The Uses of Ideological Language." In *The Form of Ideology,* edited by David J. Manning. London: Allen and Unwin.

Ridgeway, Cecilia, and Joseph Berger. 1986. "Expectations, Legitimation, and Dominance: Behavior in Task Groups." *American Sociological Review* 51: 603–17.

Ridgeway, Cecilia, and Henry Walker. 1994. "Status Structures." In *Sociological Perspectives on Social Psychology,* edited by Karen S. Cook, Gary Alan Fine, and James House. Boston: Allyn and Bacon.

Riesman, David, Nathan Glazer, and Reuel Denney. 1950. *The Lonely Crowd: A Study of the Changing American Character.* New Haven, Conn.: Yale University Press.

Riesman, David, Robert Potter, and Jeanne Watson. 1960. "The Vanishing Host." *Human Organization* 19: 17–27.

Ritzer, George. 1985. "The Rise of Micro-Sociological Theory." *Sociological Theory* 3: 88–98.

Robinson, Dawn, and Lynn Smith-Lovin. 2001. "Getting a Laugh: Gender, Status, and Humor in Task Discussions." *Social Forces* 80: 123–58.

Robinson, Russell K. 2008. "Perceptual Segregation." *Columbia Law Review* 108: 1093–1180.

Robnett, Belinda. 1996. "African-American Women in the Civil Rights Movement, 1954–1965: Gender, Leadership, and Micromobilization." *American Journal of Sociology* 101: 1661–93.

Rock, Paul. 1979. *The Making of Symbolic Interactionism.* Totowa, N.J.: Rowman and Littlefield.

Rogers, Everett. 2003. *Diffusion of Innovations.* New York: Free Press.

Rogers, Mary. 1981. "Ideology, Perspective, and Praxis." *Human Studies* 4: 145–64.

Rogers, William B., and R. E. Gardner. 1969. "Linked Changes in Values and Behavior in the Out Island Bahamas." *American Anthropologist* 71: 21–35.

Rosch, Eleanor. 1978. "Principles of Categorization." In *Cognition and Categorization,* edited by Eleanor Rosch and Barbara B. Lloyd. Hillsdale, N.J.: Erlbaum.

Rose, Edward, and William Felton. 1955. "Experimental Histories of Culture." *American Sociological Review* 20: 382–92.

Rosental, Claude. 2003. "Certifying Knowledge: The Sociology of a Logical Theorem in Artificial Intelligence." *American Sociological Review* 68: 623–44.

Ross, Andrew. 1991. "Getting Out of the Gernsback Continuum." In *Strange Weather: Culture, Science, and Technology in the Age of Limits.* New York: Verso.

Rossel, Robert Denton. 1976. "Micro-History: Studying Social Change in the Laboratory." *History of Childhood Quarterly* 3: 373–400.

Roy, Donald. 1959–1960. " 'Banana Time': Job Satisfaction and Informal Interaction." *Human Organization* 18: 158–68.

Rymond-Richmond, Wenona. 2007. "The Habitus of Habitat: Mapping the History, Redevelopment, and Crime in Public Housing." Unpublished Ph.D. diss., Northwestern University.

Sageman, Marc. 2008. *Leaderless Jihad: Terror Networks in the Twenty-First Century.* Philadelphia: University of Pennsylvania Press.

Sampson, Robert J., Jeffrey Morenoff, and Felton Earls. 1999. "Spatial Dynamics of Collective Efficacy for Children." *American Sociological Review* 64: 633–60.

Sampson, Robert J., Jeffrey Morenoff, and Thomas Gannon-Rowley. 2002. "Assessing Neighborhood Effects: Social Processes and New Directions in Research." *Annual Review of Sociology* 28: 443–78.

Sampson, Robert J., and Stephen Raudenbush. 1999. "Systematic Social Observation of Public Spaces: A New Look at Disorder in Urban Neighborhoods." *American Journal of Sociology* 105: 603–51.

Sandel, Michael J. 1996. *Democracy's Discontent: America in Search of a Public Philosophy.* Cambridge, Mass.: Harvard University Press.

Sandstrom, Kent, Daniel Martin, and Gary Alan Fine. 2009. *Symbols, Selves, and Social Reality: A Symbolic Interactionist Approach to Social Psychology and Sociology.* New York: Oxford University Press.

Sani, Fabio. 2005. "When Subgroups Secede: Extending and Refining the Social Psychological Model of Schisms in Groups." *Personality and Social Psychology Bulletin* 31: 1074–86.

Sartori, Giovanni. 1969. "Politics, Ideology, and Belief Systems." *American Political Science Review* 63: 398–411.

Sato, Ikuya. 1988. "Play Theory of Delinquency: Toward a General Theory of 'Action.' " *Symbolic Interaction* 11: 191–212.

Sawyer, R. Keith. 2005. *Social Emergence: Societies as Complex Systems.* New York: Cambridge University Press.

———. 2007. *Group Genius: The Creative Power of Collaboration.* New York: Basic Books.

Schaaf, John. 1983. "Biting Cassowaries." *Mycena News* 33(September): 37.

Scheff, Thomas J. 1966. *Being Mentally Ill: A Sociological Theory.* New York: Aldine.

———. 1994. *Bloody Revenge: Emotions, Nationalism, and War.* Boulder, Colo.: Westview Press.

Schegloff, Emanuel A. 1986. "The Routine as Achievement." *Human Studies* 9: 111–51.

Schneider, Joseph W. 1985. "Social Problems Theory: The Constructionist View." *Annual Review of Sociology* 11: 209–29.

Schnettler, Sebastian. 2009. "A Structured Overview of Fifty Years of Small-World Research." *Social Networks* 31: 165–78.

Schudson, Michael. 1989. "How Culture Works: Perspectives from Media Studies on the Efficacy of Symbols." *Theory and Society* 18: 153–80.

Schuman, Howard. 1994. "Attitudes, Beliefs, and Behaviors." In *Sociological Perspectives on Social Psychology,* edited by Karen S. Cook, Gary Alan Fine, and James House. Boston: Allyn and Bacon.

Schutz, Alfred. 1945. "On Multiple Realities." *Philosophy and Phenomenological Research* 5: 533–76.

Schwalbe, Michael. 2008. *Rigging the Game: How Inequality Is Reproduced in Everyday Life.* New York: Oxford University Press.

Schwartz, Barry. 2000. *Abraham Lincoln and the Forge of National Memory.* Chicago: University of Chicago Press.

Scott, James. 1987. *Weapons of the Weak: Everyday Forms of Peasant Resistance.* New Haven, Conn.: Yale University Press.

———. 1998. *Seeing Like a State: How Certain Schemes to Improve the Human Condition Have Failed.* New Haven, Conn.: Yale University Press.

Scott, Marvin B., and Stanford Lyman. 1968. "Accounts." *American Sociological Review* 33: 46–62.

Seckman, Mark A., and Carl J. Couch. 1989. "Jocularity, Sarcasm, and Relationships: An Empirical Study." *Journal of Contemporary Ethnography* 18: 327–44.

Sewell, William H. 1985. "Ideologies and Social Revolutions: Reflections on the French Case." *Journal of Modern History* 57: 57–85.

———. 1992. "A Theory of Structure: Duality, Agency, and Transformation." *American Journal of Sociology* 98: 1–29.

Shalin, Dmitri. 1984. "The Romantic Antecedents of Meadian Social Psychology." *Symbolic Interaction* 7: 44–65.

———. 1986. "Pragmatism and Social Interactionism." *American Sociological Review* 51: 9–29.

Sherif, Muzafer. 1935. "A Study of Some Social Factors in Perception." *Archives of Psychology* 27(187): 1–60.

———. 1954. "Integrating Field Work and Laboratory in Small Group Research." *American Sociological Review* 19: 759–71.

Sherif, Muzafer, O. J. Harvey, B. Jack White, William R. Hood, and Carolyn W. Sherif. 1987. *Intergroup Conflict and Cooperation: The Robbers Cave Experiment.* Middleton, Conn.: Wesleyan University Press.

Sherif, Muzafer, and Carolyn Sherif. 1953. *Groups in Harmony and Tension.* New York: Harper & Brothers.

———. 1964. *Reference Groups.* Chicago: Regnery.

Shibutani, Tamotsu. 1955. "Reference Groups as Perspectives." *American Journal of Sociology* 60: 562–69.

Shils, Edward. 1968. "The Concept and Function of Ideology." *International Encyclopedia of the Social Sciences* 7: 66–76.

———. 1981. *Tradition.* Chicago: University of Chicago Press.

Short, James F., Jr. 1984. "The Social Fabric at Risk: Toward a Social Transformation of Risk Analysis." *American Sociological Review* 49: 711–25.

Siman, Michael L. 1977. "Application of a New Model of Peer Group Influence to Naturally Existing Adolescent Friendship Groups." *Child Development* 48: 270–74.

Simmel, Georg. 1898. "The Persistence of Social Groups." *American Journal of Sociology* 3: 662–98.

———. 1902. "The Number of Members as Determining the Sociological Form of the Group." *American Journal of Sociology* 8: 1–46, 158–96.

———. 1950. "The Metropolis and Mental Life." In *The Sociology of Georg Simmel,* translated and edited by Kurt H. Wolff. New York: Free Press.

Simon, Herbert A. 1956. "Rational Choice and the Structure of the Environment." *Psychological Review* 63: 129–138.

Slater, Philip E. 1970. *The Pursuit of Loneliness.* Boston: Beacon Press.

Small, Mario. 2009. *Unanticipated Gains: Origins of Network Inequality in Everyday Life.* New York: Oxford University Press.

Smelser, Neil. 1962. *Theory of Collective Behavior.* New York: Free Press.

———. 1998. *The Social Edges of Psychoanalysis.* Berkeley: University of California Press.

Smith, Moira. 2009. "Humor, Unlaughter, and Boundary Maintenance." *Journal of American Folklore* 122: 148–71.

Smith, R. Tyson. 2008. "Passion Work: The Joint Production of Emotional Labor." *Social Psychology Quarterly* 71: 157–76.

Smith-Lovin, Lynn, and Charles Brody. 1989. "Interruptions in Group Discussions: The Effects of Gender and Group Composition." *American Sociological Review* 54: 424–35.

Snow, David A., and Leon Anderson. 1987. "Identity Work Among the Homeless: The Verbal Construction and Avowal of Personal Identities." *American Journal of Sociology* 92: 1336–71.

Snow, David, and Robert Benford. 1988. "Ideology, Frame Resonance, and Participant Mobilization." In *International Social Movement Research*, vol. 1, edited by Bert Klandermans, Hanspeter Kriesi, and Sidney Tarrow. Greenwich, Conn.: JAI Press.

Snow, David, E. Burke Rochford Jr., Steven Worden, and Robert Benford. 1986. "Frame Alignment Processes, Micromobilization, and Movement Participation." *American Sociological Review* 51: 464–81.

Snow, David, Louis Zurcher, and Sheldon Ekland-Olsen. 1980. "Social Networks and Social Movements: A Microstructural Approach to Differential Recruitment." *American Sociological Review* 45: 787–801.

Spears, Timothy B. 1997. *100 Years on the Road: The Traveling Salesman in American Culture*. New Haven, Conn.: Yale University Press.

Spector, Malcolm. 1973. "Secrecy in Job Seeking Among Government Attorneys: Two Contingencies in the Theory of Subcultures." *Urban Life and Culture* 2: 211–29.

Stanley, David H. 1982. "The Gospel-Singing Convention in South Georgia." *Journal of American Folklore* 95: 1–32.

Stebbins, Robert. 1979. *Amateurs*. Beverly Hills, Calif.: Sage Publications.

———. 2006. *Serious Leisure: A Perspective for Our Times*. New Brunswick, N.J.: Transaction.

Steiner, Ivan. 1974. "Whatever Happened to the Group in Social Psychology?" *Journal of Experimental Social Psychology* 10: 94–108.

Stenross, Barbara, and Sherryl Kleinman. 1989. "The Highs and Lows of Emotional Labor: Detectives' Encounters with Criminals and Victims." *Journal of Contemporary Ethnography* 17: 435–52.

Stevens, Mitchell L. 2001. *Kingdom of Children: Culture and Controversy in the Homeschooling Movement*. Princeton, N.J.: Princeton University Press.

Stewart, Susan. 1984. *On Longing: Narratives of the Miniature, the Gigantic, the Souvenir, the Collection*. Baltimore: Johns Hopkins University Press.

Stokes, Randall, and John Hewitt. 1976. "Aligning Actions." *American Sociological Review* 41: 838–49.

Stolte, John, Gary Alan Fine, and Karen Cook. 2001. "Sociological Miniaturism: Seeing the Big Through the Small in Social Psychology." *Annual Review of Sociology* 27: 387–413.

Stone, Gregory P. 1970. "Appearance and the Self." In *Social Psychology Through Symbolic Interaction*, edited by Gregory P. Stone and Harvey A. Farberman. Waltham, Mass.: Ginn-Blaisdell.

Stone, Gregory, and Harvey A. Farberman. 1967. "On the Edge of Rapprochement: Was Durkheim Moving Toward the Perspective of Symbolic Interaction?" *Sociological Quarterly* 8: 149–63.

Strauss, Anselm. 1978. *Negotiations: Varieties, Contexts, Processes, and Social Order*. San Francisco: Jossey-Bass.

———. 1982. "Interorganizational Negotiation." *Urban Life* 11: 350–67.

Strauss, Anselm, Leonard Schatzman, Rue Bucher, Danuta Erlich, and Melvin Sabshin. 1964. *Psychiatric Ideologies and Institutions*. Glencoe, Ill.: Free Press.

Stromberg, Peter G. 2009. *Caught in Play: How Entertainment Works on You.* Stanford, Calif.: Stanford University Press.

Stryker, Sheldon. 1980. *Symbolic Interactionism: A Social Structural Version.* Reading, Mass.: Cummings.

Stryker, Sheldon, and Peter J. Burke. 2000. "The Past, Present, and Future of an Identity Theory." *Social Psychology Quarterly* 63: 284–97.

Summers-Effler, Erika. 2010. *Laughing Saints and Righteous Heroes: Emotional Rhythms in Social Movement Groups.* Chicago: University of Chicago Press.

Sunstein, Cass. 2000. "Deliberative Trouble? Why Groups Go to Extremes." *Yale Law Journal* 110: 71.

———. 2001. *Republic.com.* Princeton, N.J.: Princeton University Press.

Sutherland, Edwin. 1947. *Principles of Criminology,* 4th ed. Philadelphia: J. B. Lippincott.

Suttles, Gerald. 1984. "The Cumulative Texture of Local Urban Culture." *American Journal of Sociology* 90: 283–304.

Swidler, Ann. 1986. "Culture in Action: Symbols and Strategies." *American Sociological Review* 51: 273–86.

Thayer, H. S. 1981. *Meaning and Action.* Indianapolis: Hackett.

Thelen, Herbert H. 1954. *Dynamics of Groups at Work.* Chicago: University of Chicago Press.

Therborn, Göran. 1982. *The Ideology of Power and the Power of Ideology.* London: New Left Books.

Thomas, W. I., and Dorothy Swaine Thomas. 1928. *The Child in America: Behavioral Problems and Programs.* New York: Knopf.

Thompson, Hunter S. 1967. *Hell's Angels.* New York: Ballantine.

Thorne, Barrie. 1993. *Gender Play: Girls and Boys in School.* New Brunswick, N.J.: Rutgers University Press.

Thrasher, Frederic. 1963. *The Gang.* Chicago: University of Chicago Press. (Originally published in 1927.)

Thurk, Jessica, and Gary Alan Fine. 2003. "The Problem of Tools: Technology and the Sharing of Knowledge." *Acta Sociologica* 46: 107–17.

Tolich, Martin. 1993. "Alienating and Liberating Emotions at Work: Supermarket Clerks' Performance of Customer Service." *Journal of Contemporary Ethnography* 22: 361–81.

Tönnies, Frederick. 1957. *Community and Society: Gemeinschaft und Gesellschaft,* translated and supplemented by C. P. Loomis. East Lansing: Michigan State University. (Originally published in 1887.)

Travers, Jeffrey, and Stanley Milgram. 1969. "An Experimental Study of the Small World Problem." *Sociometry* 32: 425–43.

Truzzi, Marcello. 1975. *Verstehen: Subjective Understanding in the Social Sciences.* Reading, Mass.: Addison-Wesley.

Tuomela, Raimo. 2007. *The Philosophy of Sociality: The Shared Point of View.* New York: Oxford University Press.

Turner, John C. 1987. *Rediscovering the Social Group: A Self-Categorization Theory.* Oxford: Blackwell.

Turner, Jonathan. 1988. *A Theory of Social Interaction.* Stanford, Calif.: Stanford University Press.

———. 2005. "A New Approach for Theoretically Integrating Micro and Macro Analysis." In *The Sage Handbook of Sociology*, edited by Craig Calhoun, Chris Rojek, and Brian Turner. London: Sage Publications.

Turner, Ralph, and Lewis Killian. 1987. *Collective Behavior*, 4th ed. Englewood Cliffs, N.J.: Prentice-Hall.

Unruh, David R. 1980. "The Nature of Social Worlds." *Pacific Sociological Review* 23: 271–96.

———. 1982. *Invisible Lives: Social Worlds of the Aged*. Beverly Hills, Calif.: Sage Publications.

Uzzi, Brian. 1997. "Social Structure and Competition in Interfirm Networks: The Paradox of Embeddedness." *Administrative Science Quarterly* 42: 35–67.

Vaisey, Steven. 2008. "Socrates, Skinner, and Aristotle: Three Ways of Thinking About Culture in Action." *Sociological Forum* 23: 603–13.

———. 2009. "Motivation and Justification: A Dual-Process Model of Culture in Action." *American Journal of Sociology* 114: 1675–1715.

Venkatesh, Sudhir. 1997. "The Social Organization of Street Gang Activity in an Urban Ghetto." *American Journal of Sociology* 103: 82–111.

———. 2008. *Gang Leader for a Day: A Rogue Sociologist Takes to the Streets*. New York: Penguin.

Verba, Sidney, Kay Lehman Schlozman, and Henry E. Brady. 1995. *Voice and Equality: Civic Voluntarism in American Politics*. Cambridge, Mass.: Harvard University Press.

Vinitzky-Seroussi, Vered. 1998. *After Pomp and Circumstance: High School Reunions as an Autobiographical Occasion*. Chicago: University of Chicago Press.

Vogt, Evan Z., and Thomas O'Dea. 1953. "Cultural Differences in Two Ecologically Similar Communities." *American Sociological Review* 18: 645–54.

Walsh, Katherine Cramer. 2003. *Talking About Politics: Informal Groups and Social Identity in American Life*. Chicago: University of Chicago Press.

Walzer, Michael. 1992. "The Civil Society Argument." In *Dimensions of Radical Democracy: Pluralism, Citizenship, Community*. London: Verso.

Wanderer, Jules J. 1987. "Simmel's Forms of Experiencing: The Adventure of Symbolic Work." *Symbolic Interaction* 10: 21–28.

Warren, Mark E. 1990. "Ideology and the Self." *Theory and Society* 19: 599–634.

———. 2001. *Democracy and Association*. Princeton, N.J.: Princeton University Press.

Watts, Duncan. 2003. *Six Degrees: The Science of a Connected Age*. New York: Norton.

Weber, Max. 1911. "Deutscher Sociologentag" ("German Sociology Today"). *Verhandlungen* 1: 39–62.

Weick, Karl, and D. P. Gilfillan. 1971. "Fate of Arbitrary Traditions in a Laboratory Microculture." *Journal of Personality and Social Psychology* 17: 179–91.

Wellman, Barry, Peter Carrington, and Alan Hall. 1988. "Networks as Personal Communities." In *Social Structures: A Network Approach*, edited by Barry Wellman and S. D. Berkowitz. Cambridge: Cambridge University Press.

West, Candace, and Angela Garcia. 1988. "Conversational Shift Work: A Study of Topical Transitions Between Women and Men." *Social Problems* 35: 551–75.

West, Candace, and Don Zimmerman. 1987. "Doing Gender." *Gender and Society* 1: 125–51.

White, Harrison. 1995. "Network Switchings and Bayesian Forks: Reconstructing the Social and Behavioral Sciences." *Social Research* 62: 1035–63.

White, Hayden. 1987. *The Content of the Form: Narrative Discourse and Historical Representation*. Baltimore: Johns Hopkins University Press.

White, Winston. 1961. *Beyond Conformity*. New York: Free Press.

Whittier, Nancy. 1997. "Political Generations, Micro-Cohorts, and the Transformation of Social Movements." *American Sociological Review* 62: 760–78.

Whyte, William F. 1943. *Street Corner Society*. Chicago: University of Chicago Press.

Whyte, William H. 1956. *The Organization Man*. New York: Simon & Schuster.

Wilkins, L. T. 1965. *Social Deviance: Social Policy, Action, and Research*. Englewood Cliffs, N.J.: Prentice-Hall.

Williams, Howard L. 1988. *Concepts of Ideology*. New York: St. Martin's Press.

Williams, Robin M. 1967. "Individual and Group Values." *Annals of the American Academy of Political and Social Science* 371: 20–37.

Wilson, David Sloan. 1978. *In the Presence of Nature*. Amherst: University of Massachusetts Press.

Woolcock, Michael. 1998. "Social Capital and Economic Development: Towards a Theoretical Synthesis and Policy Framework." *Theory and Society* 27: 151–208.

Worster, Donald. 1985. *Nature's Economy: A History of Ecological Ideas*. San Francisco: Sierra Club Books.

Wright, Will. 1975. *Sixguns and Society*. Berkeley: University of California Press.

Wulff, Helena. 1988. *Twenty Girls: Growing Up, Ethnicity, and Excitement in a South London Microculture*. Stockholm: Stockholm Studies in Social Anthropology.

Wuthnow, Robert. 1985. "State Structures and Ideological Outcomes." *American Sociological Review* 50: 799–821.

———. 1987. *Meaning and Moral Order: Explorations in Cultural Analysis*. Berkeley: University of California Press.

———. 1994. *Sharing the Journey: Support Groups and the Quest for a New Community*. New York: Free Press.

Yablonsky, Lewis. 1959. "The Delinquent Gang as a Near-Group." *Social Problems* 7: 108–17.

———. 1962. *The Violent Gang*. New York: Macmillan.

Yerkovich, Sally. 1977. "Gossiping as a Way of Speaking." *Journal of Communication* 27: 192–96.

Yinger, J. M. 1977. "Contracultures and Social Change." *American Sociological Review* 42: 833–53.

Zeitlin, Steven, Amy Kotkin, and Holly Cutting-Baker. 1982. *A Celebration of American Family Folklore: Tales and Traditions from the Smithsonian Collection*. New York: Pantheon.

Zerubavel, Eviatar. 1979. *Patterns of Time in Hospital Life: A Sociological Perspective*. Chicago: University of Chicago Press.

———. 1980. "If Simmel Were a Fieldworker: On Formal Sociological Theory and Analytical Field Research." *Symbolic Interaction* 3: 25–34.

————. 1997. *Social Mindscapes: An Invitation to Cognitive Sociology*. Cambridge, Mass.: Harvard University Press.

Zhao, Shanyang. 2003. "Toward a Taxonomy of Copresence." *Presence* 12: 445–55.

Zimbardo, Philip G., Ebbe B. Ebbesen, and Christina Maslach. 1977. *Influencing Attitudes and Changing Behavior*, 2nd ed. Reading, Mass.: Addison-Wesley.

Zurcher, Louis. 1968. "Social Psychological Functions of Ephemeral Roles." *Human Organization* 27: 281–97.

————. 1970. "The 'Friendly' Poker Game: A Study of an Ephemeral Role." *Social Forces* 49: 173–86.

————. 1977. *The Mutable Self*. Beverly Hills, Calif.: Sage Publications.

Zurcher, Louis, and David Snow. 1981. "Collective Behavior: Social Movements." In *Social Psychology: Sociological Perspectives*, edited by Ralph H. Turner and Morris Rosenberg. New York: Basic Books.

# Index

acid rain, 98–99
Aldrich, Howard, 113
Alexander, Jeffrey, 34
Althusser, Louis, 91
American exceptionalism, 124–25
Anderson, Benedict, 16, 96, 108, 131
Aristotle, 132
Arnold, David, 144
artists, self-taught. *See* self-taught artists
associations, 24, 179*n*2
Athens, Lonnie, 23
attitudes, 92

Bacon-Smith, Camille, 107, 116, 119
Bales, Robert Freed, 7–8, 21
Banfield, Edward, 19, 125, 137
Bateson, Gregory, 73
Becker, Howard, 29, 42
Bentham, Jeremy, 25–26
Berger, Peter, 39
Bey, Hakim, 118
Billig, Michael, 131–32
Blumer, Herbert, 35, 57, 59, 171
Boltanski, Luc, 168–69
Brake, Michael, 119
Brown, Phil, 129–30
built environment, 59–61
bureaucracy, 13–14, 64
Burke, Peter, 71
Burning Man Festival, 118–19
Burt, Ron, 148

Calhoun, Craig, 140
Camic, Charles, 169

chess players: ethnographic study of, 14; history of the game and, 65
civil society: enactment of, small groups as context for, 132–34; framing function of small groups in, 128–30; identity and, 118, 131–32; individualism *vs.* associational involvement in the United States, 124–25; mobilization function of small groups in, 130–31; small groups as a consequence of, 135–38; small groups in, centrality of, 125–28, 138–39; tiny publics and the basis of, 164
clubs, 112–15
Cohen, Stanley, 154
Cohen, Steven, 7–8
collective action, 132
Collins, Randall, 16, 23, 52–53, 164–65, 170, 180*n*1, 180*n*3
community: social order and, 111–12; virtual, 114, 179*n*1, 182*n*4; wispy (*see* wispy communities)
Comte, August, 54
constraint, 52, 54–58
contestation, groups and, 28
control, group, 26–27
Cook, Karen, 5
Cooley, Charles Horton, 5, 52, 54
Couch, Carl, 64
culinary training. *See* restaurant workers
cultural diamond framework, 71
cultural entrepreneurs, 146

215

culture: "boy," 8; building of by
fantasy-gamers, 9; creation of
through framing, 129; diffusion of,
146–51; ethnographic observation
of, 6–7 (*see also* ethnographic observation); extensions of through
interlocks (*see* interlocks); of
groups (*see* idioculture); norms
and, 70–71; organization of social
action by, 176–77; as performed,
34–35; as social relations, 162–63;
sociology of, 4–5; subcultures (*see*
subcultures); tradition and, 181*n*6;
in tribal societies, 179*n*1

Deaux, Kay, 31
democratic theory, 126
dramatism, 160–61
Dundes, Alan, 95, 97
Durkheim, Émile, 29, 54, 58, 180–81*n*4
dyads, 22

Eliasoph, Nina, 113, 138, 183*n*7
Ellickson, Robert, 21, 133
emergentist theory, 158
Emirbayer, Mustafa, 168
environment, built, 59–61
environment, natural: connection to,
182*n*7; emotional experience of,
99–100; "environmentalist" label,
debates over, 101–3; images and
ideology of, 96–99; naturework, 11
ethnographic observation: culture as
a group practice, advantages for
studying, 6–7; field studies carried
out, description of, 7–15; as a
stream of sociological research,
4; of talk, 11–12
events, 115
exteriority, 52, 54–55; belief in organizational primacy, 66–67; institutional linkages, 63–64; obdurate
burdens of tradition, 65–66; "obdurate," meaning of, 181*n*5; as obdurate reality, 58–59; physical limits
of the built environment, 59–61;
temporal and spatial effects, 61–63

family, 110, 134, 137
fantasy role-playing gamers, ethno-
graphic study of, 9–10
Farrell, Michael, 29
Fischer, J. L., 37
Foucault, Michel, 26–27
framing, 73–78, 128–30
Freud, Sigmund, 117

Gamson, William, 101
Garfinkel, Harold, 172, 184*n*1
gatherings, 115–22
Geer, Blanche, 42
Geertz, Clifford, 40, 89–90, 106
gender, status allocation and, 31
generalizeability, miniaturist
approach and, 6
Ghaziani, Amin, 37
Giddens, Anthony, 28, 61, 158
Gieryn, Thomas, 90, 181*n*2–3
Gladwell, Malcolm, 148
Gmelch, George, 49
Goffman, Erving: dramatism of, 160;
Durkheim, indebtedness to, 54;
encounters, 112; framing, model of,
9–10, 73, 101; frontstage *vs.* backstage behavior, 30; games, fun as
reason for participating in, 110,
121; group culture, referential
afterlife of, 170; group relations
and actions, explaining, 175; interaction order, the, 1, 25, 62–63, 163,
184*n*1; norms as a frame, 70; patterns of behavior, norms and, 72;
persons and groups, examining a
world of, 20; processes at work in
formal conditions of interaction,
finding, 176; reliance on theories
of, 17; situations as organizing features of social life, 23; social cartography of, 168; sociology as a study
of action, 171; standing behavior
pattern, finding a, 169
Goldfarb, Jeffrey, 164
Gordon, Milton, 36
Gould, Roger, 133
Gouldner, Alvin, 91, 96

Gramsci, Antonio, 90
Granovetter, Mark, 130, 140, 148
Griswold, Wendy, 71
Gross, Edward, 63
group extensions, 140–43, 155–56. *See also* interlocks; subcultures
group process theory, 4
groups: as an arena of action, 38–39; civic identity and, 131–32; in civil society (*see* civil society; politics); comparative analysis of, 37–38; contestation and, 28; control and, 26–27; culture of (*see* idioculture); dyads, 22; as dynamic action systems, 173; explanatory value, components that reveal, 25–26; extensions/linkages of (*see* group extensions; interlocks; subcultures); as little things that become big things, 177; meso-level analysis and (*see* meso-level analysis); networks and, 21, 24; other social forms, contrasted with, 23–25; the power of, 19–21, 32–33; representations and, 28–30; role relations and, 22–23; shared history of, 169–71; small, definition of, 21–22; social significance of, 1–3; status allocation and, 30–31; temporary (*see* wispy communities). *See also* localism; tiny publics

Habermas, Jürgen, 91, 179n2, 183n2, 183n4–5
Hall, Peter, 64
Hardin, Garrett, 181n4
Hare, Paul, 21–22
Harrington, Brooke, 17
Hechter, Michael, 26
high school debate teams: ethnographic study of, 12; innovations and the culture of, 145–46
Hirsch, Paul, 130
Hobbes, Thomas, 20
Hochschild, Arlie, 182n6
Hollingshead, August, 36
Homans, George, 34, 40, 171, 176

Horne, Christine, 68
Horowitz, Ruth, 153
humor, 83–87

identity: community response to subcultures and, 154–55; ideology and, 103–4; marks of, 143; social relations and, 168–69; subculture and, 151–53
ideology: commitment to, small groups and, 28; conception/definition of, 90–93; emotion and, 99–100, 181–82n5–6; group-based model of, 94; group identity, networks, and, 103–5; images, moral order, and, 94–99; leisure, connection to, 11; metaphor and, 97–98; political party activists, salience for, 14–15; presentation to others of, 100–103; relations and communities, based on, 89–90; resources and, 104–5; rituals and, 104; social interactions, based in, 93–94, 105–6
idioculture, 50–51; appropriate culture as criterion for inclusion in, 46–48; building, 40–50; bureaucracy and, 10–11; comparative analysis of groups and, 37–38; creating, 35–40; definition of, 36; ethnographic observation in field studies of, 7–15; functional culture as criterion for inclusion in, 45–46; group shared history as, 169–71; introduction of the concept of, 8; justifying focus on, 36–40; known culture as criterion for inclusion in, 42–43; as local cultural understandings, 3; as mediator between environment and action, 39–40; triggering event as necessary for inclusion in, 48–49; usable culture as criterion for inclusion in, 43–45; workings of the elements of, 49–50
imagined communities, 16, 108–9, 117, 131. *See also* wispy communities
information diffusion, 146–51
institutions, 63–64, 110

interaction order(s): culture/idiocul-
ture and, 35–36, 40, 51, 156; durable
and stable interaction, dependence
on, 174; exteriority and, components bolstering, 59; as fields of
performance, 5; Goffman on, 1, 25,
63, 163, 168; identity and, 84; ideology and, 94, 105–6; intersecting
tiny publics and, 3; mass media
and, 151; meso-level analysis and,
176; negotiation and, 78; norms
and, 72, 74–75, 88; of restaurants,
11; small groups and, organizing
properties of, 20; stable, maintaining a, 67–68; subcultures and, 144;
wispy communities and, 107–8. *See
also* symbolic interactionist thought
interlocks, 143, 146; media diffusion,
150–51; multiple group membership, 147–48; structural roles, 150;
weak ties, 148–50

Jamison, Ann, 182*n*1
Jenkins, Henry, 116
Johnston, Hank, 131
Joyce, James, 157–58, 174, 177

Karinthy, Frigyes, 148
Kelly, Harold, 49
Kern, Roger, 112
Kinloch, Graham, 91
Kleinman, Sherryl, 17
Koselleck, Reinhart, 183*n*2

Lebowski Fest, 107–8, 182*n*1
Lee, Alfred McClung, 36
leisure, 110–11
Lemann, Nicolas, 127
Levtzion, Nehemia, 183*n*3
Lewin, Kurt, 27
Lichterman, Paul, 113
Lipset, Seymour Martin, 125
Little League baseball teams: compar-
ative analysis of, 37–38; ethno-
graphic study of, 7–9; filtering
elements of idioculture and, 42–50

Lizardo, Omar, 150
localism, 157; arenas of action and,
165–67; conceptualizing, 157–64;
context, the significance of, 162–63;
dramatism and, 161; frames of reference, as a source of, 129; the
group, perspective on the world
through, 176–77; idioculture and, 3
(*see also* idioculture); as a lens on
action, 171–74; negotiation and,
160–62; as a particular sociology,
174–75; shared history and, 169–71;
social relations and, 167–69; as a
stage, the local as, 165–71; toward a
sociology of, 163–64
Luckmann, Thomas, 39

macrogatherings, 117–20
macrosociology: folk belief, as a form
of, 58; methodological individualism, reliance on, 157; microsociological foundations of, 16, 52–54, 67
(*see also* microsociology); organizational primacy and, 66
Maffesoli, Michel, 25, 109
Mannheim, Karl, 96, 147
Manning, David, 103
Marconi, Guglielmo, 148
Marx, Karl, 65
masses, 24–25
McCarthy, John, 128–30
McLellan, David, 90
McRobbie, Angela, 164
Mead, George Herbert, 23, 54, 56, 67
media diffusion, 150–51
meso-level analysis: central concepts
of, 54; Collins' incorporation of, 52;
context and the local in, 175; culture and, 163, 177; groups, focus
on, 17, 25, 69, 126, 157; ideology
and, 97, 106; ignoring of, 1–2;
macrosociology and microsociology, incorporation of both, 67;
points of reference of, 180*n*2, 184*n*2;
question for further research, 143
metaphors of causation, 53

meteorologists. *See* weather forecasters
metis, 164
Michigan Womyn's Music Festival, 118
microethnography, 37
microsociology: Durkheim as inspiration for, 54; human choices mediated by material reality and, 59; localism distinguished from, 157–58; macrofoundations of, 16, 52–54, 61–62, 67; methodological individualism, reliance on, 157; as miniaturist approach to sociology, 5–6; as sociological miniaturism, 3
Milgram, Stanley, 27, 148
Mills, C. Wright, 58
Minnesota Mycological Society, 11, 97, 104
Mische, Ann, 163
Molotch, Harvey, 169
monads, 23
Morris, Charles, 54
mushroom collectors: emotional experience of nature by, 99–100; environmental ideology of, debates over, 101–3; ethnographic study of, 11; framing of norms by, 75–78; ideology and, 95–97; local concerns and public policy, linkage of, 98–99; narrating of norms by, 83–87; negotiating of norms by, 80–82; the organization of norms and, 73; rituals of, 104

"narrative turn" in social theory, 12
National Weather Service: built environment of, 60–61; bureaucratic procedures of, 53; as collective actor, 64; ethnographic study at local offices of, 13–14; structure of, changes in, 62; work practices at, 168. *See also* weather forecasters
naturework, 11. *See also* environment, natural
Nee, Brett de Bary, 137
Nee, Victor, 137

negotiated order perspective, 78–80
neighborhood effects literature, 159
networks: civic engagement and, 130–31; groups and, 21, 24 (*see also* group extensions)
Nisbet, Robert, 125
norms: concept of "norm," 69–73; culture and, 70–71; framing, 73–78; interaction and, 71–73; as a local production, 87–88; narrating, 82–87; negotiating, 78–82; social order and, 68–69

obdurate reality. *See* exteriority
obdurate reality of images, 56
Oldenburg, Ray, 110, 167
Olson, Mancur, 28, 132
Opie, Iona, 147
Opie, Peter, 147
organizational primacy, belief in, 66–67
Ostrom, Elinor, 135

Parsons, Talcott, 172
Patrick, James, 147
Peterson, Richard, 112
political party activists: ethnographic study of, 14–15; localism as source of variation in civic engagement, 129; moments of group activation of, 141; social relations among, 169; temporal and spatial limits and, 63. *See also* social movements
politics, small groups and, 125–28. *See also* civil society
Portes, Alejandro, 137
Putnam, Robert: bowling alone, 127, 136; bridging *vs.* bonding relations, impact of, 135–36; civic engagement, definition of, 126; friendship and social capital, 108; groups and civil society, relationship of, 17, 19, 115, 135, 183*n*8; individualism, limits to concerns regarding, 124; wispy communities as answer to concerns of, 122

Raynor, J. D., 97
representation(s): as a component of miniaturist approach, 6; groups and, 28–30
resources: acquisition by groups for collective action, 130–31; ideology and, 104–5
restaurant workers: the built environment and, 60; constraints and social order for, 54–57; ethnographic study of, 10–11; exteriority, example of, 55; occupational culture of, 142; smaller units constitutive of the larger unit of, 53; social relations in the kitchens of, 168; temporal limits and, 61–62
Riesman, David, 19, 125
risk, humor and norms of, 83–87
rituals: ideology and, 104; social organization and, 170–71
Robinson, Dawn, 39
Rock, Paul, 74
role relations, 22–23
Roy, Donald, 36–37

Sandstrom, Kent, 16
Sawyer, Keith, 158
Schaaf, John, 77
Schutz, Alfred, 171–72
Scott, James, 164
self-taught artists: ethnographic study of, 12–13; institutional linkages and, 63–64
Sensenbrenner, Julia, 137
Sheller, Mimi, 168
Sherif, Carolyn, 41
Sherif, Muzafer, 41, 47, 71–72, 173
Shibutani, Tamotsu, 140, 147
Shils, Edward, 103
Simmel, Georg: dramaturgical theorists and, 160; on dyads, 22; as macro-/microtheorist, 54; situations as sites of broader forces, recognition of, 5; social forms as source of personal connections, recognition of, 19; sociology of action, as practitioner of, 171
situations, 23–24

Small, Mario, 126, 142, 184n1
small groups. See groups
Smelser, Neil, 48
Smith-Lovin, Lynn, 39
Snow, David, 28, 104–5, 129
social movements, 129–30
social order: community and, 111–12; constraints of local hierarchy and, 55–58; individual interests and, 68–69; as negotiated order, 79
social problems discourse, 12
social psychology, 4–6
sociological miniaturism. See microsociology
sociology: of action, 171–74; groups, the study of, 19–20, 177; local (see localism); macro (see macrosociology); micro (see microsociology); streams of research in, 4–5
status allocation, 14, 30–31
Stets, Jan, 71
Stolte, John, 5
Stone, Gregory, 152
Strauss, Anselm, 78–79, 160
structuration, 61–64, 158
subcultures, 143–45; community response to, 154–55; diffusion of information and, 146–51; groups-based model of, 145–55; identity and, 151–53; interlocks and (see interlocks). See also group extensions
Suttles, Gerald, 169
Swidler, Ann, 71, 162
symbolic interactionist thought: linkage of macro- and microelements in, 54, 56–57; meaning, social construction of, 29, 35; negotiation perspective in, 78–80; situating of others, actions dependent upon, 71; status hierarchies, individual negotiation of position in, 30. See also interaction order(s)
systematic multi-level observation of groups (SYMLOG), 8

talk, local construction of, 12
Tea Party movement, 131
technology, 59, 149–50

Thomas, Dorothy, 72, 161
Thomas, W. I., 72, 161
Thrasher, Frederic, 144
tiny publics: civil society, as the basis
    of, 164; conception of, 2–3; the
    family, 110; motivation for social
    engagement through, 162; societies
    built on, 143–44; subcultures and,
    144 (*see also* group extensions).
    *See also* groups; idioculture
Tocqueville, Alexis de, 2, 19, 24,
    124–26, 138
Tracy, Destutt de, 90
transcendence, miniaturist approach
    and, 6
Tuomela, Raimo, 1

United States, individualism *vs.* asso-
    ciational involvement in, 124–25

van den Scott, Lisa-Jo, 16
Venkatesh, Sudhir, 152
Victims of Child Abuse Laws
    (VOCAL), ethnographic study of, 15
virtual communities, 114

Walzer, Michael, 126
weather forecasters: the built envi-
    ronment and, 60–61; ethnographic
study of, 13–14; space, concern
    with arrangement of, 166; temporal
    and spatial limits and, 61–62. *See
    also* National Weather Service
Weber, Max, 3, 40, 54
"we-mode" groups, 1
White, Harrison, 140–41, 163
White, Hayden, 170
Whyte, William Foote, 47
Whyte, William H., 125
Wilson, David Sloan, 99–100
wispy communities, 107–10, 122–23;
    "club" form of, 112–15; community
    in, 111–12; events, 115; fun as the
    goal of, 110–11, 114; gatherings,
    115–17; macrogatherings, 117–20;
    microgatherings, 120–22; networks
    of self-taught artists as, 13; "occa-
    sion" form of, 112, 115–17; struc-
    tural forms/subtypes of, 111–12
Woodstock, 117–18
Wulff, Helena, 165

Yablonsky, Lewis, 141, 153
Yerkovich, Sally, 149

Zald, Mayer, 128–30
Zerubavel, Eviatar, 56, 61, 70
Zurcher, Louis, 104–5